YALE HISTORICAL PUBLICATIONS

DAVID HORNE, EDITOR

MISCELLANY 78

PUBLISHED UNDER THE DIRECTION OF
THE DEPARTMENT OF HISTORY

Dream of Empire: German Colonialism, 1919–1945

BY WOLFE W. SCHMOKEL

NEW HAVEN AND LONDON

YALE UNIVERSITY PRESS, 1964

For Varian

Preface

In the growing volume of historical research and analysis dealing with Germany under the Hitler regime, the subject of German colonial ambitions has been almost totally neglected. Part of the reason for this neglect may lie in the impression conveyed by statements of certain National Socialist leaders, especially in Hitler's *Mein Kampf*, that the rulers of the Third Reich had for ideological and strategic reasons repudiated overseas expansion as a German foreign policy goal. Part of it may also be explained by the facts that since German colonial ambitions during this period were not fulfilled, Nazi imperialism found no concrete expression, and that the documentary evidence for these ambitions and plans is relatively scarce and scattered and comparatively inaccessible.

This investigation aims to provide the first over-all survey of colonial discussion and planning in the Third Reich, both official and unofficial. It also deals with the diplomatic negotiations involving the German colonial claim, and presents for the first time, I believe, the concrete plans that existed for the creation and administration of a new German overseas empire. It aims to show that from 1933 until well into World War II there flourished in Germany a lively colonial movement. Its agitation, carried on under Party auspices and supported by the statements of almost all major Nazi leaders, reached such a pitch in the late 1930s that it not only found considerable echo in Germany but created the impression in Britain and other foreign countries that colonies were a major German foreign policy objective. For years the subject of the revision of the colonial clauses of the Versailles peace settlement played an important role in international diplomacy, and the idea of restoring at least part of Germany's pre-World War I empire to her was seriously considered by Western statesmen. In the course of our investigation we will present considerable evidence that after the outbreak of World War II the acquisition of colonies became a definite war aim of Germany's rulers.

Elaborate preparations were made for the transfer to and administration by the Reich of large African areas.

All of this must be viewed, however, against the background of Hitler's basic political and ideological conception of Germany as a primarily continental power, which involved the extension of German political sovereignty and "national settlement space" into Eastern Europe. Hitler by no means repudiated this aim in favor of an all-out policy of overseas expansion. There was thus a certain tension between National Socialist ideology and the salt-water imperialism which opportunism led the Nazi leaders to espouse. This tension is a point upon which the present study will touch repeatedly.[1]

Longer-range research might produce a fuller picture of the organization and personnel of the German colonial movement, and more work may some day be done on Hans Grimm, intellectual champion of German overseas expansion, and on the enormously difficult subject of Hitler's motivation and ultimate foreign-policy objectives, on which this study merely ventures some suggestions.

Whatever value the investigation may have it owes in large part to a number of suggestions from Hajo Holborn and Harry R. Rudin of Yale University and Harold Gordon of the University of Massachusetts. Professor Gordon's suggestions enabled me to track down the documentary evidence upon which Chapter 4 is largely based. The magnificent cooperation of the staff of the Berlin Document Center, the Institut für Zeitgeschichte in Munich, and the Bundesarchiv of the German Federal Republic made possible the evaluation of this material in the course of a relatively brief sojourn in Germany.

1. This tension between "continentalism" and Weltpolitik is one of the major themes of Henry C. Meyer's *Mitteleuropa* (The Hague, 1955). This work, which deals mainly with the World War I period, makes it quite clear, however, that the creation of a German-dominated continental bloc and overseas expansion were considered complementary, rather than mutually exclusive policy aims by many German political thinkers. This study will show that this view was also adopted by the leaders of the Third Reich. It is interesting to note that a number of personalities whom Meyer mentions as proponents of *Mitteleuropa* (especially Hjalmar Schacht and Paul Rohrbach) were also active in the colonial movement during the Nazi period.

I also acknowledge my debt to Rayford Logan of Howard University, whose pioneer study of the diplomatic aspects of the German colonial claim provided much of the factual framework of Chapter 3, enabling me to concentrate on matters of interpretation.

W.W.S.

University of Vermont
June 1963

Contents

Contents

Abbreviations

Auswärtige Politik	*Akten zur deutschen Auswärtigen Politik 1918–1945* (Baden-Baden, 1950–).
BA	Bundesarchiv, Koblenz, Germany.
BDC	Berlin Document Center.
British Documents	E. L. Woodward and Rohan Butler, eds., *Documents on British Foreign Policy* (London, 1950–).
BVP	Bayerische Volkspartei (Bavarian People's Party).
DDP	Deutsche Demokratische Partei (German Democratic Party).
DKG	Deutsche Kolonialgesellschaft (German Colonial Society).
DNVP	Deutschnationale Volkspartei (German Nationalist People's Party).
DOAG	Deutsch-Ostafrikanische Gesellschaft (German East Africa Company).
DVP	Deutsche Volkspartei (German People's Party).
FR (1937) or (1938)	*Foreign Relations of the United States —Diplomatic Papers, 1937* (Washington, 1954); *1938* (Washington, 1955).
German Documents	*Documents on German Foreign Policy, 1918–1945* (Washington, 1950–).
HO	Akten des Hauptamts Ordnungspolizei (Files of Main Office for Ordinary Police).
KORAG	Koloniale Reichsarbeitsgemeinschaft (Reich Colonial Working Group).
KPA	Kolonialpolitisches Amt (Office for Colonial Policy).
KPA, Tätigkeitsbericht	Kolonialpolitisches Amt der NSDAP, Reichsleitung, Tätigkeitsbericht, Berlin

	Document Center (copy in Institut für Zeitgeschichte, Munich).
NSDAP	Nationalsozialistische Deutsche Arbeiterpartei (National Socialist German Labor Party—Nazi).
RFM	Akten des Reichsfinanzministeriums (Files of the Reich Ministry of Finance).
RKB	Reichskolonialbund (Reich Colonial League).
SPD	Sozialdemokratische Partei Deutschlands (Social Democratic Party of Germany).

The German Colonial Movement

Overseas expansion was not originally an important part of the National Socialist program. The leaders of the Third Reich adopted it as an aim only gradually. For this reason it is essential that we consider in some detail the colonial movement that existed in the Weimar period, its leadership, activities, and accomplishments. While the Nazis changed some of the emphases of the colonial program and gave it a definite ideological coloring, the colonial idea itself can be traced back to the imperialism of pre-World War I Germany. It was kept alive during the 1920s by men who had grown up in that tradition.

Imperialism had never taken a deep hold on the great masses of the German people.[1] When Germany lost her colonial empire as a result of World War I, only a relatively few persons, most of

1. Thus the original Deutsche Kolonialgesellschaft (DKG), founded in 1888 as a combination of several earlier colonial societies, had only 16,000 members. It never grew significantly larger. For an analysis of its membership, which differed little from that of the DKG of the 1920s, see Fritz Ferdinand Müller, *Deutschland, Ostafrika, Zanzibar* (Berlin, 1959), pp. 165 ff., 190–91. For a revealing instance of self-criticism of the DKG's perpetual inability to "carry colonial enthusiasm into the masses" see *Deutsche Kolonialzeitung, 48* (1936), 167 ff.

whom had a direct and material interest in the colonies, really paid much attention to this aspect of the peace settlement. For most Germans there were more pressing problems and concerns: "The loss of our colonies was accepted by a large part of the German people with dumb equanimity," one colonialist lamented.[2]

Thus the organizations formed after the war to protest against the colonial peace settlement and to agitate for its revision consisted largely of Germans who had lost their homes and positions in the colonies as the result of that settlement. In 1918 the Reichsbund der Kolonialdeutschen was founded as the first such group. Soon colonial organizations multiplied. The most remarkable fact about them was the close similarity in their programs and attitudes, brought about in large part by a considerable overlap in their respective memberships. The most important of these groups was the Deutsche Kolonialgesellschaft (DKG). Its history dates back to the 1880s, when it gave an important impetus to Bismarck's colonial policy. After its reorganization in 1920 it went through a difficult period of financial vicissitudes during the years of inflation and political instability. By 1924 the DKG had overcome these difficulties to a sufficient degree to enable it to make its first appeal to the general public by organizing a Colonial Congress to commemorate the fortieth anniversary of the founding of Germany's empire.[3] By 1926 it had 250 branches throughout Germany, with a total of 30,000 members.

Under the energetic leadership of the former colonial governors Theodor Seitz (1920–1930) and Heinrich Schnee (1930–1936), the DKG, despite its relatively small membership, showed some lively activity, especially in the field of colonial propaganda. Until 1928 the monthly *Mitteilungen der Deutschen Kolonialgesellschaft* was its main organ. In that year it acquired the *Deutsche Übersee- und Kolonialzeitung*. A subsidiary, the *Frauenbund der DKG,* presided over by Agnes von Bömeken and, later, by Frau von Bredow, published an annual calendar, *Deutsche Jugend, Deutsche Kolonien,* designed to appeal to youth, with glamorized biographies of colonial heroes, photographs, accounts of life in the colonies,

2. G. Wüst, ed., *Kolonialprobleme der Gegenwart* (Berlin, 1939), p. 26.
3. Arthur Dix, *Weltkrise und Kolonialpolitik* (Berlin, 1932), p. 299.

colonial fiction, etc. It also helped to maintain German schools in the former colonies and supported the *Koloniale Frauenschule* in Rendsburg, which trained girls for life in overseas areas.[4]

The Youth Committee of the DKG, which was the nucleus of the future Bund Deutscher Kolonialjugend, with 8,000 members, aimed to spread the "colonial idea" among young people, especially through its monthly magazine *Jambo*.[5] In 1928 the DKG also took over the sponsorship of the Bund deutscher Kolonialpfadfinder, which had originally been affiliated with Wilhelm Föllmer's Deutscher Kolonialverein. The latter group itself, which did not confine its interests to overseas areas, favored eastern settlement and expansion. It merged with the DKG in 1933, when its organ, *Brücke zur Heimat*, was also consolidated with the *Kolonialzeitung*.

The Bund deutscher Kolonialpfadfinder had a membership of only 2,500, organized in 170 groups, including one in Southwest Africa. Nevertheless it published two periodicals, *Kreuz und Lilie* and *Der Kolonialspäher*. In 1931 it united with another group, the Kolonialbund Deutscher Pfadfinder, to form the Deutscher Kolonialpfadfinderbund. In 1933 the latter, along with other colonial youth groups, was integrated into the Hitler Youth's Kolonialscharen.[6]

Other colonial groups included the Kolonialer Volksbund of Paul Leutwein, which specialized in the training of "colonial orators" (*Kolonialredner*) and kept alive the old *Mittelafrika* dreams[7] of World War I, agitating not only for colonial revision

---

4. Ibid., p. 300. Hanswerner Nachrodt, *Der Reichskolonialbund*. Schriften der Hochschule für Politik, Herausgegeben von Paul Meier-Benneckenstein; II. Der Organisatorische Aufbau des Dritten Reiches, Heft *30* (Berlin, 1939), 17–18.

5. Adolf Dresler, "Die deutschen Kolonien und die Presse," *Forschungen zur Kolonialfrage, 11* (Würzburg, 1942), 78. Dix, p. 300. Ernst Gerhard Jacob, *Deutsche Kolonialkunde, 1884–1934* (Dresden, 1934), p. 72.

6. Dix, pp. 300–02. Dresler, p. 75. Jacob, pp. 50, 72.

7. These plans for the creation of a large German Central African Empire, stretching from coast to coast of the continent, from ca. lat. 20 north to lat. 20 south are discussed, surprisingly objectively, in Emil Zimmermann, *The German Empire of Central Africa* (London, 1918). During World War I the more liberal German politicians, e.g. Friedrich Naumann, tended to favor colonial

but for "the acquisition of colonial possessions in territorially uni-
fied form." In political orientation it was definitely far to the right
and conceived its special mission as combatting the continental
autarkic tendencies of other rightist groups, such as the NSDAP.
Quite different in this respect was the Bund für Koloniale Erneuerung, founded in 1929, which united the Bund der Kolonial-
freunde (1922) and Gesellschaft für Koloniale Erneuerung (1926).
This organization, which stressed economic arguments in its agitation, was presided over by Wilhelm Külz, a former Reichsminis-
ter and member of the Democratic Party. Its vice presidents were
the Socialist Reichstag member Max Cohen-Reuss and the labor
union official Mikausch. The Bund's organ, the *Kolonialfreund,*
contained many contributions by Socialists of the old revisionist
wing, especially Hermann Kranold and Valentin Müller, who even
before World War I had attacked the prevailing anticolonial senti-
ment within the SPD. When this group dissolved itself in 1931
"according to the desires of the Foreign Office," it suggested that
its members join the DKG.[8]

There were also a number of groups representing more specifically the interests of old colonials—who themselves commonly
carried on active propaganda for colonial revision. Foremost
among these was the Deutscher Kolonialkriegerbund (originally
named Zusammenschluss der ehemaligen Kolonialkämpfer),
founded in 1922 and headed until 1924 by General Georg von
Märcker, who had campaigned in Tanganyika and after the war
contributed greatly, as a free corps leader, to the suppression of
the Berlin Spartacist revolts. His successor as president of this
colonial veterans' association was General Franz Ritter von Epp,
another free corps leader, of whose colonial experience more will
be said later. The organ of this group was the *Kolonialpost.*[9]

Not to be confused with the Kolonialkriegerbund is the Ko-

---

acquisitions over continental annexations. The pan-Germans, despite the colonialist origin of that movement (Carl Peters, the "hero" of the German
acquisition of Tanganyika, was one of its founders), emphasized European
aggrandizement among their war aims.

8. Dix, p. 302. Dresler, pp. 75, 78–79. Jacob, p. 60.

9. Dresler, p. 75. Evans Lewin, *The Germans and Africa* (London, 1939),
p. 344. Nachrodt, p. 17. Jacob, p. 55.

lonialkriegerdank, a society founded in 1909 by Duke Adolf Friedrich von Mecklenburg, whose primary aim was to help colonial veterans in economic difficulty. This group published from 1921 to 1928 a monthly entitled *Der Kolonialdeutsche*. In 1928 the DKG acquired it and changed its name to *Übersee- und Kolonialzeitung*, to carry on the tradition of the old *Kolonialzeitung* it had published until 1919.[10]

Numerically insignificant and mainly devoted to keeping alive memories of the past were such groups as the Ostafrikanerverband, the Verein der Kameruner, the Interessenvertretung ehemaliger Südwestafrikaner, the Siedlungsgemeinschaft ehemaliger Ostafrikaner, and the Kameradschaft ehemaliger Kameruner Offiziere (which published its own periodical, the *Kamerunpost*, for a few years after 1923).[11] The Kartell Vereinigter Auslandsgeschädigten-Verbände, formed in 1932, was more oriented toward remedying the economic grievances of the old colonials by lobbying for increased compensation for property lost overseas as a result of the war and the peace treaty.[12] Some mention must also be made of charitable organizations, such as the Frauenverein vom Roten Kreuz für Deutsche Übersee, the Reichsbund der Katholischen Auslandsdeutschen, and the Evangelische Kolonialhilfe, some of which originated before the war; their main aim was to aid Germans still in the colonies and in other overseas areas who found themselves in economic distress,[13] and of the Akademischer Kolonialbund, founded by the noted Africanist Diedrich Westermann in 1924, which not only kept alive scholarly interest in the colonies but also carried on active revisionist propaganda in its *Arbeitsblatt*.[14] The Deutsche Weltwirtschaftliche Gesellschaft of the indefatigable Heinrich Schnee was specifically designed to convince economic circles of the necessity for German colonies.[15]

Almost all these various groups were coordinated in the Koloniale Reichsarbeitsgemeinschaft (KORAG), founded in 1922 as

---

10. Nachrodt, pp. 17–18. Lewin, p. 344.
11. Dresler, pp. 75–78.
12. Jacob, p. 52.
13. Dix, pp. 302–03. Nachrodt, p. 17.
14. Jacob, p. 73. Lewin, p. 344.
15. Bundesarchiv, Reichskanzlei files, file 822.

an umbrella organization. The dominant position of the DKG among the colonial groups is attested to by the fact that its president also served as ex officio president of KORAG, an organization which included, incidentally, not only the colonial organizations themselves but also business (especially shipping) firms with colonial and overseas interests and such groups as the Kolonialabteilung der deutschen Landwirtschaftsgesellschaft (colonial section of the German Agricultural Society), and Kolonialwirtschaftliches Komitee (Committee for Colonial Economics).[16] This business support undoubtedly played a major role in keeping the colonial cause alive during the Weimar period. It provided financial backing for the numerous organizations we have listed and for a number of publications not directly affiliated with any of them but largely or exclusively devoted to the "colonial question." Among them were the *Weltrundschau,* edited by the former colonial officials Hans Berthold and Josef Deeg (Berthold, interestingly enough, was an early contributor to the Nazis' *Völkischer Beobachter*),[17] and *Der deutsche Gedanke* and the *Leitartikel-Korrespondenz,* both edited by Paul Rohrbach, a former Settlement Commissar for Southwest Africa. Less inclined toward right-wing political polemics, the *Hamburger Monatshefte für Auswärtige Politik* and *Europäische Gespräche* stressed the economic arguments for German colonies. The correspondence service *Koloniale Nachrichten,* founded by the Nachrichtenbüro deutscher Zeitungsverleger, supplied the daily press with colonial items. In addition, such extreme right-wing publications as *Fridericus* and *Die Rote Hand,* which appeared in Munich from 1918 to 1920, gave more than passing attention to the colonial problem.[18] A publishing house, Süsseroth-Verlag, specializing in books and pamphlets on the German colonies, particularly for young people, seems to have had some connection with the German Nationalist Party (DNVP).[19]

Needless to say, not all periodicals devoted to the discussion of colonial and overseas affairs were propagandistic. The *Koloniale*

16. Dix, pp. 302–03. Nachrodt, pp. 17–18. Dresler, p. 75.
17. Dresler, p. 91.
18. Ibid., pp. 73–75.
19. Ibid., p. 14.

Rundschau, as the organ of the Gesellschaft für Eingeborenen-schutz, continued to appear after World War I and stressed the interests of native populations, especially in Africa, rather than German territorial ambitions. Its editor was Diedrich Wester-mann.[20] Such publications, however, also tended to keep alive German interest in colonial policy and thus gave indirect assistance to the colonial agitators.

The extent to which old colonial officials, on the one hand, and economic—especially financial—interests, on the other, dominated the colonial movement during the Weimar period is startlingly illustrated by the list of participants in a conference called by Dr. Schnee in May 1930 to work out common guidelines for the activities of the various colonial associations:[21]

Herr T. Amsinck, Chairman, Wörmann and German East Africa Lines, Hamburg

Herr G. Baltrusch, Member, Reich Economic Council, Berlin

Dr. H. Bell, former Reich Minister, Member of the Reichstag (M.d.R.) Berlin (Center Party)

Dr. M. Cohen-Reuss, M.d.R., Hamburg (Social Democrat)

Herr W. Dauch, M.d.R., Hamburg (German People's Party)

Dr. B. Dernburg, former Reich Minister, M.d.R., Berlin (German Democratic Party)

Dr. E. Emminger, former Reich Minister, M.d.R., Munich (Bavarian People's Party)

Dr. Frisch, *Geheimer Rat,* Director, Dresdener Bank, Berlin

Herr T. Goldschmidt, Member of the Presidium of the Reich Association of German Industry, Berlin

Dr. A. Hahl, Governor (ret.), Director, New Guinea Co., Berlin

Herr E. Hamm, former Reich Minister, Berlin

Dr. Kastl, *Wirkl. Geheimer Rat,* Managing Director,

20. Ibid., p. 15. Lewin, p. 344.
21. Bundesarchiv, Solf Papers, file 131.

Member of the Presidium of the Reich Association of German Industry, Berlin

Dr. M. Kempner, former State Secretary, Berlin

Dr. H. Krämer, Member, Reich Economic Council, Berlin

Dr. W. Külz, former Reich Minister, M.d.R., Berlin (German Dem. Party)

Dr. F. v. Lindequist, *Wirkl. Geh. Rat,* Governor (ret.), Macherlust bei Eberswalde

Dr. H. Luther, President, Reichsbank

Dr. L. Quessel, M.d.R., Berlin (Social Democrat)

Freiherr A. von Rechenberg, *Wirkl. Geh. Rat,* Governor (ret.), Berlin

Herr O. Riedel, Director, Hamburg

Dr. J. Ruppel, *Ministerialdirektor* in the Foreign Office, Berlin

Herr H. Sachs, *Geh. Rat,* M.d.R., Berlin (German People's Party)

Dr. H. Schacht, former President, Reichsbank, Berlin

Dr. A. Salomonsohn, President, Diskonto-Gesellschaft, Berlin

Dr. E. Schultz-Ewerth, Governor (ret.), Berlin

Dr. T. Seitz, *Wirkl. Geh. Rat,* Governor (ret.), President, D.K.G., Berlin

Dr. W. Solf, Ambassador (ret.), former Reich Minister, Berlin

Dr. E. von Stauss, Director, Deutsche Bank and Diskonto-Gesellschaft, Berlin

Dr. A. Vögler, Director, United Steel Works, Dortmund

Herr Max M. Warburg, Banker, Hamburg

Herr W. Weigelt, Director, Deutsche Bank and Diskonto-Gesellschaft, Berlin

It is noteworthy that this high-powered group included two Socialist Reichstag members of the Revisionist persuasion, but— interestingly enough in view of what we shall have to say below —not a single National Socialist. A minor point of interest, especially in connection with the tenor of later Nazi colonial propaganda, is the presence of several Jewish personalities. At a later period they were to receive little credit for their efforts from their fellow colonial enthusiasts.

The guidelines agreed upon at this meeting, as reported by Schnee to the ex-governor and Colonial Minister, Wilhelm Solf, who had been unable to attend, in a letter of June 3, 1930,[22] also furnish an insight into the aims and techniques of the colonial movement during this period:

1. Equal rights for Germans living in the former colonies, now under the mandate of foreign power.

2. Protection of German culture in the mandates, free access for German missionaries, doctors, etc.

3. Continued criticism of the "Colonial Guilt Lie."

4. Combating attempts by the mandatory powers to annex the mandates as *de jure* colonies.

5. "Our own colonies are to be sought in view of the fact that some people are not yet ready to be independent, as was admitted by the Brussels meeting of the Socialist International in August 1928." (This is an interesting point in that it shows an effort to combat anticolonial liberal and socialist opinion by citing the views of other Socialists. We may surmise that Cohen-Reuss and Quessel urged the inclusion of this point.)

6. Encouragement of attempts by the government to gain mandates, as already begun by Stresemann.

7. Engaging in propaganda, especially among workers, aimed at strengthening the position of the government in making colonial demands. (This last point again hints at the importance the colonialists attached to gaining support among the Socialist workers.)

This program may be said to be as typical of the fairly moderate character of colonial agitation in the 20s as the people who formulated it were of the leadership of the colonial movement. One notes especially that the ultimate aim was mandates for Germany, not outright restitution of the former colonial empire with full sovereignty; and that the immediate goals were simply to assure that the mandatory powers lived up to their own obligations under

22. Ibid.

the Treaty of Versailles and that the relatively limited cultural and economic interests Germany still had in her former colonies were maintained, partly perhaps in order to keep alive a valid claim for those areas.

The number of organizations concerned with colonial matters and the fairly vociferous propaganda carried on in their voluminous publications may easily lead one to overestimate the importance of the colonialists, and particularly the impact they had on public opinion and public policy. The total membership of the colonial organizations was small. The largest of them, the DKG, claimed 30,000 members in 1926;[23] in later years, when all the groups were forcibly incorporated into the new RKB, their total membership amounted to only 40,000.[24] The same persons often belonged to several of these associations. The fairly exhaustive list of the main leaders of the colonialists given above, while it suggests that their influence was greater than the number of their followers would indicate, also shows the main weakness of the movement. These were almost without exception people with past colonial experience and/or vested interests in the colonies. Even a Socialist like Quessel had been a colonial specialist before the war. There was no younger generation of leaders, or followers with a truly spontaneous interest in the colonies. By and large it is true that "nobody talked of colonial questions in Germany in the post-war years, except for direct participants,"[25] and L. S. Amery, a British observer with considerable interest in this matter, correctly concluded that, compared to other brands of revisionism, colonial agitation was unimportant in the Weimar Republic.[26]

Still, the colonialists to some extent made up by their influence and articulateness what they lacked in numbers. They were especially well represented in the Reichstag, as members of practically all parties, and missed few opportunities to strike a blow for

23. A. L. C. Bullock, ed., *Germany's Colonial Demands* (London, 1939), p. 47.

24. Josef H. Krumbach, ed., *Franz Ritter von Epp: Ein Leben für Deutschland* (Munich, 1940), p. 269.

25. Maria Holtsch, *Die ehemaligen deutschen Südseekolonien im Wandel seit dem Weltkrieg* (diss., Marburg, 1934), p. 79.

26. L. S. Amery, *The German Colonial Claim* (London, 1939), p. 14.

their cause in that forum. Under the leadership of Dr. Schnee—the last German Governor of Tanganyika, who represented the German People's Party from 1924 to 1932[27]—an Inter-Party Colonial Association (Interfraktionelle Koloniale Vereinigung) was formed in 1925.[28] This group, which was effective in maintaining a nonpartisan united front whenever colonial matters came up for discussion, included members of all parties, from the German Nationalists to the Socialists.[29] The influence of the colonialists was not equally strong in all parties, but sufficient to ensure that all of them, with the exception of the Socialists and Communists, at least paid lip service to the colonial demands in their platforms and, as we shall see, to press the various governments of the Republic to maintain the colonial claim at least perfunctorily.[30]

Of the various political parties, the German People's Party (DVP, Deutsche Volkspartei), representing mainly the interests of industry and the upper middle class, was most strongly committed to colonial revision. It is no accident that Heinrich Schnee, the most important figure among the colonialists, represented that party in the Reichstag. Many other old colonial officials and businessmen with colonial interests were members of the DVP.[31]

The German Nationalist Party (DNVP, Deutschnationale Volkspartei), while programmatically maintaining the German colonial claim, was not particularly active in this respect. As the successor of the Conservative Party of the Empire, which had been the representative primarily of landed interests, it contained fewer individuals with direct ties to the colonies. It was clear, on the

---

27. *Das deutsche Führerlexikon; 1934/35* (Berlin, 1934), p. 429.

28. Dresler, p. 71.

29. Dix, p. 298. *Deutsche Kolonialzeitung, 45* (1933), 5.

30. Dresler, p. 71. Rayford W. Logan, *The African Mandates in World Politics* (Washington, 1948), pp. 30 ff. Mary E. Townsend, "The Contemporary Colonial Movement in Germany," *Political Science Quarterly, 43* (1928), 69–75. Bundesarchiv, Epp Papers, undated memorandum by Epp on the attitudes of various political parties toward the colonial cause. Prior to the 1930 Reichstag elections the Kolonialgesellschaft elicited statements favoring colonial revision from all parties except the KPD and SPD: Dix, p. 298.

31. Townsend, pp. 71–72.

other hand, that this right-wing group would not put itself into opposition to any "national" cause.[32]

The Democratic Party (DDP, Deutsche Demokratische Partei) was divided on this issue. As a liberal party it contained among its members individuals opposed to colonialism per se and traditional free traders, convinced of the economic uselessness of overseas possessions. It also spoke, however, for business, especially banking interests with a potential stake in economic overseas expansion. Hjalmar Schacht, the main champion of colonial revisionism on economic grounds, was a member of this party until 1926.[33] The former Colonial Secretary and banker Bernhard Dernburg was one of its Reichstag deputies. The result was that the Democratic press was often cool toward the demands of the colonial societies, while the parliamentary party tended to support them.[34]

Even more equivocal was the position of the Social Democratic Party (SPD, Sozialdemokratische Partei Deutschlands). A majority within the party, whose spokesman was Rudolf Breitscheid, opposed raising the colonial argument, partly because of considerations of principle (some of the arguments used against overseas colonies by Breitscheid bear a strong resemblance to Hitler's reasoning in *Mein Kampf*),[35] partly because of expediency. There were more important tasks for German foreign policy and it was unwise to bring up all the demands at the same time.[36] There was, on the other hand, the old revisionist wing of the party with its organ, the *Sozialistische Monatshefte,* which had been decidedly procolonial before and during World War I and maintained this attitude, bolstered by the fact that in addition to its old economic arguments for colonies it could now adduce considerations of equal rights for Germany and of wounded national honor. Since the leaders of the party were very sensitive to being accused of lack of patriotism, these were unanswerable arguments. Even

32. Bundesarchiv, Epp Papers, undated memorandum by Epp—see above, n. 30.

33. Matthias Schmitt, *Kolonien für Deutschland* (Stuttgart, 1939), p. 1.

34. Dresler, p. 71. Bundesarchiv, Epp Papers, undated memorandum (n. 30).

35. Logan, p. 46.

36. Ibid., p. 54.

Breitscheid demanded equal rights for Germany in the colonial as well as in all other spheres, although it is not quite clear what concrete steps were necessary in his view to vindicate these rights.[37] The Revisionists also had the support in this matter of Socialists in other countries. In 1919 the International Socialist Congress meeting in Lucerne had specifically condemned the clauses of the Peace Treaty that deprived Germany of her colonies,[38] and, as we have seen, the German colonial movement could cite the 1928 Brussels meeting of the Socialist International as supporting the argument that the continued administration of overseas areas by the European powers was necessary because some peoples were not yet ready for independence.[39] The trade union wing of the SPD was especially noted for its support of the colonial claim, often justified by the alleged economic necessity for colonies. Thus an official publication of the Trade Union Movement stated that "the exclusion of Germany from any participation in colonial activities is considered by the parties of the Left as not only an injustice but also an obstacle to the healthy development of her economic life."[40] We have already seen that prominent Socialist leaders joined the Bund für Koloniale Erneuerung, which advocated the return of the mandates to Germany and a colonial policy in which the welfare of the natives would be the primary consideration.[41] In general, leaders of the colonial movement seem to have felt that under certain conditions the opposition of the Socialists to their program would evaporate, especially if more workers could be convinced of their personal economic interest in colonies.[42]

The Center Party (Zentrum) and its Bavarian ally, the Bavarian People's Party (BVP, Bayerische Volkspartei), seem to have taken only a slight interest in colonial revision, although in both there

37. Ibid., p. 55.
38. Dix, p. 303.
39. Above, p. 4.
40. Quoted from Townsend, pp. 72–73.
41. Ibid., p. 72.
42. Deutsche Kolonialgesellschaft und Interfraktionelle Koloniale Vereinigung des Reichstags, *Deutschland in den Kolonien* (Berlin, 1926), pp. 30–31, 94–95.

were individuals who favored the colonial demand and supported it from the tribune of the Reichstag.[43]

Of all the political parties only the Communists opposed colonialism in any form, even taking a stand against Germany's appointing a member to the League's Permanent Mandates Commission.[44] In answer to the pleas of economic necessity the Communists pointed to the alternative of close economic cooperation with Russia as potentially more fruitful than colonial exploitation.[45] It is interesting to find here on the extreme left of the political spectrum the same concept, though in different form, of *Ostpolitik* as a substitute for *Weltpolitik,* which Hitler advocated in *Mein Kampf.*

As for the National Socialists, more will be said about their views on colonies later. It is sufficient to point out that despite Hitler's scruples, Nazi speakers in the Reichstag (especially Ernst Graf von Reventlow, Otto Strasser, and Franz Ritter von Epp) continued to call for a return of the colonies as a part of their campaign against Versailles.[46] The *Völkischer Beobachter,* the party's official newspaper, also advocated colonial revision throughout the Weimar period.[47]

Party programs and occasional speeches in the Reichstag, however, do not necessarily give a fair indication of public opinion. As a matter of fact, although it is possible, by studiously assembling every reference made to the colonies in the latter forum, to depict them as an important policy concern,[48] real colonial debates were extremely rare in the Weimar Reichstag. The only important ones were triggered by the negotiations surrounding Germany's entry into the League, when there seemed to be a slight possibility of a mandate being given to Germany, and by the British attempt to unite their East African possessions with Tanganyika in a "Closer Union" in 1927–29. This raised fears in Germany of Tanganyika's being annexed by the British Empire,

43. Reichstag, *Verhandlungen, 444,* 893; *392,* 9874–75.
44. Ibid., *393,* 11,005.
45. Logan, pp. 29–30.
46. Reichstag, *Verhandlungen,* e.g. *388,* 4469, 4548–62.
47. Dresler, p. 72.
48. Logan tends to fall into this error.

thus endangering the economic rights to which Germany as a League member was entitled under the principle of the Open Door prevailing in the mandates. This threat also afforded an opportunity to reaffirm Germany's claim to its former possessions.

If the Reichstag didn't take much interest in the colonial problem, the people at large took even less. Even leaders of the colonial movement admitted privately that they had an uphill fight in keeping any spark of "colonial will" alive and that the population at large was ignorant of and not interested in their cause because of problems that seemed to be of more immediate interest. In an undated memorandum, which was probably written around 1930, Epp asserted that the colonial problem was considered by the government as well as by the people to be "a question of the third order."[49]

Even among the business community, where support of the colonial movement was perhaps strongest, some financial and economic interests opposed any efforts to regain the German colonies, on the grounds that they would entail unnecessary costs and bring few economic advantages.[50] The former Colonial Secretary, Solf, reported to Schnee in 1930 his impression that there was little colonial enthusiasm among the Hamburg business community, which felt that it could buy colonial goods and raw materials as easily in foreign as in German possessions.[51] As a matter of fact, Solf himself tended to share this opinion of the economic uselessness of colonies and recommended that the colonial organizations drop their emphasis on economic arguments, which could easily be disproved, and instead base their demands on legal rights and German honor.[52] In short, while little evidence can be found of active opposition to colonies on a point of principle,[53] the general feeling in Germany was that this question either was entirely unimportant or that Germany should not demand her colonies back for practical reasons. One argument is of interest today:

49. Bundesarchiv, Epp Papers (n. 30).
50. Townsend, p. 74.
51. Bundesarchiv, Solf Papers, Solf to Schnee, June 23, 1930.
52. Ibid., Solf to Schnee, June 14, 1930.
53. For some exceptions see Mary E. Townsend, "The German Colonies and the Third Reich," *Political Science Quarterly*, 53 (1938), 186–206, esp. 187.

Germany as a nonimperial power enjoyed a special respect and sympathy among colonial peoples, which probably affected German trade favorably and could conceivably have become a political factor.[54] The Socialist Chancellor Hermann Müller expressed this idea in an article in *Europäische Gespräche* that is typical of the position of a majority within the SPD on the colonial question:

> Although the German Reich cannot be denied the right to colonial activity, and although the colonial guilt lie has no basis in our former colonial activity, the German Reich should not seek to acquire colonies for practical reasons. The German economy suffers from lack of capital. How can it raise the capital that would have to be invested in the colonies to initiate a useful colonial policy? At this time the Germans have the greatest prestige among the colonial peoples striving for independence, just because Germany does not participate in the colonial exploitation of foreign peoples. This fact must have favorable effects on Germany's trade.[55]

The apathy of the majority of Germans on the colonial question is further attested to by a questionnaire which in 1927 was sent out to 200 government officials by the Auswärtiges Institut of Hamburg University, asking them to express their views on the desirability of the return of the mandates to Germany. Only 50 persons replied at all; half of them were opposed to colonial revision.[56]

We may thus conclude that the colonial movement during the years of the Weimar Republic, while efficiently run and extremely active and articulate, failed to gain appreciable mass support for its cause or to make colonial revision into a major political issue. By and large, it remained the pet project of a small group of former colonial officials, military officers and entrepreneurs, aided by a number of businessmen and professional patriots. Only the

54. For an attempt to refute this argument see Paul Rohrbach, *Deutschlands Koloniale Forderung* (Hamburg, 1935), pp. 168–69.

55. *Europäische Gespräche* (Hamburg, December 1927), pp. 329–35.

56. Townsend, "The German Colonies and the Third Reich," p. 187; and "The Contemporary Colonial Movement in Germany," p. 75.

influential positions occupied by some of the colonialist leaders and the general German revulsion against the Versailles settlement as a whole enabled them to keep the flame of German overseas ambition alive.

This general situation did not change immediately upon Hitler's assumption of power. Some of the old colonial leaders were, as a matter of fact, apprehensive that the new Chancellor's views on colonies, as he had expressed them in *Mein Kampf,* would make the attainment of their objective impossible. Thus Solf, in a letter to his old colleague Schnee, dated October 2, 1933, asked "how the negative attitude of the *Führer* can be squared with the statements of the opposite tendency at colonial rallies" that had been made by various Nazi leaders.[57]

This was indeed a baffling contradiction. Hitler's "negative attitude" toward the colonial cause pervades the pages of *Mein Kampf.* He condemned "the totally impracticable, purely fantastic babble of inflated parlor patriots and bourgeois café politicians" who looked back to the glories of the Second Reich:

> On calm reflection no one will seriously deny that screaming for a new battle fleet, for recovery of our colonies, etc., is in reality nothing but silly gossip, without so much as a thought of practical application. The way in which the senseless outpourings of these knights of the protest meeting, some of them innocent, some of them insane, but all of them in the silent service of our mortal enemies, are exploited in England cannot be characterized as favorable to Germany.

We see here that colonial agitation was condemned primarily because it was likely to strain relations with England, which, according to Hitler's conception of foreign policy, had to be won as an ally by a Germany whose expansionist ambitions were to be satisfied in Eastern Europe. But even aside from this foreign policy consideration, the Führer felt that colonies could never be a substitute for European expansion: A territorial policy designed to "make the subsistence of the people as a whole more or less

57. Bundesarchiv, Solf Papers, file 131.

independent of foreign countries" in his view could not "be fulfilled in the Cameroons, but today exclusively in Eastern Europe." A colonial policy founded on an insufficient home base was considered by Hitler to be conducive to national weakness rather than strength: "Today many European states are like pyramids stood on their heads. Their European area is absurdly small in comparison to their weight in colonies, foreign trade, etc. We may say, summit in Europe, base in the rest of the world. . . . And from this comes . . . the weakness of most European colonial powers."

Part of this weakness, in Hitler's view, was caused by racial factors. Thus France had become "the hunting ground of African Negro hordes."

> Not only that she complements her army to an ever-increasing degree from her enormous empire's reservoir of colored humanity, but racially as well, she is making such progress in negrification that we can actually speak of an African state arising on European soil. . . . An immense self-contained area from the Rhine to the Congo, filled with a lower race gradually produced from continuous bastardization.[58]

No wonder some of the colonialists were apprehensive of the new government's policy in regard to their hobbyhorse. But even in Hitler's own statements there were also grounds for optimism: One passage in *Mein Kampf* clearly indicates that opposition to colonialism, like so much else in Nazi ideology, was not an absolute but was dictated merely by opportunism: "The orientation of the German national strength towards [*Weltpolitik*]," Hitler had written, "*without the most thoroughgoing previous securing of our position in Europe* was an absurdity."[59] This passage seems to indicate that a time might come, after Germany's continental ambitions had been achieved, when the Reich could become active overseas. Hitler went even further. In a statement issued before the 1930 Reichstag election he had, while maintaining his

58. Adolf Hitler, *Mein Kampf* (Boston, 1943), pp. 138, 139, 635, 644; cf. pp. 626, 645.
59. Ibid., p. 626. Italics in original.

18

position that Germany's primary goals lay in Eastern Europe, also taken a stand in favor of a new overseas empire:

> We stand for the return of the colonies, in the first place because we do not recognize as legal the theft of our colonies, and because we reject as an impertinent attack on our national honor the lying and monstrous assertion that the German people lack the ability to administer colonies, which served as an excuse for this theft.

> Our position regarding the colonial question in general is fixed by the third point of the National Socialist program: "We demand land and soil (colonies) for the feeding of our people and the settlement of our population surplus."

> In the first place we strive for the enlargement of our living space, necessary for the hemmed-in German people, by means of acquisition of territory in Europe adjoining the existing Reich. Such acquisition of territory is immensely more necessary for the preservation and healthy development of our national substance and for the power-political position of the German Reich than the acquisition of territory overseas.

> We do not deny the value which overseas colonies can have for settlement and for the supply of our national economy with raw materials.

> We also do not by any means oppose any possible future new colonial acquisitions, as far as they are useful for the purpose mentioned.

> But we must guard against the attention of the German people being diverted by colonial endeavors—perhaps intentionally—from more important things.

> As long as the German Reich itself remains a tributary exploitation colony of foreign countries and of international high finance, colonial endeavors must take second place to the necessity to regain, first of all, our national independence. And more important than the supply of overseas products remains the possibility of

feeding the German people in Central Europe in case of war.

Possible colonial acquisitions must never be bought by giving up such vital necessities of the German people.

(Signed) Adolf Hitler[60]

In addition, as Solf pointed out, various prominent figures in the Nazi Party had always endorsed the colonial claim. Most of the colonialists, moreover, were conservative in their political sympathies and thus quite ready to embrace a regime, which, for the time being, emphasized its conservative side. The National Socialists also had at all times been among the most vociferous groups in condemning the Versailles "Dictate." How could they therefore accept permanently what Hitler himself had characterized as "the rape of our colonies"?[61] The *Kolonialzeitung* expressed its hope that the new regime's "rejection of internationalism" in economics and politics would lead it to embrace the colonial claim and would also stimulate new colonial interest among the people at large,[62] and Heinrich Schnee, who had an interview with Hitler in March 1933, hailed the establishment of his government as the "dawn of a new era from which we may expect the final attainment of our colonial goal."[63]

To show their readiness to cooperate with the government the colonialists revamped their organizational structure to conform to the Nazis' Leadership Principle. The DKG reorganized its subdivisions so that they would coincide with the NSDAP *Gaue* and gave its president almost absolute power. The president (still Schnee) now appointed a Working Committee, which carried on the affairs of the organization. The Presidium (*Vorstand*) was composed of this Committee, twenty-one members appointed by the President, twenty-one appointed by a delegates' convention, and the honorary members of the DKG. Representatives of the

---

60. Berlin Document Center, file 1294. This statement is undated, but seems to date from 1930.

61. Hitler, p. 626.

62. *Deutsche Kolonialzeitung, 45* (1933), 98.

63. Townsend, "The German Colonies and the Third Reich," p. 194.

most important branches of the new structure of the National Socialist State were members.[64] All colonial youth organizations were first united in a Jungkolonialer Ring in June 1933 and later in the year were incorporated in the Hitler Youth as Kolonialscharen, with which the DKG retained only a loose connection in an advisory role. The new Kolonialreferent of the Hitler Youth, Captain von Ötzen, an old colonial himself, was appointed to the standing committee of the new cover organization of the remaining colonial associations, Reichskolonialbund (RKB).[65]

This was essentially the old KORAG, suitably refurbished in line with the Führerprinzip and dominated, like its predecessor, by the DKG and its president.[66] For the first few years of the Third Reich the colonial movement thus continued to exist as a group of private citizens. Clearly, however, its position as a private group with political aims was an abnormal one in a totalitarian state, and it is not surprising that the Party soon began to take an official interest in the colonial problem. In May 1934 the Party established a Kolonialpolitisches Amt (KPA) by separating the Kolonialpolitisches Referat of the Wehrpolitisches Amt from the latter agency. The former chief of the Wehrpolitisches Amt, General Franz Ritter von Epp, was named head of the KPA.[67] The new organization was divided into three sections: Section I, Personnel and Business, was originally headed by SA Sturmbannführer Dillmann; Section II, under SS Standartenführer Paul Schnöckel, an old colonial soldier, was responsible for indoctrination; and Section III (NSKK Obersturmführer Himmelreich) handled press matters. The KPA was responsible for colonial indoctrination within the Party, and for supervising and "guiding" all colonial discussion within the German press.[68]

The leader of the new office, General Franz Ritter von Epp, had been a colonial enthusiast long before he joined the Nazi

64. *Das deutsche Führerlexikon*, 1934/35 (Berlin, 1934), p. 136.

65. *Deutsche Kolonialzeitung*, 45 (1933), 167.

66. Ibid., p. 140. Josef Viera, *Kolonien in Blickfeld von heute* (Düsseldorf, 1940), p. 136. Townsend, "The German Colonies and the Third Reich," p. 193.

67. *Verordnungsblatt der Reichsleitung der NSDAP* (Munich, 1934), p. 160.

68. Krumbach, *Franz Ritter von Epp*, pp. 264–65. KPA, Tätigkeitsbericht (1942), pp. 54–59.

Party. In this respect he is typical of the leaders of the colonial movement during the Third Reich. For the most part, they were men with some overseas experience, often military, who were active in the colonial movement during the Weimar period and joined the Nazi Party when it appeared to take a more uncompromising stand against the Versailles settlement than any other political group and was therefore most likely to raise the colonial claim. The colonial grievance was, after all, primarily a part of the whole complex of national grievances created by Versailles. It is not surprising, then, that most of the colonialist leaders of the 20s were nationalists on other issues as well, and that for many of them joining the most radical nationalists of all was a natural step. Still, they were basically conservatives, primarily interested in restoring the glories of the Second Empire, and were not always comfortable among their new comrades and not quite in agreement with the more radical and novel aspects of the Nazi Weltanschauung. Epp's career demonstrates all this rather well.

Epp was born in Munich in 1868. He gained his colonial experience with the German Expeditionary Corps sent to China following the Boxer Rebellion. During his stay in the Far East he tended to follow his Emperor's advice to put the fear of God into the Chinese by acting like the Huns of old a bit too literally. He narrowly escaped a court-martial for plundering and beating up a Chinese policeman. Epp was bitter that others did not share his conviction that "these people must ruthlessly be shown who is master."[69] Following his stint in China, he served in German Southwest Africa during the Herero and Hottentot Wars of 1904–07. Like so many colonialists of the old school, he seemed to like natives better the more primitive they were. In occasional reports written for German newspapers, he had many kind words to say about his enemies, the Hereros, their bravery and the intelligence with which they carried on their resistance to the German army.[70] Also typical of many Germans with overseas experience was his high opinion of the British, whom he got to know during a leave spent in Capetown. He commented on their quiet manners and the absence of barrack-room mannerisms among British

69. Krumbach, *Franz Ritter von Epp*, p. 161.
70. Ibid., p. 198.

officialdom. "The official is here to help, not to control or even to give orders."71

Epp's military record during World War I was outstanding. Serving on all the major fronts in Europe, he rose to the rank of general and corps commander. For his valor he was decorated with the Maximilian Order, which carried with it a patent of personal nobility. Epp's popularity among his men, in whose welfare he took an exceptional interest at all times, stood him in good stead after the war, when he raised one of the free corps that liberated Munich from its short-lived Soviet regime. Most of the members of Epp's unit were veterans of his old corps. During this brief campaign he seems to have gotten on exceptionally well with his superior, the Socialist War Minister Gustav Noske.

While still in active service Epp became involved in right-wing politics. As early as December 1920 he gave financial aid to the *Völkischer Beobachter* out of his private fortune. During the Nazis' short-lived uprising in November 1923 he played as ambiguous a role as most of his fellow officers in Munich. Originally he seems to have encouraged the conspirators to count on his support. On November 9, however, while trying to prevent bloodshed, he took action against them. At any rate, he was among the officers retired from the army following this episode, which at the same time alienated him temporarily from the National Socialists. During the mid-20s he joined the BVP. In 1924 he succeeded General Märcker as President of the Colonial Veterans' Organization, the Kolonialkriegerbund. In that capacity he was one of the most vocal advocates of colonial revision. He also vigorously defended the interests of the army. Feeling that these interests were neglected by the governments of the day, Epp conceived a special resentment against Foreign Minister Gustav Stresemann (who, by the way, shared the General's views on the colonial question to a far greater extent than any of the other leading Weimar politicians) and thus readily agreed when the Nazis in 1928 offered him an opportunity to oppose Stresemann for a Bavarian Reichstag seat. Epp joined the NSDAP for this particular purpose, openly explaining his motives and reservations in the *Völkischer*

71. Ibid., p. 237.

Beobachter.[72] In particular, he made no secret of his royalist leanings, refused to be critical of "other national parties," and expressed mild aversion to the "edges and roughness" of the Nazi movement, which, however, he ascribed to its "youthful" character. On another occasion in 1928 Epp sharply contradicted the Nazis' main foreign policy demand, eastward expansion,[73] which he lampooned as "Ostlandreiterei."

Epp's personal popularity in Bavaria helped him gain a Reichstag seat as one of only twelve Nazi members. As one of the few high-ranking officers of the old army who had joined the Party at that time, he became its official military policy spokesman, while not neglecting colonial agitation within and outside the NSDAP. In 1932 the Party established an Office of Military Policy to plan rearmament measures. Epp became the head of that agency and in that capacity attended the Geneva disarmament talks as the NSDAP representative in the German delegation. He also established a colonial section within the office.

After the Nazis' advent to power and the beginnings of *Gleichschaltung,* Epp was appointed Reichsstatthalter of Bavaria, in reality a figurehead position with few responsibilities. Epp, in whose politics Bavarian particularism always played a certain role, so misjudged the real situation as to stress "Bavarian rights" in his inaugural speech and to refer to the "Bavarian Fatherland."[74] How powerless he was became apparent in the following year, when he vainly tried to smooth some of the "edges and roughness" of the Nazi movement by preventing the murders of the so-called SA-Purge.

We have already mentioned that in 1934 Epp also became head of the new KPA (colonial office) of the NSDAP. (The Military Policy Office was dissolved in 1935, ostensibly because its work had been completed with the achievement of "military sovereignty.")

Throughout the prewar years Epp continued to sound the colonial theme within Germany and during several visits abroad. He established particularly close relations with the colonial agencies

72. May 10, 1928.
73. Bundesarchiv, Epp Papers, file 24/1.
74. Krumbach, *Franz Ritter von Epp,* pp. 115–16, 125.

of Fascist Italy, whose regime and policy were perhaps really closer to Epp's personal political convictions than Hitler's. Despite his nominally high rank in the Nazi hierarchy as a Reichsleiter, Epp never was a member of the inner circle around Hitler; in fact, he was seldom in Berlin. These facts must be borne in mind when appraising the real position of the German colonial movement within and vis-à-vis the Nazi Party. After a relatively brief moment of glory in 1940–41, when the power over an empire as Nazi Germany's first colonial minister seemed almost within Epp's grasp, he subsided again into such obscurity that the Allies did not even attempt to arraign him before one of the postwar trials of Nazi leaders. Toward the very end of World War II, in April 1945, Epp seems to have been implicated in the abortive revolt of the "Freedom Action Bavaria," an anti-Nazi resistance group, and was arrested by Gauleiter Paul Giesler. Shortly thereafter he came into the custody of United States forces, where he died on the last day of 1946.[75]

The founding of the KPA within the Nazi Party structure still left the old colonial organizations functioning alongside it as voluntary associations of private citizens. The agitation carried on by them was not openly endorsed by state or party, even though the KPA supervised and to some extent directed their activities, especially as far as publications were concerned. The cordiality of relations between local party leaders and the colonial organizations depended upon the personal views of the leaders. Thus, at a rally of the RKB in Frankfurt in 1933, at which Epp was the main speaker, the local party authorities manifested their full support of the colonial cause. SA, SS, and Hitler Youth formations were sent to participate, and there was talk of a "Colonial and National Socialist fighting brotherhood." On that occasion, incidentally, as on a number of others during the early period of Nazi rule, Epp had to appease the unspoken impatience of the colonialists: "The hour will come when we shall unfurl the colonial banner. Until then the German people must entirely fill themselves with colonial will." The patent meaning of this pas-

---

75. For a brief biography of Ritter von Epp see *Neue Deutsche Biographie*, herausgegeben von der Historischen Kommission der Bayerischen Akademie der Wissenschaften (Munich, 1955–), *4*, 547–48.

sage was that the colonial organizations were to confine themselves, at least for the time being, to drumming up enthusiasm
within Germany. In Bremen, also, the local party leader,
Gauleiter Carl Röver, strongly supported the colonial movement.[76]

In Hamburg, however, the colonial leaders had no such support
from the authorities. In 1935 they therefore invited Epp to address their annual colonial rally, hoping that he, as a high party
official, would produce "a decisive impression on State and Party
in Hamburg, which in colonial matters had heretofore been very
much reserved." Epp insisted upon full cooperation from the
authorities as a condition for his coming, and, in a conference
with the Lord Mayor and the local office of the Propaganda Ministry, it was finally agreed that the rally would have "friendly
support" from state and party agencies, although it was not possible, "for political reasons," to have it officially sponsored. We
must remember that the Anglo-German Naval Agreement had
been concluded only recently and that Hitler's political tack of
the moment called for friendly relations with England. Thus we
find Epp's speech quite moderate in tone: "We cannot take colonies from another country. The earth is distributed from pole to
pole. But to our old colonies we have an indisputable legal
right."[77]

Two documents illustrate the position of the colonial movement during the early years of the Nazi period rather well. The
first is a letter dated May 31, 1933, from Dr. Karl Jung, who was
to become Epp's deputy at the KPA, to Major Weigel, a German
leader in Southwest Africa:

> The position taken by the Reich Chancellor towards
> the colonial problem is, at present, a very circumspect
> one, especially as the influence of the Party over the
> Foreign Office is not very strong.
>
> An endeavor is, however, being made to give colonial
> thought an unofficial impetus, that is, purely from the
> Party. With this end in view the various colonial organi-

76. *Deutsche Kolonialzeitung, 45* (1933), 139–40.
77. Bundesarchiv, Epp Papers, file 22/5.

zations were combined, that is, within the DKG. [Actually, this refers to the RKB.] I sincerely trust that this union will shortly be complete . . .[78]

And in a speech delivered in the spring of 1933 Epp explained the situation even more clearly:

Many surely thought: Now, with the national government in power, the big negro drum of colonial propaganda will surely be beaten; only military music will be heard from now on.

But it isn't happening that way; the national government conducts itself very cautiously. This is due to a situation which we simply have to face: Those who surround us have not after all changed their wholly hostile attitude toward us. It is not surprising that a nationally minded people receive hostile treatment when it refuses to be plundered any longer. The ring around us has become tighter, as it did for Italy when it became Fascist.

But you must not lose sight of the guidelines of colonial propaganda. If we want to achieve our aim, we must have a source of power, a means of applying pressure. We must, if we want to get something, also offer something in return. Our government is not yet in the position to be able to offer anything or to apply strong pressure . . . In four months or a year one cannot regain what has been systematically ruined during fourteen years. Thus the Reich government can approach the colonial question only cautiously, for [to raise it] would mean [to ask for] a revision of the Versailles Treaty.

But the free political associations are not bound to this cautious treatment of the colonial question and precisely now, when the Reich government is obligated . . . to put the colonial question behind other problems, it is the task of our people and of the natural bearers of the colonial movement to keep this thought alive and not allow the impression to arise that the whole German

78. Benjamin Bennett, *Hitler over Africa* (London, 1939), p. 179.

people has given up the colonies and has forgotten this question. . . .

It is the task of the associations . . . not to let the enemies assume that their plunder is now secure. This work we have to keep up until [the government] is in a position to raise the claim and to back it up. Having a government like the present one . . . we must not lose our confidence in it if for once it acts with restraint . . . In good time it will put on its military boots and act differently . . .[79]

We may conclude that in the early years of its rule the National Socialist government found it advantageous for its foreign policy to allow colonial activity to be carried on by private organizations, under some control by a party agency (the KPA). Thus colonial propaganda that offended British sensibilities could be disavowed, if necessary, as not reflecting governmental thinking. We shall see in discussing the foreign policy aspect of the colonial problem that this thinking was not yet by any means definitely fixed.

In 1936, however, the rulers of Germany began to push the colonial claim in international discussions. At the same time, the colonial movement ceased to be even nominally a private affair and became a segment of the party apparatus—which at that point of the development of German totalitarianism was only formally distinguishable from the state machinery. We shall see how in later years Epp wanted Germany's leaders to go even further and to make his growing colonial bureaucracy an official part of the Reich administration. In the event, this was never done, even though during the early war years the KPA definitely worked for the state. But this belongs to a later chapter of our story.

The new phase of colonial agitation began with the formation of a new Reichskolonialbund (RKB) on May 12, 1936.[80] Unlike the organization that had existed under the same name since 1933, the new League was open to individual members, rather than being a cover organization for various colonial groups. Moreover, it was to monopolize all colonial activity in Germany. The DKG

---

79. Krumbach, *Franz Ritter von Epp*, pp. 261–63.
80. *Deutsche Kolonialzeitung, 48* (1936), 195.

dissolved itself in June to join the new League, its leaders admitting their essential failure in making the colonial grievance a popular cause and expressing their hope that the RKB would be "better able to impart colonial enthusiasm to the masses of the people."[81] The other colonial groups still in existence received, in September 1936, a "suggestion" from the Gestapo to dissolve themselves "voluntarily" by November 15 of that year. "Should these organizations not comply with the demand, they are to be dissolved compulsorily."[82] An exception was made for the Kolonialkriegerbund, whose president, General von Epp, now became the Bundesführer of the RKB, thus having complete charge of all colonial activities.

CHART 1

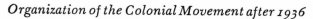

Organization of the Colonial Movement after 1936

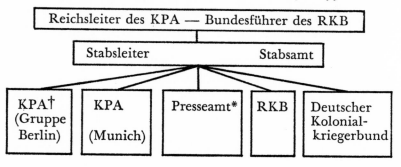

†Liaison with government
*Responsible for all publications of the colonial organizations and
for treatment of the colonial problem in the daily press

A retired rear admiral and SS Standartenführer, Wilhelm Rümann held the position of Stabsleiter until 1938. Like most of the higher leadership of the movement, including his successor,

81. Ibid., pp. 167–68.
82. Berlin Document Center, Reichskolonialbund, Ordner 212, letter from Geheime Staatspolizeiamt Darmstadt to local police authorities of September 19, 1936.

Korvettenkapitän Richard Wenig, he had personal experience in the colonies, having participated in the Herero campaign.

While the RKB had been founded by the direct order of Hitler,[83] it was not until April 1937 that its status within the Party-State and the scope of its activities were clearly defined. The interval, during which the RKB built up its Gau and Kreis organizations and embarked upon a vigorous membership campaign,[84] was marked by a relative absence of colonial activity, since the various agencies of the party had been ordered by Bormann in a directive of October 15, 1936, to desist from "any colonial propaganda or other assistance to the Kolonialbund" until further orders.[85]

These orders were issued by the Führer's deputy, Rudolf Hess, on April 3, 1937:

> The Führer has decided on the new regulations, referred to in directive 131/36, as follows:
>
> 1. The membership of the RKB shall be limited to 1,000,000.
>
> 2. The task of the RKB includes, in general, colonial indoctrination and enlightenment at home, as well as the cultural and welfare tasks in the colonies delegated to it.
>
> 3. The Bundesführer will take steps in matters touching on foreign policy only in agreement with Ambassador von Ribbentrop. Liaison officials have been appointed for both sides.
>
> 4. The work of the RKB among women is to be reorganized in such manner that the philosophical [weltanschauliche] indoctrination of the women will be under the control of the Reichsfrauenführerin and that their indoctrination and training for colonial tasks may be accomplished only in cooperation with her.

83. Hans Ulrich Freiherr von Wangenheim, *Kolonien des Dritten Reiches* (Berlin, 1939), pp. 9–10.

84. The documents in Ordner 212, Reichskolonialbund, Berlin Document Center, provide insight into these purely organizational activities.

85. Ibid.

5. The officials, both male and female, of the RKB, which, incidentally, does not possess the privileges of an organization of the Party, are to be appointed with the consent of the officers of the Party.

The Party, its substructure, and its member organizations will aid the Bund in the accomplishment of its tasks according to directives to be issued by the Reichs-propagandaleiter.

(Signed) Hess[86]

The directive indicates some of the reasons for the long delay in its formulation. Apparently the jealousies of the leaders of various other party agencies who feared that the new RKB might encroach upon their domains was a major factor. There is evidence, however, that Hitler himself still did not want to go all out with a colonial campaign. Despite the absence of objections from the Party's Foreign Policy Office (Ribbentrop) and from the Minister of Interior, he refused, as late as March 1937, to grant the RKB the right to show a swastika flag.[87] The membership limitation to one million and the status of the RKB as an associated organization rather than as a branch of the Party are other indications that Hitler was not yet quite ready to fully unleash the colonialists. But the restrictions were removed in short order. By October 1937 the leadership of the Colonial League rejoiced in a swastika flag and in the fact that "at the same time the barriers have been removed which heretofore hindered the RKB in dealing with foreign nations."[88] We shall see how, during this period, the colonies came to play an ever greater role in the foreign policy of the Third Reich. As for the membership restriction, it fell as soon as the RKB reached the million mark set for it

---

86. Ibid.

87. Correspondence about this matter in Bundesarchiv, Reichskanzlei files, file R43II—130.

88. Berlin Document Center, Reichskolonialbund, Ordner 212, letter from Kreisverbandsleitung Neustadt a.d.S., of the RKB to local groups, dated October 25, 1937.

in 1938.[89] When the League ceased its activities in early 1943, it had 2,100,000 members.[90]

The formal distinction made between the RKB and the official Party apparatus proved to be of no importance. In effect the RKB acted and was treated as an arm of the Party. Thus local organizations were instructed to make use of SA leaders in establishing new groups, and the SS provided for wounded veterans among its members by assigning them positions as RKB organizers.[91] Other party agencies laid down in detail the guidelines for the propaganda activities of the League.[92] Party organizations such as the SS, SA, and HJ were urged to aid the RKB's propaganda efforts by furnishing posters, bands, and personnel for the distribution of propaganda material, etc. In short, after 1937 the RKB became, for all practical purposes, an instrument of the totalitarian Party-State, carrying out the purposes of the latter.

The organizational scheme of the League provided for a Colonial Council (Kolonialrat) and a Members' Committee to advise the Bundesführer. The former consisted of twenty-seven outstanding personalities of the old colonial movement, the party, the state, the economic community, and the sciences. Its president was the former governor and colonial secretary Friedrich von Lindequist. Its tasks were largely technical-scientific ones, subcommittees being formed for Tropical Hygiene and Medical Affairs, Native and Labor Problems (under another former governor, Dr. Albert Hahl, who had gained his colonial experience in the Pacific), and Colonial Communications. As a matter of fact, very little was heard of the Kolonialrat or its members after its formation. Its main use seems to have been as a dead-end spur on which to park the old non-Nazi colonialists.

The Membership Committee, composed of certain appointed

89. Nachrodt, p. 25.

90. Berlin Document Center, Reichskolonialbund, Ordner 212, Aktenvermerk of March 5, 1943.

91. *Mitteilungsblatt der Bundesführung des Reichskolonialbundes* (Munich, June 15, 1937), p. 22; Circular from SS Oberabschnitt Fulda-Werra to local SS units of May 20, 1941. Both in Berlin Document Center, RKB, Ordner 212.

92. Undated memorandum from Dienststelle Ribbentrop [1937], Berlin Document Center, Hauptarchiv, file 1294.

representatives in addition to the leaders of the Gau organizations and the members of the Kolonialrat, also was purely advisory in function and played a very minor role.

While the Business Office of the League was located in Berlin, Epp himself stayed in Munich, where he was aided by a fairly large staff section. The Business Office, as the executive of the League, was subdivided as follows:

Section I. Propaganda

Section II. Colonial Training and Indoctrination, Science and Scholarship (this section was responsible for the large Colonial Library, "inherited" from the DKG)

Section III. Organization and Personnel

Section IV. Cultural Tasks

Section V. Colonial Welfare

Section VI. Treasurer

Section VII. Publications

These sections performed their tasks in close cooperation, frequently in personal union with the corresponding sections of the KPA. The differentiation between the KPA as an official Party organ and the RKB as a voluntary association within the Party was, as we have already pointed out, mere fiction.

The work of Section I, Propaganda, included the largest part of the RKB's activities. The whole rationale of the RKB was, after all, that it was necessary to instill in the German people a strong desire and enthusiasm for colonies which would strengthen the government's hand when the time came to take steps (the exact nature of which was seldom discussed) to regain them. The RKB was to create a basis of "colonial will," a favorite phrase in RKB publications, "to which the Führer, as the great molder of German foreign policy, will one day show the way and direction, when the time for it has come."[93] We find occasional optimists who believed that a strong "colonial will" was all that was needed to make Great Britain and the other mandatory powers willing to hand over the colonies.[94] Epp was more realistic and admitted, once war had come, that the colonial problem was a question of power: "When Germany is master in Europe, the question of

93. Nachrodt, p. 40.
94. Rohrbach, p. 182.

33

colonies will solve itself." He believed, presumably, although we will never find such an idea expressed under the Nazi regime, that "colonial will" was necessary to force the German government, i.e. Hitler, to demand colonies at some future conference table.

Propaganda among the general population was carried on in various ways. Frequent colonial rallies, staged with all the pomp and circumstance typical of Nazi gatherings, provided a forum for Epp and other RKB leaders, as well as for old colonials like Governor Schnee and General von Lettow-Vorbeck, the one bona fide colonial hero World War I had produced. Such rallies generally received wide press coverage, which carried their effect beyond the immediate participants.[95] Another favorite propaganda device was traveling exhibitions, designed to spread the colonial gospel by showing samples of the goods that the colonies could supply Germany with, as well as graphs, pictures, and other visual material. By 1939 three such exhibitions were touring cities throughout Germany.[96] Such activities were arranged in close cooperation with the Propaganda Ministry.[97] For groups throughout the country the RKB provided specially trained "colonial speakers," as well as pictorial material.[98] Needless to say, these speakers were held to an exact official line, annually laid down by the KPA. The 1939 version of this "speaker's guide" outlined the scope of colonial agitation as follows:

I. There can be no colonial policy for its own sake. German needs must be the measuring stick for all foreign policy. Germany's "own" colonial empire is the "basis of consideration" for territorial demands.

II. Colonies are needed because of Germany's lack of space. They are to provide raw materials and markets. The four-year plan can be no substitute for colonies. Mass settlement is not among the reasons for Germany's colonial claim, although the colonies might provide a

---

95. See, e.g., *Deutsche Kolonialzeitung, 47* (1935), 93, 145 ff.; Bundesarchiv, Epp Papers, files 23/1, 23/3; Krumbach, *Franz Ritter von Epp*, p. 272; Townsend, "The German Colonies and the Third Reich," p. 195.

96. *Deutsche Kolonialzeitung, 51* (1939), 207–32, 260.

97. Townsend, "The German Colonies and the Third Reich," p. 195.

98. Nachrodt, pp. 29–30. *Deutsche Kolonialzeitung, 50* (1938), 13.

suitable area to resettle German overseas communities under the flag of the Reich. Aside from their material value, colonies must be sought by the Reich in order to provide German youth with a testing ground for character. [This argument, as farfetched and absurd as it seems, was one of the staples of colonial agitation, which will be further analyzed below.]

III. There must never be any reference to "former" colonies. [Among the individuals who broke this commandment was the Führer himself!] The return of Germany's rightful possessions must be brought about peacefully. [This point is supported by quotes from Hitler speeches.] The following reasons must be stated for the colonial demand: (1) National honor. (2) Equality of rights for Germany. (3) Legal claim to colonies taken from Germany under the justification of the "colonial guilt lie," which had been conclusively disproved. (4) Economic necessity. (5) "Ethical reasons": Germany must be allowed to contribute its share to the work of civilization.

IV. An account should be given of the prewar history of the German overseas possessions.

V. The war in the colonies and their loss as a result of the Versailles Treaty should be discussed by stressing especially the "swindle" surrounding Point 5 of Wilson's Fourteen Points, the fact that the whole Versailles settlement was forced upon a helpless Germany, the setting up of the mandate system, and the instances in which the Allies had broken the rules laid down under it. It must be pointed out that what Germany wants are its own colonies, as it possessed them in 1914. "Under no circumstances may colonies of foreign powers, least of all specific ones, be mentioned as desiderata."

VI. Colonial Guilt. Allegations against the German colonial regime must be rejected. The "colonial guilt" of "the others" must be stressed: Nonobservance of the Congo Act at the outbreak of World War I,[99] militariza-

99. The German colonialists propagated a myth that the Allies had broken the Congo Act by initiating military operations against the German overseas

tion of the natives, attack on private property through confiscation of German colonial holdings after the war, etc.

VII. Development of the colonies after the war. Here it must be pointed out that the colonies have been neglected by the mandatory powers and that Germany would be far more willing and able to realize their economic potential.

VIII. Germany and the European colonial tasks. The so-called "race guilt lie," i.e. the allegation that Nazi racial doctrines made the Reich unfit to rule over non-Aryan populations, must be attacked and its racial policy described as one which especially qualifies Germany as a colonial power.[100]

The guidelines were followed with remarkable faithfulness, not only by colonial speakers but also by the authors of books and pamphlets on the colonial problem, scores of which appeared during the prewar years, remarkable chiefly for their sameness and the unending repetition of arguments identical to the ones laid down in the Richtlinien.

A special concern of the RKB's propaganda apparatus was to keep alive colonial interest among Germany's youth by means of agitation in the schools. The old DKG had always paid a certain amount of attention to this field and had scored some remarkable successes: As early as 1919 the Socialist Prussian Minister of Education, Konrad Hänisch, had directed school authorities to see to it that the former colonies continued to be given room in the public school curricula.[101] The Foreign Office of the Weimar Republic encouraged the education authorities to keep alive and

---

possessions. As a matter of fact, the Act merely provided that the colonies within the Conventional Congo Basin could be declared neutral, by mutual consent, in the event of a European war.

100. "Richtlinien für die Kolonialpolitische Schulung," *Deutscher Kolonial-dienst; Ausbildungsblätter der Reichsleitung des Kolonialpolitischen Amtes der NSDAP* (Munich, January 1939), pp. 12–16. MS in Institut für Zeitgeschichte, Munich.

101. Jacob, pp. 72–73.

strengthen the realization of the importance of overseas possessions among German youth.[102] A later Prussian minister of education, Adolf Grimme, took an anticolonial position, but his policies were revoked when Prussia came under Reich administration in 1932.[103] The DKG, through its Colonial Youth Committee, stood ready to supplement the regular curriculum by providing schools with speakers, films, and other propaganda material.

Nazi educational authorities were friendly to the colonial cause from the outset. Minister Bernhard Rust published a decree in August 1933 which required schools to aid in the "fight for German living space" by scheduling special talks on the colonies and encouraging the circulation of *Jambo,* the DKG's periodical for young people, among their pupils.[104] Hans Schemm, the leader of the National Socialist Teachers League, declared in a speech in June 1934 that "one of the most important tasks of the school and of the German educator is to continue to awaken and to strengthen the colonial interest of our children."[105]

It was felt that much remained to be done in overcoming the lack of knowledge about the colonies that prevailed among German youth.[106] To this end, generous doses of colonial propaganda were included in the curriculum, especially of secondary schools,[107] and the colonial organizations aided the educational authorities by supplying speakers, literature, visual aids, pictures, and films for special programs.[108]

Colonial propaganda among young people was also carried on by the Hitler Youth, whose chief, Baldur von Schirach, considered colonies as important to Germany, though in a different way, as eastward expansion. HJ boys and BDM girls were told that the

102. Ibid., p. 72.

103. Ibid., p. 73.

104. H. W. Bauer, *Kolonien im Dritten Reich, 1* (Cologne, 1936), 184. *Deutsche Kolonialzeitung, 45* (1933), 100. Schmitt, p. 1.

105. Schmitt, p. 1.

106. Bauer, 2, 209–10.

107. *Deutscher Kolonialdienst* (November 1938), pp. 11–12. Heinrich Schnee, *Geschichtsunterricht in Völkischen Nationalstaat* (Bochum, 1936), pp. 104–09. (The author is not the former Governor and President of the DKG.)

108. KPA, Tätigkeitsbericht (1942), p. 57.

"task of our policy in regard to population is the concentration and rooting of the German in his home soil, especially in the East. Colonial property overseas, on the other hand, is important as a raw material source, as a field for training in world experience, and as a visible sign of our equal right in the world."[109] Special Kolonialreferenten were responsible for colonial agitation in Hitler Youth units, and some HJ leaders were sent to the colonies to gain overseas experience.[110]

Colonial agitation in the Hitler Youth as well as in other party branches was technically a responsibility of the KPA's Indoctrination section. In practice, however, that section was almost identical, with respect to personnel and activities, with the RKB's Section II,[111] and the activities of the two offices may be discussed together.

"Colonial training and indoctrination" covered a number of activities. The RKB's own functionaries were trained through regular courses (Kolonialpolitische Reichslehrgänge) at the RKB's school at Ladeburg-Bernau.[112] Originally these courses merely trained them as agitators according to the Richtlinien cited above. Later, especially during the war years, regular training courses for colonial officials were also held at Ladeburg, and elsewhere; we shall discuss them later. The Indoctrination section saw to colonial "schooling" in local party branches, for which special Kolonialreferenten were appointed on the Gau level of the Party hierarchy.[113] A circular from the Oberste SA Führung to all SA units of November 30, 1938, stressed the necessity for greatly intensified colonial propaganda in the SA and requested that SA leaders be sent to KPA training courses.[114] Colonial

---

109. Bauer, *1*, 18. Schmitt, p. 1.

110. Bauer, *1*, 184–86.

111. Paul Rohrbach, ed., *Afrika—Beiträge zu einer praktischen Kolonialkunde* (Berlin, 1943), p. 280.

112. Ibid., p. 281.

113. Circulars from Reichsorganisationsleiter, Hauptschulungsamt, dated November 2, 1937, and March 20, 1939, Berlin Document Center, Reichsorganisationsleiter, Ordner 311.

114. Berlin Document Center, Kolonialpolitisches Amt, Ordner 211.

propaganda work was also undertaken in the Labor Service, some camps of which were named for colonial heroes,[115] and in the armed forces and police units.[116] On a local level, the RKB offered lectures and courses of various sorts—in African languages, for example—to which members of Party branches, such as the SS, were specially invited.[117]

Section II was also responsible for liaison with the many colonial scientific and scholarly institutions in Germany, ranging from an Institute for Colonial Mining to the "Academy for German Right," a politicolegal group.[118] It also had charge of the fine colonial library which the RKB had taken over from the DKG.

Section IV (Cultural Tasks) maintained or aided sixteen German schools in Tanganyika and Southwest Africa. It also ran a school for the children of overseas Germans in Bad Harzburg (later Blankenburg) and cooperated with the Koloniale Frauenschule in Rendsburg, which trained girls for life in the colonies through a curriculum ranging from midwifery to the making of wine, and from blacksmith work to "raciology" (*Rassenkunde*).[119] For the graduates of this institution, as well as for other qualified persons, the RKB found jobs in the mandates, provided financial aid to defray travel costs, and assisted with the immigration formalities.[120]

Section V also did most of its work in the colonies, providing aid for distressed German settlers, as well as Christmas gifts, radio sets, etc. The purpose of these actions was to maintain a link be-

---

115. Karl Brüsch, ed., *Kolonien—Grossdeutschlands Anspruch,* Das Deutsche Koloniale Jahrbuch (Berlin, 1939), pp. 133–36.

116. Nachrodt, pp. 32–33.

117. Berlin Document Center, Reichskolonialbund, Ordner 212, letter from Kreisverbandsleiter Unna of RKB to Sturmbannführer of local SS unit, dated August 11, 1940; circular from same, dated August 7, 1940.

118. For a complete list of such institutions, demonstrating the considerable academic interest in overseas areas, see *Koloniales Taschenbuch 1942,* Herausgegeben von der Bundesführung des Reichskolonialbundes (Munich, 1942), pp. 115–53.

119. Paul H. Kuntze, *Das neue Volksbuch unserer Kolonien* (Leipzig, 1942), pp. 155–56.

120. Ibid., p. 156. Nachrodt, pp. 26–27.

tween the Germans in the colonies and the mother country, and thus to strengthen the national consciousness of the settlers.[121]

Section VII (League Literature) was responsible for the publications of the RKB, produced in its own publishing house in Munich.[122] These included the monthly *Deutsche Kolonialzeitung*, whose official edition, destined for colonial functionaries, carried a special supplement, *Der Koloniale Kampf;* an illustrated monthly (later biweekly), *Kolonie und Heimat*—created in 1937 to appeal to a wider popular audience; *Die Frau in den Kolonien,* an illustrated monthly for women; and *Jambo,* a periodical for young people. In addition, the Press section of the RKB's Siamese twin, the KPA, published *Deutscher Kolonialdienst,* a monthly for official use only, and, as of 1938, the *Kolonialer Informationsdienst,* a correspondence service for German newspapers. A biweekly (later quarterly) survey of the world press, *Kolonialpolitik in der Weltpublizistik,* which was mailed by the KPA to all German diplomatic and consular missions abroad, was remarkable chiefly for its strongly anti-American bias, apparent long before the United States came into the war; a regular feature was headed "American World Aggression."[123]

The Press section of the KPA also reviewed all books dealing with colonial subjects and classified them as Positive, Positive with Reservations, Unimportant, Negative, and Negative with Reservations. This evaluation was to "guide" the general press in its reviewing.[124] Aside from this, the KPA would also give its official seal of approval to certain books submitted to it before publication, provided they conformed to the guidelines referred to elsewhere. The whole colonial discussion in Germany was thus regimented. Thereby it was assured that all agitation would reflect the official viewpoint.

This is not to say that the work of the RKB was unsuccessful

121. Louise Diehl, *Die Kolonien warten* (Leipzig, 1939), pp. 76 ff.; Deutsche Kolonialgesellschaft und Interfraktionelle Koloniale Vereinigung des Reichstags, *Deutschland in den Kolonien* (Berlin, n.d.), p. 12.

122. Nachrodt, pp. 27–28.

123. Dresler, pp. 92–94. Nachrodt, passim.

124. Bundesarchiv, file 4990a.

in arousing widespread popular attention for its cause and support for the colonial claim. Aside from the membership figures already cited, we have other evidence that the agitation was successful in creating a fairly significant and spontaneous echo in the population at large. The RKB did not approve of all these manifestations: In 1940 an article in the *Deutsche Kolonialzeitung* by Paul Ritter, a colonial veteran and KPA official, deplored the excesses of colonial enthusiasm coming to the fore at that moment when "colonial morning air" was being sniffed by many. Singled out for criticism were "a colonial boom literature . . . blooming luridly" and the ignorance and half-baked ideas of " 'colonial experts' who are inundating the press with their products," such as a seriously meant proposal to introduce the study of Kisuaheli into the curriculum of German schools as a mandatory subject.[125] As early as 1938 the colonies had become something of a fad, manifest in such absurdities as a musical review entitled "Ki-Sua-Heli," which featured a chorus line impersonating colonial raw materials (e.g. diamonds) and Germany's female stunt pilot, Hanna Reitsch, buzzing around the hall in an airplane.[126]

Typical of the literary outgrowths of "Kolonial Kitsch" were a book of colonial songs, containing such gems as "Afrikana, Insulana," sung to the tune of "Deutschland Über Alles,"[127] and a book by R. Küas, *Tessu und die Tänzerin,*[128] whose heroine, a

---

125. *Deutsche Kolonialzeitung, 52* (1940), 178–79.

126. *Deutscher Kolonialdienst* (March 1938), pp. 14–17. Another manifestation of colonial enthusiasm was the rash of books glorifying German "colonial heroes," especially Carl Peters, who was often treated (perhaps rightly) as a forerunner of National Socialism. In September 1937 Hitler granted a posthumous pardon to Peters, who, in 1897, had been convicted by a disciplinary court for misuse of his authority in East Africa. His activities there had earned him the name of "Hanging Peters." For a list of works on this dubious pioneer of German colonialism, see Fritz Ferdinand Müller, *Deutschland, Ostafrika, Zanzibar* (Berlin, 1959), pp. 24–25. Reichskolonialbund, *Kolonien im deutschen Schrifttum* (Berlin, 1936) and Kolonialpolitisches Amt der NSDAP, *Koloniales Schrifttum in Deutschland* also list numerous biographies of Peters, Wissmann, Lüderitz, and other "colonial heroes." Emin Pasha, however, being Jewish, received no eulogies after ca. 1936.

127. *Deutscher Kolonialdienst* (March 1939), p. 21.

128. Reviewed in *Deutsche Kolonialzeitung, 104* (1942), 231.

native girl, is kidnapped by Fetish priests and taken to a "secret monastery," there to learn the "terrible and mysterious snake dance." Escape is hopeless, until she is rescued by "the German protective power and young Tessu, who, as a German noncommissioned officer, is armed against the terrors of the fetish." Aside from these outgrowths, however, the volume of colonial literature

CHART 2

Distribution of Colonial Literature with a Propagandistic Bias
1919–1941

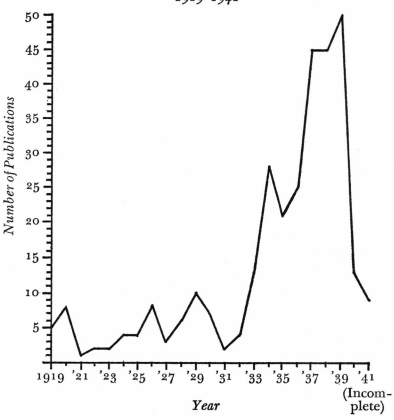

indicates that there existed a considerable interest. The graph compiled from two bibliographies of colonial literature does not take into account purely scientific or technical works, works of travel and description, and memoirs without any propagandistic character. It also does not include adventure stories for juvenile consumption, except those which are openly propagandistic. All of these, of course—and their total number is several times greater than that of the books tabulated below—at least stimulated interest in the colonies, if not active colonial revisionism.

The graph shows clearly the rapid rise in the number of publications dealing with colonial questions in the years after the Nazis came to power and before the outbreak of the war. The drop in 1940 is explained by the paper shortage and technical difficulties brought on by the war. The slight drop in 1935 reflects the uncertain status of the colonial movement at that time, after the first illusions about a speedy fulfillment of colonial wishes by the national government had been shattered and before the Nazis openly embraced the colonial line. The impact of the work of the RKB on public opinion is also attested to by some foreign observers. One Englishman reported that on a boat to Tanganyika in 1938—admittedly a somewhat special case—"one could smell the colonial claims of Germany in the air. [Everyone on board] wanted to talk about them."[129]

Aside from the RKB-KPA, some other agencies were concerned with colonial activity to a minor extent. One of these was the Foreign Office, whose colonial section was a sort of liquidation agency for the old Colonial Office, abolished in 1920.[130] Most of its activities were rather innocuous; among other things it shielded from the Party's race fanatics a number of pathetic Africans, who, as former members of the German colonial military forces, had been exiled from their homelands. In order to enable them to make a living, the Foreign Office organized and subsidized a traveling "Africa Show," which went through various vicissitudes before the Party forbade all non-Aryans to appear as entertainers. Eventually, these loyal African subjects were supported by a dole

---

129. G. L. Steer, *Judgment on German Africa* (London, 1939), p. 7.
130. Erich Kordt, *Nicht aus den Akten* (Stuttgart, 1950), p. 42.

which the Foreign Office arranged to have paid them by the Kolonialkriegerdank.[131]

The Foreign Office colonial section also had a number of financial interests in German colonial business concerns, such as the Deutsch-Ostafrikanische Gesellschaft (DOAG), the Überseeische Gesellschaft and the Lupa Studiensyndikat, a group interested in gold-mining possibilities in Tanganyika. Through a company wholly owned by it, the Überseeische Industrie und Handelsgesellschaft, the Foreign Office supported the German settlers in Southwest Africa and Angola and tried to acquire additional land in the former for German settlement. During the Weimar period, the Foreign Office also had a hand in the re-acquisition—by German owners, whom it continued to support—of confiscated cocoa plantations in the British Cameroons. Finally, it gave some rather modest financial aid to a number of colonial organizations and publications, such as the DKG and later even the RKB (until 1939, when the latter became self-supporting); the Koloniale Rundschau; the Afrikanachrichten; and the Kolonialwirtschaftliches Komitee, an economic study group going back to pre-World War I days (until 1939, when the Economics Ministry took over that responsibility).

That all these activities were extremely modest in scope is attested to by the fact that the highest budget the Foreign Office ever submitted for colonial purposes was 871,000 Reichsmarks, in 1938. In other years the sums were considerably lower. The total capital invested by the Foreign Office in colonial enterprises amounted to RM 5,473,375 (of which RM 3,644,000 represented the Foreign Office share in the Deutsch-Ostafrikanische Gesellschaft); to this may be added RM 6,769,088 in outstanding loans to such enterprises (figures as of 1938).[132]

The Kolonialschule at Witzenhausen, which trained young men for various positions in colonial and overseas areas and had its origins in the 1890s, was supported throughout the Weimar and Nazi periods by Reich funds, either through the Foreign Office

131. Correspondence relating to this matter in Bundesarchiv, Reichsfinanzministerium, file 11,632.
132. Ibid., files 11,632–49.

or the Ministry of the Interior. It remained, however, a private institution and still exists, under a different name, at this time. The Koloniale Frauenschule at Rendsburg, on the other hand, was founded in 1926 under the joint aegis of the Reich Ministries of the Interior and of Education and was supported entirely by these agencies.[133]

133. Bundesarchiv, Reichsministerium für Wissenschaft, Erziehung und Volksbildung, file 21/176. Cf. Rohrbach, ed., pp. 283–88.

2

The Colonial Argument

Underlying the whole colonial crusade in its various aspects were certain assumptions that we must survey and analyze in order to understand colonial revisionism. Why did the men and organizations of which we have spoken feel that Germany needed colonies? What benefits would the restoration or acquisition of overseas possessions, in their opinion, entail for the Reich?

We shall find that some of their arguments were identical to those that had been used to support the original acquisition of colonies by Bismarck's Empire and, in fact, were similar to the classical nineteenth-century imperialist argument used in all European countries. Thus they give an insight into the whole phenomenon of European colonialism. On the other hand, there are special emphases in the colonial agitation of the Nazi period that are due to the nature of Nazi Weltanschauung and are helpful in understanding it and the policy goals of Hitler's Germany.

It is extremely helpful to divide the arguments used by the colonial agitators into two large groups, economic and noneconomic. Neither group was more important. Both lines of argument, however, had their special champions. We have already quoted the opinion of ex-Governor Solf that the political and legal arguments had more validity and should therefore be stressed in colonial agitation. Solf was not alone in this opinion.

At the other extreme we find Hjalmar Schacht, who throughout the period between the wars was one of the most important figures of the colonial movement and whose influence on Hitler was decisive in motivating the Führer to introduce the subject of colonies officially into international discussions.[1] Schacht felt that the colonial demand should be based on economic necessity, pure and simple. Political considerations, such as the legal form under which German overseas possessions might be restored, were entirely secondary to him. What mattered was that Germany

> have territories under German management and included in the German monetary system.
>
> All the other questions involved—sovereignty, army, police, law, the churches, international collaboration—are open to discussion. They can all be solved by means of international cooperation so long as nothing unworthy is imputed against the honor of Germany. The German colonial problem is not a problem of imperialism. It is not a mere problem of prestige. It is simply and solely a problem of economic existence. Precisely for that reason the future of European peace depends upon it.[2]

The fact that a person of Schacht's economic astuteness subscribed to the theory that colonies were necessary to Germany's national prosperity—Schacht maintains this thesis even in his post-World War II memoirs[3]—would suggest that this argument should not be dismissed out of hand. It is possible that, given the Alice in Wonderland international economics of the 1920s and '30s, Schacht and those who copied his arguments had at least a talking point.

The basic assumption of the economic argument for German

1. Hjalmar Schacht, *Account Settled* (London, 1949), pp. 93–95. Cf. below, pp. 95 ff.

2. Schacht, "Germany's Colonial Demands," *Foreign Affairs*, *15* (January 1937), 223–34.

3. *Account Settled*, pp. 92–93, 290, 292.

colonies was identical with that of Hitler and others who argued for Eastern expansion as the necessary basis for German prosperity: The population of the Reich was considered to be too large to be supported by the agricultural and mineral resources of its postwar territory; Germans needed more Lebensraum. Thus Schnee wrote in 1925:

> The German Reich is too small for the mass of its population. It is able to feed only ⅔ of its inhabitants from the products of its own soil. . . . Our fatherland is relatively more overpopulated than it was before the war, and accordingly needs more imports from outside. After the theft of our colonies, we have our work as the only equivalent with which to pay for imported food and raw materials. The loss of our overseas possessions means more work and a limitation of the standard of living of our people.[4]

This passage contains the economic argument for colonies in its most primitive and unsophisticated form. It assumes that mere political sovereignty over a given territory in some mysterious way diminishes the necessity for the economy of the mother country to produce an equivalent for the raw materials and other goods it wishes to import from that territory—in other words, that the possession of a colonial empire automatically increases the wealth of the mother country. A good deal of the popular colonial literature is devoted to arguments on this level; a favorite device was the graphic portrayal of a "rich Englishman" standing on a huge square representing his "living space" (i.e. the total area of the British Commonwealth, including the Dominions, divided by the population of Great Britain) and a "poor German" with only a tiny square to stand on.[5]

It is hardly necessary to point out that this comparison of national territorial possessions with private real estate holdings has validity only if we assume that the resources of the colonies would

4. G. Zastrow, ed., *Deutschland braucht Kolonien* (Berlin, 1925), p. 5.

5. See, e.g., Paul Leutwein, *Die deutsche Kolonialfrage* (Berlin, 1937), pp. 31–38; Robert Baravalle, *Deutschland braucht seine Kolonien* (Graz, 1939); and Dix, *Weltkrise und Kolonialpolitik* (Berlin, 1932), pp. 320 ff.

be appropriated by the mother country or its citizens without any equivalent being returned to the colonies, i.e. under a system of pure exploitation and virtual slavery. It would be unfair and unjustified to infer that Schnee and other conservatives in the colonial movement advocated such a system. They wrote passages like the one quoted above either because their own economic thinking was hazy or because they wished to appeal to a broad unsophisticated audience. There are, on the other hand, examples of Nazi writers consciously and openly advocating just such a colonial system—which, after all, is exactly what Nazi leaders had in mind for their projected East European Empire:[6] "If, to make an extreme formulation, the colonies could produce without buying anything, i.e. perform slave labor, this would be satisfying, for they would be increasing production and at the same time lowering its cost."[7]

The frequent use of the term "living space" by the colonialists should not lead us to suppose that they envisaged mass emigration of Germans from the overcrowded mother country into the colonies. It is true that such ideas were advocated by a few enthusiasts as a solution to Germany's economic problems, especially in the earlier part of the period here under discussion. A remarkable example is the article by Rudolf Böhmer in the Hamburg Wirtschaftsdienst of August 1933, which suggested that Tanganyika alone might receive a million white immigrants.[8] Böhmer arrived at that figure by equating conditions in East Africa to those in, of all places, Württemberg!

For the most part, however, the colonialists were cautious in discussing the settlement potential of overseas areas. There were two reasons. Individuals with firsthand overseas experience pointed out that land suitable for large-scale white settlement was severely limited in the old German possessions. Overseas settle-

6. For a discussion of Nazi plans and policies for that area see Alexander Dallin, *German Rule in Russia* (New York, 1957).

7. Herbert Haag, *Kolonien und Industriewirtschaft,* Forschungen zur Kolonialfrage, 11 (Würzburg, 1940), 71. For other suggestions in the same vein see ibid., p. 11; J. H. Krumbach, *Kolonialpolitik Heute,* Tornisterschrift des OKW, Abt. Inland, 25 (Munich, 1941), 60; and Rohrbach, pp. 160 ff.

8. Wüst, ed., *Kolonialprobleme der Gegenwart,* p. 57.

ment, moreover, clearly contradicted Nazi ideology, which demanded the concentration of German *Volkstum* in a single continental bloc[9] of *Blut und Boden*, i.e. through eastward expansion. Few of the colonialists were so bold as to challenge that conception, although Epp, for one, was certainly opposed to it and had said so before Hitler came to power. In a speech delivered in 1928 the General pointed out that Eastern expansion was not a realistic alternative to a colonial policy "because it is based on historical phenomena whose bases no longer exist." The countries to the east of Germany now were not much less densely populated than the Reich, and their peoples had developed a national consciousness and expansionist ambitions of their own.[10] Moreover, the East European states had the political support of France, which made German expansion in that area extremely hazardous.[11] It is interesting to note that Paul Rohrbach, who did not entertain any exaggerated notions of the possibilities of German emigration to the colonies, nevertheless condemned the Eastern alternative, for reasons similar to Epp's, in a book published in 1935, which received party approval by being included in the National Socialist Bibliography.[12] It must be remembered, of course, that plans for aggression in Eastern Europe were being soft-pedaled at that time.

For the most part, however, the colonialists and the Eastern European enthusiasts within the Party came to agree on a formula which provided for both forms of expansion: "Ostpolitik and Kolonialpolitik are not opposites but complement each other logically for the welfare of the Third Reich, for which we have all

---

9. Ibid., pp. 49–66. Matthias Schmitt, *Funktion und Bedeutung der Kolonien*, Forschungen zur Kolonialfrage, 95 (Würzburg, 1940), 140. Hitler, *Mein Kampf*, pp. 138–39.

10. There was an active colonial movement in Poland led by Orlicz Dreszer. The German colonialists, for the most part, discussed these Polish ambitions with sympathy. *Deutsche Kolonialzeitung*, 45 (1933), 76; 50 (1938), 76. *Deutscher Kolonialdienst* (November 1938), p. 24; (December 1938), pp. 23–24. G. Kurt Johannsen and H. H. Kraft, *Germany's Colonial Problem* (London, 1937), p. 16. Bauer, *Kolonien im Dritten Reich*, 2, 86–87.

11. Bundesarchiv, Epp Papers, file 24/1: undated draft for a speech.

12. Rohrbach, *Deutschlands Koloniale Forderung*, esp. p. 168.

fought and will ceaselessly continue to fight."[13] "The solution cannot be one-sided, e.g. only in the idea of Eastern settlement, but in combined expansion on either side of the water."[14]

In this scheme the colonies were to provide those raw materials still lacking in the Greater German sphere in Europe, for which purpose a limited number of Germans would live in them, perhaps on only a temporary basis.[15] Mass settlement, however, with the possible exception of Germans from other overseas areas, e.g. Brazil, who might be transferred to German colonies, was to take place in Europe, where "God and Hitler [would] see to it" that new land became available.[16]

The formula "Kolonialpolitik und Ostpolitik"—the one to provide raw materials, the other space for agrarian settlement—became a staple of colonial agitation about 1936, i.e. after the Party took full control of the colonial movement. From that time overt discussion about the desirability of overseas possessions came to an end.[17] The colonial cause had been officially adopted by the Party, but the scope of colonial ambition had been somewhat restricted. The colonies were considered no longer as potential outlets for Germany's surplus population but merely as a means to help feed that population, which would stay in Europe and expand its settlement space there.

An article by Hermann Behrens in *Deutscher Kolonialdienst* of

13. *Deutsche Kolonialzeitung, 46* (1934), 116.

14. Dix, *Weltkrise und Kolonialpolitik*, p. 28.

15. RKB, *Koloniales Taschenbuch*, p. 22.

16. Joachim Seegert, *Die dritte Heimat* (Berlin, 1933), passim. Wangenheim, *Kolonien des Dritten Reiches*, p. 62. Kuntze, *Das neue Volksbuch unserer Kolonien*, pp. 175–78. Edmund Schmid, *Deutsche Siedlung im I., II. und III.* Reich Nationalsozialistische Bibliothek, 48 (Munich, n.d.), 100.

17. For evidence of such discussion and diverging views within the Party see *Deutsche Kolonialzeitung, 46* (1934), 113–16, which attacks anticolonial views expressed in the *NS Landpost*, Agriculture Minister Richard W. Darré's organ. Also of interest in this connection is an exchange of correspondence between Epp and Ley in 1935 (Berlin Document Center, Reichsorganisationsleiter, Ordner 768). Ley objected to a film based on Hans Grimm's colonialist epic *Volk ohne Raum*, on the ground that its doctrine might "run counter to policy." Ley's anticolonial position is also attested by an order emanating from his Politisches Organisationsamt, forbidding the establishment of KPA branches on the Gau level (dated August 6, 1934, BDC, Ordner 768).

October 1937, "Ost-und Kolonialpolitik: Ihre ergänzende Notwendigkeit," sums up the new official view. The author pointed out that it had been the "ideologists" who had upheld the concept of expansion and settlement directed exclusively to the East, while the "technologists" had advocated a new colonial empire in addition. Denying that the colonialists were dreaming "of a greater Germany overseas," involving the establishment of large German populations there, he nevertheless castigated the "mad delusions of intellectual Eastern ideologues" who would "decline natural opportunities"—a highly significant phrase—for the sake of abstract theory and who neglected to consider the factors of climate and economic geography, which allowed tropical colonies to produce certain raw materials not available in Europe.[18]

What prevented Germany from buying those raw materials in countries not under her political control? The colonialists replied that Germany's lack of foreign exchange made this impossible. Hjalmar Schacht and others never tired of arguing that the economic position of the Reich had vastly changed from that of the days before World War I, when it had been able to buy wherever it wanted, and when, as they admitted, the economic potential of its colonies had been neglected.[19] Germany's foreign investments had been lost during and after the war, her foreign trade had been destroyed, she had been deprived of certain trade privileges previously enjoyed in a number of countries by provisions of the Versailles Treaty, and even if she wanted to finance her imports by credits, international credit was not available. (As a matter of fact, however, Hitler, in a speech in February 1938, sharply rejected suggestions that the Reich accept credits in lieu of colonies.) Germany also found herself unable to earn enough foreign currency through exports because of high tariffs and other restrictions imposed by most nations. Therefore Germany needed colonies, areas within her own currency system where she could buy needed imports with marks.[20] As a matter of fact, foreign observers,

18. *Deutscher Kolonialdienst* (October 1937), pp. 1–6.

19. See, e.g., Karl Brüsch, ed., "Kolonien, ein Kapitel deutscher Ehre," *Das deutsche koloniale Jahrbuch* (Berlin, 1938), pp. 8–9.

20. H. W. Bauer, *Deutschlands Kolonialforderung und die Welt* (Leipzig, 1940), pp. 59 ff. Joachim H. Schultze, *Der Wirtschaftswert unserer Kolonien*

critical of the German colonial claim, often admitted that here was the most valid of the arguments in favor of it, even if the German foreign exchange problem were aggravated by such policies as the artificially high pegging of the mark, German trade restrictions, and re-armament efforts, all of which increased the need for imports.[21]

Along with the foreign exchange argument went the complaint that the trade of foreign colonies was consciously monopolized by their mother countries in order to exclude Germany from these raw material sources. As evidence of this allegation, the German colonialists cited trade figures which showed the great share the mother countries held in the trade of their respective colonies and the loss of Germany's primary position among the trade partners of most of her former colonies. It was alleged that high customs duties and export taxes were closing the open door in the colonies of the European powers.[22] The old imperialist argument that trade follows the flag was refurbished with new statistics,[23] and it was pointed out that even a colonial administration which scrupulously maintained the Open Door trade policy—as the mandatories were by treaty bound to do in the former German colonies—was advantageous to the business interests of the administering country: Colonial officials would mainly buy the goods produced in their native land, and the common language factor would aid the trade of the mother country, as would the tendency to let public contracts there.[24] Germany thus could not expect to sell her goods as easily in territories under foreign administration as she could in colonies of her own, and consequently would find it difficult to earn the foreign exchange to purchase needed tropical raw materials.

(Berlin, 1940), p. 11. P. Josef Maria Abs, *Der Kampf un unserer Schutzgebiete* (Düsseldorf, 1930), p. 16. Johannsen and Kraft, p. 44. Franz J. Scheidl, *Deutschlands Kampf um seine Kolonien* (Vienna, 1939), pp. 180 ff.

21. See, e.g., Bullock, pp. 65–66.

22. Bauer, *Kolonialforderung*, pp. 61–64. Schmitt, *Funktion und Bedeutung*, pp. 99–104.

23. See, e.g., C. Gini, "Trade Follows the Flag," *Weltwirtschaftliches Archiv*, 47 (1938), 181–227.

24. Bauer, *Kolonialforderung*, pp. 65 ff.

These arguments are perfectly reasonable insofar as they point out the difficulties created by the high trade barriers characteristic of the 1930s for a country whose economic well-being depended on a large volume of imports and, therefore, exports. It was (and is) true enough that Germany "must obtain more raw materials than she could produce at home to supply her population with work and with food."[25] The obvious fallacy in the belief that colonies would solve this problem for Germany lay in the fact that economically they were relatively unimportant, as pointed out by a League Committee appointed to study the question of access to raw materials. This committee, which published its report on September 7, 1937,[26] pointed out that only 3 per cent of the supply of certain basic raw materials were produced in all areas under colonial rule. The former German colonies could not possibly add much to Germany's raw material base or to her trade position. The value of their total exports (in 1936) amounted to around RM 200 million.[27] Germany, in 1938, bought from them goods valued at RM 25,376,000. Germany's total imports from all of Africa in that year amounted to RM 356,906,000,[28] or about 7 per cent of all German imports.[29] The mandated areas produced none or very little of the raw materials which Germany claimed to need most, e.g. mineral oil, rubber, iron ore, and other minerals. Clearly, Germany's economic problem could be solved only by steps to unfreeze world trade, which were indeed recommended by the League.[30] The autarkic tendencies universal in the economic practices of the period were the real causes of Germany's problems, along with the re-armament measures which ate up a good deal of her foreign exchange earnings.[31]

Many of the German colonialists, however, saw autarky as a

25. Edward Norman Peterson, *Hjalmar Schacht—for and against Hitler* (Boston, 1954), p. 193.

26. League Document A27 (1937), IIB.

27. Schmitt, *Funktion und Bedeutung*, p. 150.

28. *Deutscher Kolonialdienst* (March 1939), p. 81.

29. Schultze, p. 7.

30. Royal Institute of International Affairs, *Germany's Claim to Colonies*, Information Department Papers, 23 (London, 1939), p. 50.

31. For a negative point of view on the economic value of African colonies to the economy of Germany (and other colonial powers) see Grover Clark, *The Balance Sheets of Imperialism* (New York, 1936), esp. pp. 3, 9–13, 15–17, 36, 43.

desirable goal for Germany herself and despite the plain facts of the matter continued to argue that with the acquisition of an overseas empire Germany could achieve that goal. They maintained that the mandates, while economically unimportant at the present, partly because of the mandatories' neglect in developing them,[32] had a great economic potential which Germany, driven by necessity, would develop to the fullest. Her form of government would make such intensive development possible. Thus Hitler himself, in a speech delivered at the 1936 Party Congress, said: "The leadership of a state which is able to achieve the economic results which today are undeniable in Germany will certainly be able to administer the colonies in an economically useful manner."[33] Any comparison of the economic role the colonies were to play after their restitution, with their actual insignificant contribution to Germany's wealth and trade before 1914, was rejected as an attempt to prove "that the prize dairy cow is worthless for the reason that she didn't provide us with any milk as a calf."[34] Under prewar conditions of universal free trade and with Germany as a creditor nation, there had been no necessity to depend on the colonies or to rush their development. Moreover, in the view of Nazi colonialists, Germany had at that time been hindered in her colonial efforts by lack of experience and the absence of a truly dynamic colonial policy.[35] Nevertheless, they pointed out, the overseas territories had experienced a steady economic upswing, which, by 1913, had already made some of them a paying proposition rather than a liability.[36]

The author marshaled impressive statistics in an effort to prove that the African possessions of most European powers, Germany included, had yielded little wealth in return for the sums spent on them. He considered it unlikely that this situation would change. More sympathetic to German Lebensraum arguments was the demographer Warren S. Thompson in *Danger Spots in World Population* (New York, 1929).

32. See, e.g., Kuntze, pp. 127 ff., and Schmitt, *Kolonien für Deutschland*, pp. 57 ff.

33. Scheidl, p. 171.

34. Schmitt, *Funktion und Bedeutung*, p. 124.

35. Ibid., pp. 122–32.

36. See, e.g., Rohrbach, *Afrika*, pp. 11–14; Kuntze, pp. 127 ff.; and Bauer, *Kolonialforderung*, pp. 49 ff.

The expectations held regarding the future economic value of the colonies to Germany were generally stated with caution and seldow expressed in actual figures. The 1936 version of the KPA Richtlinien[37] in fact cautioned speakers to be careful in their use of such figures so that future disappointments might be avoided. In terms of capital value one author estimated the value of the German colonies to be equal to ⅓ of the total German national wealth, or at least RM 50 billion.[38] In terms of production, we find mentioned, as a minimum figure, the amount of RM 400–700 million annually, this being based on the actual output of territories adjoining the mandates owned by the same countries which administered—and allegedly neglected—the former German territories.[39] Another estimate considered that German colonies should be able to supply 10 per cent of all German imports, thus saving a considerable amount of foreign currency.[40]

What was expected by the more restrained colonial writers was not that the colonies would make Germany a fully self-sufficient economic unit, but that they would lessen the country's dependence on foreign trade and break the monopoly of a few producers over certain raw materials. They would make "Germany at least partially independent of . . . political and speculative influences."[41] For her part, the Reich would pursue in its overseas possessions the exact policies it accused other colonial powers to have employed against it, and establish within them "a complete monopoly" through appropriate currency measures, which would vitiate any official Open Door policy.[42]

The whole colonial economic argument was strongly influenced by the idea of economic autarky. Occasionally, German economic self-sufficiency, made possible through the acquisition of tropical areas producing raw material, was seen as a positive ideal to be striven for.[43] The Germans' experience of being cut off from

37. Berlin Document Center, Reichsorganisationsleiter, Ordner 311.
38. Dix, pp. 257–60.
39. Schmitt, *Funktion und Bedeutung*, p. 150.
40. Bauer, *Kolonialforderung*, p. 58.
41. Hjalmar Schacht, *The End of Reparations* (New York, 1931), p. 236.
42. Haag, *Kolonien und Industriewirtschaft*, pp. 125–26.
43. Fritz Zadow, *Koloniale Revision* (Leipzig, 1941), pp. 15–16. Wüst, pp. 10–11.

raw materials in World War I was sometimes cited (incongruously, because Germany's colonies had certainly not helped her then) as an argument in favor of such self-sufficiency.[44] More often autarky was considered not a desirable goal but simply a necessity imposed by the prevalent tendencies of the world economy, which were traced back to the provisions of the Versailles Treaty, and especially reparations. In this view the time of a true world economy and more or less free international trade was irrevocably past—the "effectiveness of economic laws" had been limited and "the boundaries of political activity extended . . . We are living today in a time of Neomercantilism."[45] The law of supply and demand and considerations of cost had no place in such a system: "Even if the exploitation of raw materials in the German colonies may require twice or even three times as much labor as elsewhere, this isn't important for Germany today, since she has no opportunity at all to buy the necessary raw materials elsewhere, even if they are as cheap as can be."[46]

A special version of the autarkic view was propounded by those who saw all of Eurafrica, not merely Germany and her colonies, as the ideal self-sufficient economic unit. Such writers as H. W. Bauer, an official in the KPA, considered that the development of African resources was a task to be carried out by the common effort of all European countries; German participation, in his view, was needed to make this effort succeed for the benefit of all.[47] Economic cooperation between "Little Europe" (presumably he meant that the Soviet Union was not to be included in such a scheme) and Africa would produce an economic bloc similar in potential to the Greater East Asia Co-Prosperity Sphere and the Western Hemisphere.[48] It was understood, especially

44. Schmitt, *Funktion und Bedeutung*, pp. 1–2.

45. Haag, p. 1. Wüst, p. 10. Cf. Bauer, *Kolonien im Dritten Reich*, 2, 33–37; Rudolf Karlowa, *Deutsche Kolonialpolitik* (Breslau, 1939), pp. 46 ff.; Scheidl, pp. 159 ff.

46. Scheidl, p. 172.

47. Bauer, *Kolonien im Dritten Reich*, 2, 115–20.

48. RKB, *Koloniales Taschenbuch*, pp. 51–80. It is interesting to note that this conception is not too far removed from the present realities of the European Common Market, with its African associates.

during the early war years, that Germany would have the leading role in such a bloc.

If the majority among colonial writers considered overseas territory necessary in order to allow Germany to achieve the goal of economic self-sufficiency, there were some, especially among the older colonialists, who argued that on the contrary the success of their cause would revive international trade and make autarky unnecessary. Paradoxically, Schacht, whose fiscal policies had had much to do with a creation of a largely autonomous German economy, was no adherent of the theory of self-sufficiency, which he characterized as "abhorrently primitive."[49] Schacht argued that circumstances beyond Germany's control had forced her to embark on policies of trade controls and restrictions, and that those controls had not brought about the decline of world trade and autarkic tendencies but had been caused by these factors.[50] Schacht and those who followed his arguments declared that the increase of German purchasing power resulting from the return of her colonies would enable Germany to repay part of her foreign debt. It should be noted that (possibly in order to impress foreign opinion) this view of autarky as an evil forced upon Germany from the outside was also the official line of the regime. Hitler,[51] as well as such high Nazi officials as Göring, Goebbels, Funk, and Frick, stressed the desirability of expanding foreign trade,[52] picturing the German Four Year Plan as merely an attempt to secure for Germany an iron ration and to make her able to withstand economic blackmail—i.e. sanctions directed against her on account of her foreign policy.

The colonial agitators took pains to point out that the Four Year Plan should not by any means be considered a substitute for German colonies.[53] They pictured it as merely a stopgap measure, designed to minimize the economic consequences of Germany's lack of space and to secure an iron ration in case of war. Synthetic

49. Peterson, p. 229.
50. Ibid., pp. 193–98, 229–30.
51. See, e.g., the speeches of May 21, 1935, and January 30, 1937, quoted in Scheidl, pp. 202–04.
52. Bauer, *Kolonialforderung*, pp. 99–105.
53. Ibid., pp. 105–10.

raw materials, it was pointed out, because of their production costs,[54] could be considered only a partial solution for Germany's shortages. In the long run, the Führer himself pointed out, "the economic security of German life cannot be achieved solely within its European space."[55] The colonies' role would be "to produce all that which is needed to satisfy the demands of an advanced civilized nation above and beyond the absolutely essential, the iron ration."[56] It should be noted that in such a concept the argument that the colonies would be cut off from Germany in a war becomes pointless; the mother country could survive without the colonies. The fact that this was admitted, however, helps to explain the relatively low priority that the colonial demand held, as we shall see, among Nazi foreign policy goals.

We have already seen that the primary economic role of the overseas possessions of the Third Reich was to have been that of raw material suppliers. Colonial propaganda painted a bright picture of the amounts and varieties of such materials to be found in the mandates and tried hard to prove that an overseas empire would produce especially those goods for which the greatest need existed in Germany. Thus great hopes were expressed that the colonies, through their palm products, would be able to close Germany's fat gap, the greatest problem in her food supply.[57] There were also predictions that the colonies would meet "a considerable part of [Germany's] need for copper, zinc, and tin and, later on, probably iron."[58] In reality, the mineral production of the former German colonial possessions was negligible. Even today these areas cannot be said to be among the mineral-rich parts of Africa. By far the greatest share of such minerals that Germany's Empire had produced was derived, in the form of phosphates,

---

54. Haag, pp. 133–37. Schmitt, *Kolonien für Deutschland*, p. 57.

55. Speech of February 20, 1938, quoted from Schmitt, *Kolonien für Deutschland*, p. 54.

56. Schmitt, *Funktion und Bedeutung*, p. 72.

57. Ibid., p. 153. Schmitt, *Kolonien für Deutschland*, pp. 63–64. Haag, p. 56. (Following World War II Great Britain made an attempt to solve her fat shortage by developing large-scale groundnut plantations in Tanganyika. For various reasons, this scheme proved a failure and had to be abandoned.)

58. Haag, p. 53.

from the Pacific Islands, which, as we shall see, were not included in most of the projects for a new German overseas empire.

Hopes were also entertained that the colonies would contribute significantly to the German economy through their production of cotton and other fibers, bananas, cocoa, and coffee. Rubber, it was pointed out, was no longer a crucial item, since it could be produced synthetically in Germany. As a matter of fact, the rubber production of the mandates was insignificant. In other fields, however, it was argued that synthetics could never substitute entirely for colonial raw materials, since they might need a colonial base, especially wood, which was undoubtedly the one major raw material plentifully available in the African mandates.

It is amusing to note, incidentally, that expectations as to the variety and the amount of raw materials to be found in the German colonies varied in direct proportion to the individual writer's enthusiasm for the idea of autarky. Fairly sober appraisals of the actual facts of colonial production might show, for instance, that Germany could expect, if her prewar African empire were returned to her, to import from them 60 per cent of the bananas, 60 per cent of the cocoa, and 15 per cent of the vegetable fats she required, and sisal 60 per cent in excess of her requirements.[59] On the other hand, there were enthusiasts who flatly stated that the colonies could supply all or most of Germany's needs of rubber, cotton, cocoa, phosphates, vegetable oils, and wood,[60] or even that the colonies could fully meet all of Germany's needs for raw material.[61] To get around the plain fact that the projected German empire, which for most of these writers clearly meant the African mandates, did not produce any minerals worth mentioning (and these were among the most important of the materials Germany was short of), such writers would quote the theories of the geographer Adolf Wagner, according to whom minerals were distributed more or less evenly over the earth's surface. In other words, there had to be some in the German colonies.[62] But here

59. Schmitt, *Funktion und Bedeutung*, pp. 140 ff.
60. Karlowa, pp. 48–50.
61. Baravalle, p. 66.
62. Leutwein, p. 47.

we arrive at a point where any semblance of rationality in the colonial claim wears thin.

In all discussions of the economic benefits which a colonial empire would entail for Germany, the emphasis was almost always placed on the goods these colonies could produce for the mother country. We have already seen that the raw-material argument was officially stressed as more important than the idea of colonies for mass settlement of surplus population. It also far outweighed in importance the allegedly classical imperialist argument that colonies are needed as markets for the goods and capital of the mother country. It is true that we still find that notion expressed from time to time in colonialist literature, although mainly by those representatives of the colonial movement whose economic ideas were still grounded in nineteenth-century liberal imperialism, and exclusively during the earlier part of the period under discussion. Thus Schacht considered colonial trade and investment an important means of gaining greater prosperity, not only for Germany but for other countries.

> Again and again it must be stressed that German activity in the overseas and colonial areas is one of the most important means of overcoming the economic crisis— not merely in Germany but in the world. The re-admittance of Germany into colonial activity is an unavoidable precondition for any peaceful progress in world economic relations. This would not, furthermore, do harm to anyone and would be advantageous to other countries as well.[63]

For the most part, however, the ability of the colonies to absorb German exports was seen as merely a means to achieve Germany's real purpose, the obtaining of colonial raw materials.[64] In order to do this, however, it was maintained that overseas areas producing raw materials had to be prevented from building their own manufacturing industries; this could only be done by keeping them politically, as well as economically, wholly under the control

63. Hjalmar Schacht, *Grundsätze deutscher Wirtschaftspolitik* (Oldenburg, 1932), pp. 68–69.
64. Bauer, *Kolonien im Dritten Reich*, pp. 66–67. Baravalle, pp. 68 ff.

of the mother country.[65] Some National Socialist opinions were even more direct in openly admitting that the colonial policy of the Third Reich would work, economically as well as politically, exclusively for the benefit of the mother country. The idea of increasing the demand of the native population for finished goods, thereby opening new markets for German industry, was opposed as irresponsible and as an expression of the individualistic economic ideas which, in this view, had marred German colonial policy before World War I.[66] The Deputy Führer, Rudolf Hess, put the matter even more clearly and denied specifically that Germany had any intention of using "her national labor power to provide some savages with all sorts of things which they previously didn't know and didn't need." This doctrine of economic slavery, it should be pointed out, has roots not only in neomercantilist economics but also in the Nazis' concept of native policy, which we shall discuss.[67]

A final, minor, economic argument sometimes adduced to support the German demand for an overseas empire was that it would provide a large number of jobs for officials and thus solve the problem of "unemployment of brains," providing suitable careers for Germany's academic youth.[68] By and large it must be said, in concluding this section of our investigation, that an examination of the literature of German colonial agitation clearly shows, from an economic point of view, that the desire for raw material sources overshadowed all other arguments as its main theme.

It is doubtful that all the economic arguments the colonialists could muster would have succeeded in creating considerable popular opinion in favor of their cause, or even in convincing Germany's Nazi leaders to include the re-acquisition of colonies among their foreign policy objectives. We shall see that Hitler was never fully convinced of their validity, even though he himself used them in his public speeches. His Minister of Economics, Funk, agreed with him. When asked by a French reporter in 1938

65. Schmitt, *Funktion und Bedeutung,* pp. 49 f.
66. Scheidl, p. 165. Krumbach, pp. 58 ff.
67. Rudolf Hess, *Reden* (Munich, 1938), p. 206. See below, pp. 166 ff.
68. Wangenheim, p. 28. Haag, p. 153.

whether in view "of the opening of South-Eastern Europe to economic exploitation, he considered that Germany still needed colonies," Funk "replied that it was a mistake to view the German colonial claims purely as part of their economic needs. For them the colonial claim was first and foremost a question of national prestige."[69] The confusing Nazi technique of shifting the basis of their argument to their own purpose, i.e. whenever the validity of the thesis of the economic necessity for colonies was seriously questioned abroad, is further evidenced by the following statement of another Nazi economic expert, Nonnenbruch, the financial editor of the Party's official newspaper, the *Völkischer Beobachter:*

> The German standpoint—that her colonies have been taken by an act of force and therefore belong to her by right—is one of law. As such it has little to do with economic considerations, even if, as is self-evident, we promise ourselves economic advantages from the possession of colonies. One thing is clear: the execution of the Four Year Plan will not be affected in any way by the colonial question, and, conversely, the colonial question is not affected by the execution of the Four Year Plan. That means . . . the German right to colonies remains, even if the problem of raw materials is solved for German industry.[70]

One writer finally went so far as to characterize foreign statements questioning the economic value of colonies for Germany as red herrings designed to detract attention from Germany's real case, which he considered a legal and political one.[71]

This noneconomic side of the German colonial claim helps us understand why, quite in contrast to Schacht's attitude, the more ardent National Socialists among the colonial agitators rejected all alternatives to the restoration of full German sovereignty

---

69. *British Documents,* Third Series, *3,* 246. Brüsch, ed., *Kolonien—Grossdeutschlands Anspruch,* p. 84.

70. Royal Institute of International Affairs, p. 37.

71. Schmitt, *Funktion und Bedeutung,* pp. 7 ff.

over her former colonial empire, such as guaranteed free access to raw materials, a mandate for Germany, or extension of the mandate system to include all colonial possessions.[72]

The colonial agitators gained support not only by promising material wealth if their program were realized but through the usual sentimental attraction that far-flung empire has exercised over the people of so many European countries that trod the paths of imperialism. They also found strong backing for their cause in the near-universal resentment against the *Diktat* of Versailles.

The clause of that treaty, Article 119, by which Germany had been deprived of her colonial possessions, had foolishly been justified by the Allies in terms designed to wound German national pride and, moreover, reasonably easy to disprove. Just as the perhaps most unfortunate clause of the treaty, Article 231, which was widely understood to accuse Germany of sole responsibility for the war, became the lever with which German nationalists tried to upset the validity of the whole peace settlement, so the "Colonial Guilt Lie," embodied in the Allied reply to the German observations on the Treaty of June 16, 1919, became a prime target of the colonial agitators, who argued that by disproving it they established Germany's moral right to colonial revision.[73]

The colonialists, in short, alleged that the colonies had been taken from Germany under cover of a lie. Stressing a legalistic point of view,[74] they maintained that by disproving these "lies which were crowned by the taking of the German colonies with the allegation that the Germans are not capable and worthy to

72. See, e.g., Bauer, *Kolonialforderung*, p. 7 (foreword by Rudolf Karlowa); Haag, pp. 26 ff.; and Johannsen and Kraft, pp. 67–73.

73. For the text of the pertinent part of the Allied note of June 16, 1919, see Scheidl, p. 119.

74. Among the literature of German colonial revisionism there exists a special category of works dealing with the mandates, their status, and the question of the locus of sovereignty over them from the viewpoint of National Socialist "positive international law." Examples include Friedrich W. Winkelmann, *Die deutsche Kolonialfrage als Völkerrechtsproblem* (Diss., Göttingen, 1936). Harro Brenner, *Wem hat Deutschland seine Kolonien aufgrund des Versailler Diktats überlassen?*, Völkerrechtsfragen, 45 (Berlin and Bonn, 1938).

administer colonies,"[75] they established a positive legal right to colonial revision. The extreme formulation held that "if Germany, in view of this clear legal position, takes her colonies by force, then the annulment of the wrong created at Versailles on the colonial question is permissible self-help. Resistance against such force, however, would be wrongful under international law."[76] Generally, we do not find the colonialists advocating forceful measures to achieve their end prior to the outbreak of World War II. The assumption was, rather, that by undermining the moral position of the mandatories, the restitution of the mandates to Germany could be brought about peacefully. "It must be the task of the whole German people to take up the fight against the colonial guilt lie by all means available and to continue it until the truth triumphs in this field and until, as a result of this struggle for the truth, the right [of Germany] to own colonies is universally recognized."[77]

The term "Colonial Guilt Lie" was originally coined by Heinrich Schnee in an article that appeared in the Munich *Süddeutsche Monatshefte* in January 1925. The facts and arguments he used in denying the truth of the Allied allegations of German misgovernment in the colonies—suppression of their populations, and militarization of the natives—were not new. They had already been marshaled in 1919 in two official publications of the Reich Colonial Office,[78] which had been hurriedly produced to back up official protests against the colonial clauses of the Versailles Treaty and the justification given for them in the Allies' note of June 16, as well as in the so-called covering note handed to the Germans along with the Treaty.

Schnee's phrase and his argumentation became a stereotyped ingredient of all German colonial agitation. They were used in

75. Diedrich Westermann, ed., *Beiträge zur deutschen Kolonialfrage* (Essen, 1937), p. 17.

76. Wilhelm Mellem, *Der deutsche Kolonialanspruch* (Diss., Erlangen, 1938), p. 68.

77. Zastrow, p. 43.

78. Reichskolonialministerium, *Deutsche und französische Eingeborenenbehandlung* (Berlin, 1919). RKM, *Die Behandlung der einheimischen Bevölkerung in den kolonialen Besitzungen Deutschlands und Englands* (Berlin, 1919)

much the same form by Nazis as well as conservatives in the colonial movement. In order to be effective, they obviously had to be brought to the attention of public opinion outside Germany, and especially of the victor nations. The colonialists succeeded in doing so. A book by Schnee, *German Colonization Past and Future,* appeared in Britain in 1926.[79] In it the ex-governor expressed the German case in much the same way as in his original article. He was strongly seconded by the English historian William H. Dawson, who wrote the preface and who, over the years, became virtually the agent of German colonial revisionism and its main mouthpiece in Britain. Dawson considered the colonial clauses of the Versailles Treaty and the justification given for them "the most ungenerous act ever perpetrated in the name of the British Crown, government, and people," and held that this settlement, if not revised, must inevitably lead to another war, thus terming the return of her colonial empire to Germany "a matter both of honour and of policy for our own country."[80] However that may be, there is no doubt that the Allied statesmen at Versailles, by their needlessly vindictive and insulting language and their continued use of wartime propaganda as facts, had supplied the German colonial revisionists with their strongest arguments. By the 1930s even the most outspoken foreign opponents of their cause, such as former British Colonial Secretary L. S. Amery, who had had much to do with the Versailles colonial settlement, admitted the baselessness of the charges that had been made against Germany as a colonial power and were obviously embarrassed by them in stating their case against revision.[81]

Following Schnee, the German colonial revisionists attacked the Colonial Guilt Lie from two sides. On the one hand they pointed out that abuses and shortcomings existed in the record of all colonial countries, while on the other they stressed the positive accomplishments of Germany in her former colonies and belittled her failures. Thus much was made of the fact that all of

79. Heinrich Schnee, *German Colonization Past and Future* (London, 1926).
80. Ibid., pp. 22, 23.
81. L. S. Amery, *The German Colonial Claim* (London, 1939), passim, and *My Political Life* (London, 1953–55), Vols. 2 and 3 passim.

Germany's possessions had originally been acquired peacefully,[82] by treaties with native rulers. The later colonial wars were explained as the result of Germany's legitimate efforts to introduce law and order and to control abuses, such as slavery,[83] which had been blown up out of proportion by a meddling Reichstag, and particularly by such "traitors" as the "Jew" Erzberger and the Socialists Bebel and Noske, passages from whose speeches furnished the Allies with some of the material for the Colonial Guilt Lie.[84] In actuality, it was alleged that "nowhere in the colonial history of white peoples has so little blood been spilled as by the Germans."[85] German achievements, especially in the field of tropical medicine and in native education, were stressed heavily.[86]

The most obviously absurd of the Allied charges, that Germany had militarized its natives—the very course of the war in the colonies argued against its plausibility—received its share of rebuttals, often linked with attacks against France's policy of recruiting African soldiers for use in Europe as well as in Africa.[87] Insofar as shortcomings were admitted to have existed at all in the Empire's colonial policy, they were explained as the result of Germany's lack of experience as a colonial power and of the penny-pinching policies and wrong-headedness of the Reichstag. By 1914 the colonialists claimed, such "children's diseases of colonialism" had been largely overcome, and the colonies were at the beginning of a period of rapid peaceful development.[88]

One of the standard devices of the colonialist writers was to quote favorable views expressed by prominent figures on the sub-

82. E.g. Abs, pp. 58 ff.; and Zastrow, pp. 27–28.

83. E.g. Walter von Schön, *Deutschlands Kolonialweg* (Berlin, 1939), p. 206. Baravalle, p. 20, even alleged that Germany was alone among the colonial powers in combating this evil energetically.

84. Baravalle, pp. 28–29. Schultze, p. 63. Paul Ritter, *Der Kampf um den Erdraum* (Leipzig, 1936), pp. 282 ff.

85. Joachim Seegert, *Koloniale Schicksalsstrunde der weissen Rasse* (Berlin, 1934), p. 41. Jacob, p. 34.

86. E.g. Ritter, pp. 239 ff. (where Albert Schweitzer becomes a German "colonial hero"). Schmitt, *Kolonien für Deutschland*, pp. 16 ff.

87. Schnee, *Colonization*, pp. 74–91. Scheidl, pp. 144–47.

88. Ritter, pp. 281 ff. Schmitt, *Kolonien für Deutschland*, p. 12. Scheidl, p. 125.

ject of German colonialization. The usual list of such references included Lord Milner, Theodore Roosevelt, the British colonial administrator Harry Johnston, Cecil Rhodes, and, of course, William H. Dawson, along with many others.[89] Schnee himself also made a telling point when he recalled that in 1914 Great Britain had been negotiating with Germany about a possible division of the Portuguese possessions. Surely, he argued, Britain would not have done so if the German colonial record were as black as her propagandists and statesmen subsequently claimed.[90] The clinching argument of the colonialists, however, was the loyalty of African natives to the German regime, documented by their actions during the war, especially in Tanganyika, and subsequently on a number of occasions by petitions to the League of Nations and by other public expressions. Out of this the colonialists developed the theses that the principle of the self-determination of peoples had been thwarted by the colonial clauses of the Versailles Treaty, and, somewhat more questionable, that under this principle the mandates should be returned to German rule.[91] Schnee felt that the loyalty of the natives imposed an obligation upon Germany to insist upon colonial revision: "Can it surprise anyone . . . that the German nation will never forget such fidelity, nor renounce the right to return to the territory where it was shown, whatever formal declarations to the contrary were exacted under pressure of military menace, suffering, and starvation?"[92]

This passage also indicates that the colonial agitators by no means neglected to make use of the more general German complaint, that the whole of the Versailles settlement was morally invalid because it had been imposed by force after Germany had been made helpless by the trickery of the 14 Points and the breach

89. See, e.g., Haag, p. 138; Rohrbach, pp. 114 ff.; and Brüsch, *Kolonien—ein Kapitel deutscher Ehre*, pp. 52 ff.

90. Schnee, *Colonization*, p. 66.

91. Bauer, *Kolonialforderung*, pp. 70 ff. Lothar Kühne, *Das Kolonialverbrechen von Versailles*, pp. 12, 28 ff. Winkelmann, pp. 27 ff. Viera, pp. 50 ff. All these works cite examples showing African desires for the return of German rule and point out that the principle of self-determination had in any event been violated when the African populations had not been asked for their opinion on their transfer to the administration of the mandatory powers.

92. Schnee, *Colonization*, p. 169.

of the pre-armistice agreement. In their view, then, the colonial settlement of 1919 was invalid not only because it was based on an outrageous and unjustifiable attack on German honor, but also because the whole treaty, having been imposed on a helpless Germany, could not be considered binding.[93]

In its attack on the Colonial Guilt Lie revisionist propaganda also freely used *tu quoque* arguments, not merely in order to show that the colonial practices of which the Germans had been accused—use of unreasonable force in the pacification of their overseas empire, the employment of corporal punishment and of forced labor, etc.—were also used by other colonial powers, but also in an effort to prove that the colonial practice of those other powers was actually far worse than that of Germany. A kind of Colonial Guilt Lie in reverse was very much a part of German colonial propaganda. Attacks against the French practice of militarizing the natives[94] and the alleged neglect of the mandatory powers in the field of medical care for native populations[95] were especially frequent. Raw material for atrocity stories is not hard to find in the colonial history of any European power, and such incidents were a staple in German propaganda.[96] Even the position of Negroes in the United States was cited to prove the guilt of "the others."[97] Britain especially was indicted for merely exploiting her colonies, exacting from them high salaries for officials, without doing enough for their development. Conditions in the mandates, particularly, were described as far from satisfactory and, in fact, as regressing from the high standards set under German rule.[98] For all these reasons, one writer concluded in 1941, Great Britain "has lost [*verwirkt*] the right to be active in the community

---

93. Viera, pp. 65 ff. Scheidl, pp. 76 ff.

94. Dix, pp. 147 ff. Baravalle, p. 32. *Deutsche Kolonialzeitung, 50* (1938), 138–43.

95. *Deutsche Kolonialzeitung, 45* (1933), 221–23; *50* (1938), 359–60. Baravalle, p. 12.

96. *Kolonialzeitung, 52* (1940), 4–5, 45–47. Abs, pp. 172–78. Rohrbach, pp. 110 ff.

97. *Kolonialzeitung, 51* (1939), 90.

98. H. W. Bauer, ed., *Koloniale Wende* (Berlin, 1942), pp. 17–23. Diehl, *Die Kolonien Warten,* pp. 17 ff. Schultze, pp. 34–119.

of European colonial nations and to appeal to this community."[99] The wheel had indeed come full circle! A more moderate view widely expressed by the German colonialists held that the comparative neglect of the former German colonies by the mandatory powers showed conclusively that the latter had neither need of them nor any great interest in their development and that it was therefore a matter of common sense as well as justice to return them to Germany, which would make better use of them.[100]

The immense propaganda effort that was made in the face of the Colonial Guilt Lie was based on the assumption that the only way in which this slur against German honor could be repaired was by the actual restoration of the German colonies. In other words, the German colonial claim in this version was based, mainly, on prestige grounds. A number of German colonialists, especially those who were also National Socialists, went so far as to assert that Germany needed colonies for no better reason than that others had them and the Reich must strive for equality in all things: "As all national questions are primarily matters of emotion and not of reason, so it is also with the question of the colonial activity of a nation. Rational and practical arguments and economic statistics are not of any overriding importance here, since colonies mean more to a nation and its pride than merely business."[101] Colonial activity was seen as "a manifestation of the greatness of peoples,"[102] and Joachim von Ribbentrop, later Foreign Minister of Germany, declared in 1937 that "Germany claims the right to colonial possessions in principle, for this is a right which belongs to every nation, even to the smallest in the world."[103]

Colonial possessions were, according to this school of thought, not merely a right but a duty. They were the old White Man's Burden, of which Germany must shoulder a share.[104] "Primitive

99. Zadow, p. 307.
100. E.g. Bauer, *Kolonialforderung*, pp. 36–44.
101. Scheidl, p. 157.
102. Schmitt, *Funktion und Bedeutung*, p. 174.
103. Royal Institute of International Affairs, p. 32.
104. Diedrich Westermann, *Der Afrikaner heute und morgen* (Berlin, 1937), pp. 3–4. Bauer, *Kolonien im Dritten Reich*, 2, 141. Schmitt, *Kolonien für Deutschland*, p. 35.

peoples" were seen impatiently awaiting the advent of the German colonizer.[105] However, colonies were also a part of the Nazi's Burden of combating Bolshevism wherever it raised its head. In order to save Africa for Europe[106] white solidarity had to be restored.[107] Nazi Weltanschauung, far from hindering Germany in taking her place among colonizing powers, was of particular value in Africa, for it would enable Germany to combat Jewish influence there. This Jewish influence was behind the growth of Bolshevism in that continent. Bolshevism, in turn, was the moving force in a world conspiracy of colored peoples.[108] The theme of the Bolshevist peril, so often sounded in connection with Germany's European policy, was also a staple of the Nazi colonialists. The KPA's official *Deutscher Kolonialdienst* contained a regular column entitled "World Enemy No. 1 Overseas." National Socialism, moreover, in view of its economic doctrine of "Common Use before Private Profit" and its respect for the difference between races, had definite positive values to contribute to the common European task of African development.[109]

In at least one quarter the Nazis found agreement with these claims. The South African Minister of Defense, Oswald Pirow, in a speech delivered before the crew of the visiting German warship *Emden* on January 4, 1935, concurred wholeheartedly: "At a time like the present, when the colored tide rises higher and higher, the active resistance of a strong Germany is indispensable to [us].

"For us in South Africa and for every white man who has created a home for himself on African soil, the preservation and constant expansion of white civilization is a vital question. I therefore wish to express the hope that Germany may soon become a colonial power again."[110]

105. RKB, *Koloniales Taschenbuch,* p. 7.

106. Kühne, p. 41.

107. Westermann, *Beiträge,* p. 21.

108. Constantin von Gilwicki, *Die Enteignung des deutschen Kolonialbesitzes* (Hamburg, 1937), p. 96. Holtsch, p. 81.

109. Hans Bender, ed., "Kolonien—ein Kraftfeld Grossdeutschlands," *Das deutsche Koloniale Jahrbuch* (Berlin, 1942), pp. 41–56. Karlowa, pp. 42–43. Schmitt, *Kolonien für Deutschland,* p. 71.

110. Johannsen and Kraft, p. 54.

We shall have further opportunity to remark on the notable affinity of the proposed German colonial policy to South African ideas. Elsewhere the virtues of Nazism as a basis for colonial policy were generally judged less benevolently. Even those in England who had long condemned the old Colonial Guilt Lie and were not opposed in principle to returning the mandates to Germany were not inclined to give them to Nazi Germany: "Herr Hitler's racial theories in themselves show that his Government and Party are utterly unfitted to be trusted with the fate of subject peoples."[111] Such assertions were dubbed by German colonial propaganda "the new colonial lie"[112] and, of course, roundly rejected as prejudiced.

Overseas empire, in the view of the colonial enthusiasts, would provide Germany with more than material economic benefits and a balm to her wounded national honor and her desire for equality. It would have a very real effect on the German psyche. Overseas colonies were needed to make a true master race out of the rather pedestrian inhabitants of the Reich. Life in the colonies would train fighters, strong natures, leaders.[113] It would particularly sharpen the racial attitudes of those sent out, by giving them "sufficient opportunity to put the value of [their] own race head and shoulders above the racial value of the colored man,"[114] thus correcting the usually tolerant German attitude toward the Negro. To prove this point the colonialists cited the high percentage of good Nazis among Germans with colonial experience, who were "among the first to connect a strong national feeling with social emphasis and the racial pride of the white man."[115] Even those who stayed at home in Germany would reap a psychological reward from a German overseas empire: "The effect on national feeling is altogether one of the most valuable gifts which colonial

111. Noel-Baker, quoted from Granville Roberts, *The Nazi Claims to Colonies* (London, 1939), p. 90.

112. Scheidl, pp. 250–55.

113. Bauer, *Kolonien im Dritten Reich, 2,* 203 ff. Bender, pp. 119–21. Brüsch, *Kolonien—ein Kapitel deutscher Ehre,* pp. 101–02. Scheidl, pp. 213–15.

114. Ernst Gerhard Jacob, ed., *Das koloniale Deutschtum* (Bayreuth, 1939), p. 68.

115. Jacob, *Kolonialkunde,* p. 75.

activity can bestow on a people. The proud national feeling of the Briton has grown with the growth of his world-wide Empire."[116]

The admiration for the British character expressed in this passage casts doubt on the claim that old colonials were necessarily good Nazis. There is no doubt that such persons as Schnee, Lettow-Vorbeck, Seitz, Solf, and even Epp were strong German nationalists who found themselves on the same side as the Nazis when it came to demands for the reparation of national grievances. On the other hand, their colonial experience had given them a certain breadth of outlook, an outgrowth of which was their general respect for the British (Schnee, incidentally, was married to an Englishwoman), which contrasts strongly with the essentially parochial prejudices of the National Socialists. As a matter of fact, these old colonials considered this wider outlook one of the benefits to be gained by colonial activity: "The colonies are a bitter necessity in the political sense as well. We must break out of our continental narrowness and gain the wide political views which large-scale colonial activity and continuing work with alien races and peoples have given other nations which were luckier in this respect."[117] In this view colonial activity, far from creating prejudice and belligerence, bred tolerance and the ability to cooperate with others. It would give the Germans the elbow-room they needed in order to avoid a psychologically explosive situation in their cramped homeland.[118]

If Hjalmar Schacht was the chief advocate of colonies for economic reasons and Schnee the unceasing crusader against the Colonial Guilt Lie, the fairly original prescription of colonies as a balm to the troubled German soul goes back to the writings of Hans Grimm. This literary hero of the German colonial movement was not primarily concerned with raw materials or mass settlement in the colonies when he coined the phrase *Volk ohne Raum*[119] as the title of the most massive of his numerous fictional

116. Wüst, p. 48.
117. Zastrow, p. 6 (foreword by Heinrich Schnee).
118. Kuntze, pp. 220–22. Gilwicki, *Die Enteignung Des Deutschen Kolonialbesitzes,* p. 8.
119. Berlin, 1926.

accounts of German colonization. His advocacy of colonialism was based, in the words of a Nazi critic, "on the knowledge of the danger that arises when the German is forced by narrowness to become a cripple, physically and spiritually, instead of developing his full capacities in large spaces and in freedom." Evicted from South Africa after World War I and impoverished by the inflation raging in Germany, Grimm came to believe that "the German unhappiness of every single German is a consequence of our lack of space."[120] This proponent of a new German frontier believed that "colonial land is as necessary for a people as a sports ground is for a school,"[121] leaving us to infer from the general tone of violence in his fiction that he meant that colonies were useful as places where national feelings of aggression could be harmlessly expressed. Another interesting aspect of Grimm's work, also to be found in the books of his conscious imitator Bernhard Voigt, is the pathological love-hate relationship between his white and colored characters, almost invariably with sexual overtones.[122] Miscegenation was treated as an unspeakable evil, which, however, never failed to tempt the heroes of these works.

There is no question that Grimm made a major contribution to the colonial movement. His works, especially *Volk ohne Raum,* attracted widespread attention during a period when the audience for straight colonial propaganda was quite limited. The colonialists continued to praise him as one of the fathers of their cause.[123]

British opposition to the colonial claim was frequently couched in strategic terms. The Germans were accused of wanting their colonies mainly as springboards for further expansion in Africa and as bases for a future war against the British Empire.[124] It must be noted here that it is almost impossible to find, either in

120. Edgar Kirsch, *Hans Grimm und der nordische Mensch* (Munich, 1938), pp. 5, 15.

121. Quoted from Bauer, *Kolonien im Dritten Reich,* 2, 206.

122. See esp. Grimm's short stories: *Südafrikanische Novellen* (Munich, 1913) and *Was suchen wir alles* (Munich, 1933).

123. *Kolonialzeitung, 42* (1935), 83. Bauer, *Kolonien im Dritten Reich, 1,* 233 ff. Gilwicki, pp. 7–8. Kirsch, passim. Alfred Hoffknecht, *Hans Grimm, Weltbild und Lebensgefühl* (Diss., Münster, 1939), passim.

124. See, e.g., Bullock, pp. 140 ff.; Lewin, passim; Bennett, passim; Amery, *Colonial Claim,* pp. 157–74.

the public pronouncements of the German colonialists or in more restricted discussions, anything to justify these suspicions. On the contrary, German propaganda never tired of disavowing any such intentions. In view of Hitler's expressed opinion on the strategic value of colonies in wartime and his strong opposition to raising African armies,[125] there is no reason to doubt that these disavowals were sincere. The argument that German colonies would merely furnish a hostage to Great Britain for the friendly behavior of Germany was repeatedly heard, and the Anglo-German Naval Agreement of 1935 was hailed by the colonialists as a wise step in convincing England that Germany's modest colonial desires were not designed to undermine the British position in the overseas areas. Ribbentrop asserted at the Leipzig Fair of 1937: "Quite apart from the fact that from the military point of view every colony means for Germany a position lost in advance, the Naval Agreement concluded between Germany and England is the most striking proof of the hollowness of the argument" [that Germany's colonial ambitions were a danger to the British world position].[126] Only after World War II had actually broken out did the colonialists occasionally allude to the strategic and military value of the colonies, but even then they stressed mainly the negative aspect—the lessons of the war were showing that Great Britain must never again be given the opportunity to monopolize Africa's resources in wartime.[127] The concrete colonial plans worked out for the postwar period in Epp's KPA, and described in Chapter 4, paid very little attention to the strategic aspects of the projected German Empire, though perhaps only because the planners envisaged a future when Germany would have no more powerful enemies.

125. See esp. Hitler, *Mein Kampf,* pp. 644–45.
126. Royal Institute of International Affairs, p. 36. Wangenheim, pp. 10–11. Bauer, *Kolonialforderung,* pp. 74–77.
127. E.g. Bauer, *Koloniale Wende,* p. 40; and Haag, pp. 6–7.

3

The Diplomacy of Colonial Revisionism

Clearly all the efforts of the best-organized and most vocal colonial movement would have been in vain if it had not been able to gain governmental support for its cause. Even the most valid arguments the colonialists could bring forward would have remained without substantial effect, at least abroad, had they not been adopted and frequently voiced by Germany's political leadership and particularly by the makers of German foreign policy. Territorial changes are generally brought about not by popular agitation but by diplomacy, or by its classical extension, war. It will become clear in this part of our investigation that from 1919 to 1938 there is no evidence that any German government ever considered the latter as a means to vindicate the colonial claim. The colonial question did, however, play an important role in the diplomacy of the period.

The governments of the Weimar Republic, with the vocal encouragement of the colonial associations and their spokesmen in parliament,[1] endeavored to raise the issue on several occasions.

---

1. Cf. above, pp. 10–14.

In general, German policy on the colonies during that period had two objectives: the maintenance of all rights the mandate system afforded Germany with respect to equal access, while making it understood that Germany did not regard the colonial settlement of Versailles as final.[2]

The first of these objectives explains the extreme German watchfulness for any tendency of the victor powers to annex the mandates or any part of them, either de facto or de jure. The official German protest against the manner in which the mandates were distributed—in effect the principal Allied powers allocated the territories among themselves, with the League having no choice but to ratify the fait accompli—is to be seen in this light. In a note of November 12, 1920, the German government branded this procedure as a violation of the true character of the mandatory system and therefore of the peace settlement, and explicitly reserved Germany's right to raise future claims based on this alleged violation.[3] Prodded by Schnee[4] and the colonial associations, the German government also protested, in a note of September 25, 1925, against Belgian measures tending toward an administrative integration of Ruanda-Urundi in the Belgian Congo. This protest was rejected by Belgium on the grounds that Germany, as a non-member of the League of Nations, had no standing in the matter.[5] Belgian policies in Ruanda-Urundi continued, however, to be watched critically by the German colonialists.[6]

After Germany had joined the League, she was in a better position to insist on the inviolability of the mandates. She also benefited now by the principle of equal access, guaranteed to League members, which enabled German citizens to return to their former homes in the colonies, although economically, of course,

---

2. No attempt will be made here to describe in detail the role of colonial questions in the 1919 peace negotiations. The topic has been fully covered by G. L. Beer in *African Questions at the Paris Peace Conference* (New York, 1923), which contains the full text of the correspondence between the Allies and the German government on the question of the colonies.

3. The full text of this note is in Zadow, *Koloniale Revision*, pp. 275–84.

4. Dresler, *Die Deutschen Kolonien und die Presse*, p. 26.

5. Schmitt, *Kolonien für Deutschland*, p. 26.

6. *Kolonialzeitung*, 47 (1935), 280.

they had to make a fresh start. This principle was zealously guarded by Germany and gave rise to some controversy, especially with France.[7]

During the Weimar period the greatest amount of concern over a colonial matter was aroused by the British plans to create a "Closer Union" between the mandate of Tanganyika and the neighboring British territories. This plan, which originally envisaged merely economic cooperation between these areas, was developed by the 1927 Hilton Young Commission. A subsequent study by Sir Samuel Wilson expanded it into a scheme for a loose political federation. L. S. Amery, then Colonial Secretary, admitted that one of the objects was to "dispel the notion that the British Government was only a tenant of the League of Nations" in Tanganyika and that the mandate was merely a temporary one.[8] This, however, was precisely the German point of view. The matter was raised in a full colonial debate in the Reichstag, popular protest meetings were called by the colonial associations,[9] and both Stresemann and Curtius, his successor as Foreign Minister, in public pronouncements opposed Closer Union. Curtius informed the Reichstag that he was determined to maintain the "claim to renewed colonial activity, the more since [Germany's] former colonial possessions were taken from [her] with a justification which reflected upon her honor," and added that "about the question of when and in what form this demand is to be pressed, nothing definite can . . . yet be said."[10] Opposition to the plan was also expressed by Germany's representative on the Permanent Mandates Commission, Ludwig Kastl, and that league body condemned the plan as contrary to the principle of the mandate system. Closer Union was not achieved, since it was opposed not only by Germany and the League but also by the natives of Tanganyika, who feared that a federation would adopt the native policy of Kenya, a white settler colony. (There were similar fears in Uganda.) Moreover, Lord Passfield (Sidney Webb), the Colonial Secretary in the new MacDonald government, was unconvinced

7. *Verhandlungen, 392,* 9087–88.
8. Amery, *Life, 2,* 360 ff.
9. Jacob, *Kolonialkunde,* pp. 63–64.
10. *Verhandlungen, 428,* 5888–89; cf. *444,* 881.

of the advantages of Closer Union and of its legality.[11] In Germany, however, the colonial movement continued to raise alarums, not only over alleged renewed British efforts to incorporate Tanganyika in her East African empire,[12] but at similar French tendencies with respect to Togo,[13] and supposed Rhodesian designs on the northern part of former German Southwest Africa.[14]

The National Socialist government continued to insist on the distinct difference between mandates and conquered territories in its negotiations with South Africa about the status of the German community in that territory.[15] It protested the virtual annexation of the so-called Caprivi-Zipfel by South Africa in the summer of 1939[16] and went so far as to address, on December 30, 1939, a formal note to the powers at war with Germany, protesting the steps by which they had involved the mandates in the war.[17]

All these minor diplomatic actions were undoubtedly taken not only to safeguard the immediate German interest in equal access to the mandates, etc., but also to stress the peculiar, and in the German view temporary, character of the mandates as territories under international supervision. The German colonialists felt that colonial revision would be achieved more easily if the mandatory powers were not allowed to look on the mandates as their property. Aside from this consideration, there was the legalistic point, brought out in the German note of November 12, 1920, that any breach by the victor powers of the individual provisions of the Versailles Treaty invalidated that settlement and gave Germany a legal right to demand revision.

This demand was maintained by virtually all of Germany's chancellors and foreign ministers of the Weimar period.[18] On

---

11. Amery, *Life*, 2, 362. Bernhard Pfister, *England und die deutsche Kolonialfrage*, pp. 46–51.

12. *Kolonialzeitung, 45* (1933), 29–30; *46* (1934), 130–31, 154–55.

13. Ibid., *47* (1935), 167.

14. Ibid., *46* (1934), 206–07.

15. E.g. Zadow, pp. 294–95; and Bernhard Pfister, "Die Britische Kolonialdiskussion," *Zeitschrift für die gesamte Staatswissenschaft, 99* (Tübingen, 1939), 23–63, esp. 35 ff.

16. *The Times*, London, August 2, 1939.

17. Zadow, *Koloniale Revision*, pp. 322–23.

18. Dix, *Weltkrise und Kolonialpolitik*, pp. 290 ff.

several occasions it found formal diplomatic expression. We have already seen that the German government, while the Treaty was in preparation, attempted to discredit the allegations made against German colonial policy by comparing it favorably with that of France and Britain in two official publications.[19] The object was obviously to forestall any possibility that these accusations would be used to deprive Germany of her colonies. In March 1919, long before the contents of the Treaty were officially made known to the Germans, the National Assembly passed a resolution protesting against the Allied intention to deprive Germany of her overseas territory:

> The contents of Article 19 of the draft of the statutes of the League of Nations [Article 22 of the final Covenant] with regard to the German colonies cannot be brought into accordance with the peace conditions laid down in Point 5 of the Wilson Program.
>
> The National Assembly solemnly protests a unilateral change of these conditions, which were accepted by Germany and the Allies as the common basis for peace, and demands the restitution to Germany of her colonial rights.[20]

Also, on March 1, the former Colonial Minister, Wilhelm Solf, voiced a strong protest against the Allied intentions:

> Germany's demand for the restitution of its colonial property is unassailable and cannot be renounced . . . as a necessity for the life of a nation of 70 million . . . A forcible exclusion of Germany from colonial tasks would be an unbearable moral degradation of Germany and would constitute a wrong as fraught with doom for world peace as cutting economic arteries by preventing necessary colonial imports and exports.[21]

When it became clear that the Allies were determined to persist in their plans to deprive Germany of her overseas possessions, the

19. Cf. above, p. 65, n. 78.
20. Scheidl, *Deutschlands Kampf*, p. 39.
21. Ibid., p. 33.

Reich government, in May 1919, appealed in desperation directly to the American people in a radio message. A similar appeal was broadcast to the British people over the signature of General Lettow-Vorbeck, the hero of the East African campaign. Officially, the German point of view was submitted to the Allies as part of the major German reply to the draft treaty of May 29, 1919. This communication, which expressed Germany's willingness to accept the mandate principle if it were applied to all colonies and if Germany were made a mandatory power, did not sway the Allies from their colonial plans. The Big Four's reply to it, of June 16, 1919, added insult to Germany's colonial injury by its official formulation of the Colonial Guilt Lie, whose subsequent importance we have already discussed.[22]

After the signing of the Treaty, aside from occasional statements by government figures[23] and the German protest against the distribution of the mandates of November 1920,[24] the colonial problem disappeared from the diplomatic arena until the Locarno era. The architect of the partial reconciliation between Germany and the Western Allies, Gustav Stresemann, was greatly interested in the cause of colonial revisionism, particularly since he believed, perhaps under the influence of Hjalmar Schacht, that colonies would solve Germany's foreign exchange problem and put the Reich back on a sound economic basis.[25] Nor did he scorn the prestige arguments, declaring in a speech in 1925 that Germany could not be permanently excluded from the "great life tasks of a great people."

> When we shall again possess our own colonies I cannot say. But there is no doubt that the re-acquisition of the colonies is an aim, and an acute aim, of German policy. If there are advanced nations [Article 22 of the Covenant of the League stated that the mandates should be administered by the "advanced nations"] then we belong to

22. Ibid., pp. 36–42. Zadow, pp. 132–36, 246–48.
23. E.g. Dix, p. 290.
24. Cf. above, p. 77.
25. Dix, pp. 293–94.

the advanced nations. We have a right to be counted among them on the basis of our colonial history.[26]

In a newspaper article of the same year Stresemann described colonial revision as one of his foremost policy goals: "The aim of German foreign policy must continue to be progress toward the revision of the Eastern frontier. . . . It must further consist of pressing Germany's claim to colonial activity in order once again to gain colonial possessions."[27]

In accord with these views, the Foreign Minister made an energetic attempt to introduce the colonial claim into the discussions that eventually led to the Locarno Pacts and to the entry of Germany into the League of Nations. In the German note of September 20, 1924, to the governments of the powers represented on the League Council, he made the satisfaction of the Reich's colonial demands one of the conditions for its entry into the League; the phrasing of the condition was, however, quite careful: "Germany, which since her defeat has been excluded from all colonial activities, expects that in due time she will be given an active share in the working of the mandates system of the League of Nations."[28] In a conversation with the British Ambassador, Lord D'Abernon, Stresemann pointed out that entry into the League involved a risk for Germany, in the form of Soviet hostility, which justified the Reich in asking for a colonial concession as an appropriate price.[29] This demand was reiterated in a letter to the Secretary-General of the League dated December 12, 1924.[30]

The immediate results of the feeler were modest. The League Council "took note" of Germany's point of view.[31] The replies of the individual member powers were summed up by Stresemann in a Reichstag speech on January 3, 1925:

> Our demands for colonial activity have been very warmly and cordially supported by one party. Another party

26. Gustav Stresemann, *Vermächtnis*, 2 (Berlin, 1933), 334–35.
27. Ibid., p. 172.
28. Logan, *The African Mandates in World Politics*, p. 32.
29. Stresemann, 2, 102.
30. Logan, p. 32.
31. Ibid.

has welcomed them at least in this respect: that it stated that England had too many colonies. One smiles about the faces the English would make at this passage. There has been no official protest.[32]

The actual discussions at Locarno were significant with respect to the colonial problem in that the Western Powers implicitly withdrew their allegations of Germany's moral unfitness to be a colonial power. In the session of October 3 the colonial question came up in connection with Germany's proposed entry into the League. Briand, the French Foreign Minister, declared on that occasion that "there was nobody who in any way wanted to deny this moral right of Germany [to own colonies]."

"Chamberlain was silent on this; he was certainly privately inclined to cede us the French colonies, just as Briand was inclined to do with those of his English ally."[33] The British government later, through a statement in the House of Commons, associated itself explicitly with this repudiation of the Colonial Guilt Lie. The Undersecretary for Foreign Affairs, Geoffrey Locker-Lampson, declared that "once Germany was admitted to the League she could become a candidate for a mandate, just as could any other member of the League."[34]

On the substantive issue of colonies, however, Britain was not inclined to make concessions:

> Very unpleasant and painful was the entirely negative position taken by Chamberlain in the colonial question with reference to an alleged statement by Luther. [The German Chancellor had expressed hopes for colonial revision as a result of Germany's joining the League.] England could not dispose of the colonies which are actually the property of the Dominions, but also couldn't give up any of its own colonies.[35]

Back in Germany, the Foreign Minister had to defend himself against the colonial lobby who accused him of failing to do his

32. Stresemann, 2, 135.
33. Ibid., 2, 196. Dix, p. 294.
34. Logan, p. 39.
35. Stresemann, 2, 251.

utmost to gain colonial concessions. In a letter to Schnee, Stresemann denied the allegation "that within the Foreign Office there
was only small interest in the colonial matter. I have always found,
especially among those closest to me in the Foreign Office, the
greatest understanding for the importance of the colonial question."[36] Stresemann attempted to appease the demands of the
colonial movement that he make the return of the colonies an
absolute condition for joining the League[37] by pointing to the
moral success achieved at Locarno.[38] He also specifically denied,
in a statement before the Reichstag, that Germany's entry into
the League could be construed in any way as a recognition of the
permanence of the status of the mandates.[39]

Membership in the League of Nations gave Germany at least
a limited influence on the fate of her former Empire. Stresemann
succeeded, despite some difficulties created by the British Dominions, in getting a German member appointed to the Permanent
Mandates Commission in 1927. The post was filled until 1929 by
Geheimrat Kastl, who was then succeeded by Julius Ruppel. Both
had colonial experience and did their utmost to maintain German rights in the mandates, especially by emphasizing the right
of Germans to immigrate, to acquire or re-acquire property, and
to be active in missionary work. The German colonial lobby did
not neglect to outline their duties[40] any more than it ceased to
keep up a continuous pressure on the various governments to assure that the colonial grievance would not be forgotten. Thus
Schnee, in 1931, led a delegation to interview Stresemann's successor, Curtius, on his attitudes on the colonial question. The
DKG pressed Chancellor Brüning to bring up the colonial claim
at the Lausanne Conference. Brüning actually seems to have intended to do so, but lost office before the Conference took place.[41]

36. Ibid., 2, 296.

37. Royal Institute of International Affairs, *Germany's Claim to Colonies*,
pp. 24–25. Jacob, *Kolonialkunde*, p. 63.

38. Stresemann, 2, 213. Dix, p. 294.

39. Mellem, *Der Deutsche Kolonialanspruch*, p. 51.

40. Stresemann, 2, 148 ff.; 157 ff. Dix, pp. 294 ff.; Royal Institute of International Affairs, p. 25.

41. Townsend, "The German Colonies and the Third Reich," pp. 188–89.
Rohrbach, *Deutschlands koloniale Forderung*, pp. 174–75.

His successor, Papen, made a strong statement in favor of colonial revision at a press interview of July 1932, but failed to raise the issue diplomatically. Nevertheless, the British Ambassador, Sir Horace Rumbold, reported to London in that year "that the colonial question was receiving prominence in German official circles as it had never enjoyed in previous years." He added that "if Germany can succeed [at Lausanne] in obtaining the cancellation of the war guilt clause, she will no doubt endeavor to use this moral reinstatement to strengthen her claim to readmission into the ranks of the colonial powers."[42]

The strong interest of governmental circles in the colonial question was also manifested by the frequent attendance of President Hindenburg, Papen, and Neurath at colonial meetings.[43] Despite such interest, however, the only attempt after Locarno to raise the colonial question in diplomatic negotiations was made without Foreign Office sanction and was disavowed by the German government.

It was Hjalmar Schacht who in 1929 saw an opportunity to link his colonial enthusiasm to his other field of interest, economic policy. As the German delegate to the Conference of Experts, which met in Paris to discuss an adjustment in the German reparations payments (which finally produced the Young Plan), Schacht tried to make German annual payments of 1650 million marks dependent on colonial concessions, as well as on an adjustment of Germany's Eastern boundary. It should be noted that Schacht asked not for colonial cessions per se but for some system under which Germany would have access to colonial raw materials. At the time Schacht was toying with the idea of chartered companies, to operate purely in the economic sphere. "We expressly did not raise any questions of sovereignty."[44] Nevertheless, Schacht's feeler produced an unpleasant impression in London, the more so because Schacht apparently had put former Foreign Minister Kühlmann up to sounding out Winston Churchill and Sir William Tyrrell, the British Ambassador to Paris. Upon inquiry by the British Ambassador in Berlin, Stresemann denied any knowledge

42. *British Documents*, pp. 980–81.
43. Royal Institute of International Affairs, p. 25.
44. Schacht, *The End of Reparations*, p. 73.

of or responsibility for the "Kühlmann mission" or Schacht's feeler, thereby causing a bitter falling out between himself and the economist, who felt that he had been attacked from the rear.[45]

Stresemann tried to calm Schacht by pointing out that he agreed with him on the substance of the matter and had said so to the British Ambassador:

> As for the question itself, the Reich has always taken the view and has stressed it, for instance, on the occasion of our entry into the League of Nations, that Germany, like every other power, was entitled to colonial activity and that the justification with which one had at the time [of the peace settlement] denied our right to colonial activity was wholly baseless. I also share your view that Germany must be given a greater degree of participation in the exploitation of raw materials. In spite of this I had to state, in reply to the question put to me by Mr. Chamberlain, that Herr von Kühlmann was in Paris neither in an official nor in a semi-official capacity, and that his steps had not been inspired by the Foreign Office, and therefore had neither an official nor a semi-official character.[46]

Disavowed by his government, Schacht had no choice but to surrender his position.[47] One of Schacht's biographers raises the question whether he ever expected his demands to be taken seriously and suggests that Schacht may simply have been looking for an excuse to break off the Young Plan negotiations.[48] In view of Schacht's firm convictions on the importance of colonies to the German economy, which he reiterated even in his postwar autobiography,[49] this writer is inclined to believe that he was probably sincere in making his démarche.

45. Stresemann, *3*, 395 ff. Peterson, *Hjalmar Schacht—For and against Hitler*, pp. 88 ff. Schacht, *The End of Reparations*, pp. 63–71.

46. Stresemann, *3*, 398.

47. Ibid., *3*, 399–400.

48. Peterson, p. 89.

49. Schacht, *Account Settled*, pp. 92–93, 290, 292.

Summarizing the diplomatic accomplishments of the governments of the Weimar Republic with respect to the colonial question, it may be said that they had brought about the official repudiation of the Colonial Guilt Lie and, through Germany's entry into the League, had given Germany some influence on the administration of her former possessions. As for the substantive question of territorial revision, however, they had not been able to make any progress. In fact it is doubtful that they had done everything in their power to make the victor powers aware of the existence of the colonial grievance, and to make them understand that colonial revision was an acute aim of German foreign policy. Such a realization would have been reflected in public discussions, especially in Great Britain—where, instead, the press made virtually no mention of the question. We must suspect that for the leaders of the Weimar Republic, and even for Stresemann, who had the greatest colonial interest among them, this was essentially a secondary question,[50] even though, under the pressure of the colonial associations and right-wing opinion in general, they had to deny this and pay lip service to the colonial cause.

Hitler's rise to power brought no immediate change in this situation. As a matter of fact the diplomatic career of the National Government began, so far as the colonial question is concerned, with another disavowal of a démarche by one of its members. This time it was Alfred Hugenberg, the Minister of Economics and leader of the Nazis' Nationalist coalition partners, who felt that the time had come to strike a blow for colonies. As a German delegate to the London Economic Conference, Hugenberg on June 14, 1933, made a statement to the press which foreshadowed the later accommodation of the Eastern and the Colonial schools of German expansionists. This statement, which had originally been prepared for delivery as a speech before the Economic Commission of the Conference, called for both kinds of expansion in order to restore Germany's solvency: "One of these steps would be to give Germany a colonial empire again in Africa, out of which she would build large works and installations that would otherwise not be constructed, all over this new continent. The

50. Cf. the Reichstag debate on Locarno, esp. *Verhandlungen, 388,* 4558.

second step would be to open up, to a nation without space, areas in which it could provide room for the settlement of its vigorous race, and construct great works of peace."

The Western Powers did not react officially to this restatement of the colonial claim. Russia, however, felt that "space for settlement" meant her own territory, and that Hugenberg, who had been known as a promoter of eastern settlement schemes even before 1914, had now introduced such "Rosenberg ideas" (actually, of course, they were also Hitler's ideas) into the realm of diplomacy. Accordingly she protested sharply to the Wilhelmstrasse. In reply, the German Foreign Office disclaimed any German designs on the Soviet Union. In a press statement, it characterized Hugenberg's démarche as merely an expression of his personal opinions.

Hugenberg protested bitterly at this betrayal; he felt that his statement had expressed the views of the entire German delegation. The matter caused a row in the cabinet, from which Hugenberg resigned, though primarily for other reasons, on June 27.[51]

This episode would seem to indicate clearly that in 1933 the German government was not yet ready to raise the colonial issue in an official manner. It was apparently felt that a more propitious climate for such a demand must first be created by propaganda and the improvement of Germany's political bargaining position. Thus at a cabinet meeting in April 1933 the Foreign Minister, in the course of an over-all survey of the German foreign policy position and objectives, defined the status of the colonial problem as follows: "In the colonial question . . . we must restrict ourselves for the time being to propaganda that is directed in the main against the undermining of the principle of exercising rule by mandate. In all colonial questions we must make sure in advance of Italy's agreement."[52]

The early years of Hitler's rule are thus characterized, with respect to the colonial question, by a peculiar "diplomacy by press interviews." By frequent but unofficial statements the leaders of the Third Reich eventually succeeded in impressing upon the

51. *German Documents,* Series C, *1,* 562–608.
52. Ibid:, p. 258.

public and the governments of the victor powers the seriousness of the German colonial grievance, without risking a rebuff by making an official demand.

Only a few days after he came to power, on February 11, 1933, Hitler said to the representative of the British *Sunday Express:* "As far as our overseas colonies are concerned, we have by no means given up our colonial desires; this problem, too, will have to be solved justly. There are a great many things which Germany must import from the colonies and we need colonies just as much as other nations."[53]

It must be noted, however, that the Führer always stressed that colonial revision must be brought about peacefully and that his statements on the question, at least in these early years, lacked any belligerent edge. Clearly he still believed in the policy of friendship with Britain that he had outlined in *Mein Kampf.* Thus on October 18, 1933, Hitler told his favorite British newspaperman, Ward Price of the *Daily Mail,* that "we shall never go to war to get colonies. We are convinced that we are as capable as any other nation of administering and developing colonial territories, and we regard this as a matter for negotiation."[54] The following summer Hitler emphasized this peaceful nature of the colonial claim even more when he said, again to Ward Price, "that he would not sacrifice the life of a single German soldier in order to recover the colonies."[55] This statement, as a matter of fact, was so pacific that it was widely understood, both abroad and among the German colonial circles, to mean that the Führer had given up the colonial claim. These misapprehensions were destroyed, however, the following September, when his deputy, Rudolf Hess, in a speech at the Party Congress again stressed the necessity of colonies for Germany. He added, however, that "the foreign political situation is not propitious for us to press our claims at present."[56]

Despite the moderate tone of such pronouncements, quite

53. Bauer, *Kolonien im Dritten Reich, 1,* 163.
54. Johannsen and Kraft, *Germany's Colonial Problem,* pp. 34–35.
55. Logan, p. 70.
56. Steer, *Judgment on German Africa,* p. 12. *Kolonialzeitung, 46* (1934), 202.

similar to those made by leaders of the Weimar Republic, they had a considerable impact on the Western Powers.[57] The government and public of Great Britain, especially, followed with close attention everything the new leaders of Germany had to say which might throw any light on their future policy. It was mainly this attention now given to any German statement on the colonial question which distinguished the general situation, with respect to this matter, from that which had prevailed during the Weimar period. Some indication of this change may be seen in the fact that the London *Times* in 1932 published only two items dealing with the German colonial claim. In 1933 there were fifteen; in 1936, when the real campaign of colonial agitation was beginning in Germany, 160. England was beginning to take colonial revisionism seriously.

In January 1934 the British Ambassador in Berlin, Sir Eric Phipps, appraised the foreign policy aims of Germany's new rulers and opined that they definitely included "the recovery of some colonial foothold overseas" as well as "some outlet for German energy to the South or the East."[58] In a memorandum to the Foreign Secretary of April 5, 1934, Sir Robert Vansittart endorsed this view: "There are two views now in Germany on the 'colonial question.' I think it may roughly be said that the older party would like to solve it 'with England,' and the younger 'in spite of England.' But they both want colonies."[59]

This appraisal, as a matter of fact, was not quite correct. The "younger party," i.e. the ideological National Socialists, were not yet agreed in their views on colonies. Insofar as they favored overseas expansion, and the majority probably did, they envisaged it as possible only "with England." Thus Alfred Rosenberg, the Nazis' chief theoretician, editorialized in the *Völkischer Beobachter* on January 21, 1933—only a few days before Hitler became Chancellor—that Germany should seek to combine *Ostpolitik* and *Weltpolitik* in order to create outlets for both the "peasant"

---

57. For more statements by leaders of the Third Reich during its early years see Bauer, *Kolonien im Dritten Reich, 1,* 174–75.

58. *British Documents,* Second Series, *6,* 977.

59. Ibid., p. 115.

and the "Viking" drives of its people. The overseas objective, however, must be approached diplomatically: "A solution of this problem not against but with Great Britain would be a task within a still larger circle of world political questions."[60]

This seems to have been the prevailing attitude, implicit also in Hitler's various pronouncements. Despite Vansittart's assertions to the contrary, however, there were in the Nazi Party some figures whose attitude toward colonies was essentially negative, among them Robert Ley and the party's agricultural expert, Walther Darré.[61] Despite his personal background—he was born in Argentina, went to a British public school, and attended the *Kolonialschule* at Witzenhausen—Darré as the chief of the SS office for racial and settlement affairs espoused the mythology of *Blut und Boden* in its purest form: "The essence of National Socialism lies in the concentration of the powers of the nation on the home soil, their renewal out of the blood spring of the settled peasant population."[62] Even such *Blut und Boden* enthusiasts, however, admitted that, through the Allied allegations of 1919, colonial revision had become a matter of national honor for Germany, and they therefore paid reluctant lip service to this cause.[63] After 1934, at any rate, a more procolonial attitude became dominant in the Party, and by 1936 *Blut und Boden* ideology had wholly given way to the opportunism of imperialism.[64]

Quite in contrast to Vansittart's views, moreover, it was the conservative older element in Hitler's original coalition (along with Göring) that put the greatest emphasis on the colonial claim and was perhaps a little more inclined to be Anglophobic than the orthodox Nazis. This difference should not be exaggerated. It is possible to quote statements in favor of colonies by all members of the Nazi-conservative coalition as well as by practically all

---

60. Bauer, *Kolonien im Dritten Reich, I*, 149.

61. For a brief biography of Darré, one of the lesser known among the Nazi leaders, see *Das Deutsche Führerlexikon 1934/1935* (Berlin, 1934), pp. 21–22.

62. Georg Fritz, *Kolonien?* (Berlin, 1934), p. v (introduction by Darré).

63. E.g. ibid., passim.

64. On this intraparty discussion see *Kolonialzeitung, 47* (1935), 34; *Deutscher Kolonialdienst* (October 1937), pp. 1–7; Bullock, *Germany's Colonial Demands*, p. 48; and Peterson, pp. 243–44. Cf. above, Chapter 2, n. 17.

National Socialist leaders. Most of them were notable for their moderate tone, at least in the early years.[65]

This moderation, along with the occasional expressions of *Blut und Boden* opposition to colonies, worried the leaders of the colonial movement, who had evidently hoped for a more forceful advocacy of their cause by a "national government." Epp tried to keep up sagging spirits: "We do our work quietly and undiscouragedly because this is the way the Führer wants it and because we are convinced that he will lead us to that goal, too, because Germany needs it."[66] On the other hand, the colonialists tried to put pressure on the government to proceed a little more energetically. One of their arguments was that the German communities in the colonies, especially in Southwest Africa, must be given new reasons for hope if they were to keep up the struggle.[67] On March 20, 1935, Dr. Schnee submitted a memorandum on "Germany's Equality of Rights and the Colonial Question" to Hitler and Neurath, in which he outlined the desires of the DKG. Schnee recommended that the main emphasis be put on demands for the restoration of "the big African colonies and New Guinea," less on Togo, Samoa, and the islands under Japanese mandate, which, in fact, he was willing to relinquish. This memorandum is quite amusing for the schoolmasterly tone in which Schnee lectured Hitler on the simple facts of the geography of the colonies, their economic importance and their political status.[68] Schacht, who was in a unique position among the old colonialists in that as Minister of Economics he had direct entrée to the Führer also "often attempted to persuade Hitler to show more interest in the colonial problem . . . particularly as it had found a place in the Party Programme." (Point 3 of the 25-point program of the NSDAP of 1920 called for "land and soil (colonies) for the nourishment of our people and for the settlement of our surplus population.")

Quite aside from such pressures on Hitler, however, changes in the internal and international situation of Germany which strengthened the position of her National Socialist rulers made

65. *Kolonialzeitung, 45* (1933), 93–94. Bauer, *Kolonien im Dritten Reich, 1,* 174–75.
66. Schmitt, *Kolonien für Deutschland,* pp. 26–27.
67. *Kolonialzeitung, 46* (1934), 95–96. Bennett, *Hitler over Africa,* p. 160.
68. *German Documents,* C, *3,* 1033–37.

it possible for them by 1935 to go beyond propagandistic maintenance of the colonial claim and to introduce it, gingerly at first, as a subject of diplomatic discussion. Even Epp realized that "the colonial question will not be ripe until Germany is once more great and strong in Europe."[69] By 1935 Hitler had achieved almost complete internal mastery of Germany, had successfully defied the victors of World War I by rearming and leaving the League, and had strengthened his European position by the non-aggression pact with Poland. He judged that these accomplishments gave him a sufficient bargaining position to achieve the dream of *Mein Kampf,* an alliance with England that might give Germany, among other benefits, some colonial satisfaction. Thus, when Hitler introduced the subject of colonies in the discussions with Sir John Simon and Anthony Eden that took place in Berlin in March 1935, he was still thinking of a solution *with* England.[70] In return for a colonial settlement, which would give Germany the "necessary and reasonable minimum" of living space and which might enable her to return to the League, in which she would then no longer have to play the role of a second-class power, Hitler offered Britain Germany's help in defending her empire, an offer which, incidentally, he was to repeat on the very eve of World War II. Hitler pointed to the colonial problem as the only remaining point in his program of restoring to Germany the "equality of status" of which she had been deprived in 1919.

Sir John Simon responded in a wholly negative fashion to this feeler. He rejected the whole concept of closer relations between Britain and Germany than between Britain and France and described the question of the mandates as a matter for the League, not for the British government, to decide on. "Simon remarked that he did not wish to leave us under the misapprehension that he was holding out hopes to Germany that the British Government could do anything about the colonial question, but he would report the German statements to his Government."[71]

---

69. Steer, p. 13.

70. Cf. Kordt, *Nicht aus den Akten,* pp. 95, 109, 112, 160.

71. *Auswärtige Politik,* Series C, *3,* 1043–80 (quotation from p. 1064). Cf. Amery, *The German Colonial Claim,* p. 124; and Bauer, *Kolonien im Dritten Reich, 2,* 134–40.

The relative importance of the colonial subject in the Simon-Eden discussions must not be exaggerated. Neurath specifically denied, in response to British comments on the talks, that there was an intention to make the adjustment of the colonial grievance an absolute condition for Germany's return to the League of Nations.[72] Nevertheless, Hitler found the British government anxious enough to deal with him—the Anglo-German Naval Agreement grew out of the discussions—that henceforth he felt he could demand a price for any agreements. By December 1935 Germany declared that her willingness to negotiate an air disarmament pact—which Hitler himself had first proposed to Eden and Simon—was dependent on "practical recognition" of Germany's colonial claim,[73] and from that time this claim was almost unfailingly raised whenever the Western Powers approached Germany with any proposals for a European settlement. Unlike the governments of the Weimar Republic, Hitler felt that he was in a position to make effective demands on the Allies, who became more and more willing to pay for what they had failed to enforce —peace in Europe.

In this spirit, the Belgian Prime Minister Van Zeeland said in a conversation with Hitler's foreign affairs adviser Ribbentrop in the fall of 1935 that Belgium "would create no difficulties at a comprehensive adjustment of all questions . . . this attitude also applied to the colonial question." The statement strongly implies a willingness on Belgium's part to use Ruanda-Urundi, her share of the colonial spoils of World War I, to pay for peace with Germany. Hitler calculated on this willingness of the Western Powers to pay any reasonable price for peace when on March 7, 1936, after his successful move into the demilitarized zone of the Rhineland, he made them a peace offer in which he dangled the promise of Germany's return to the League before them, provided Germany's "equality of rights" was recognized in the colonial sphere:

> Since the equal status of Germany and the rehabilitation
> of the full sovereignty over the entire German Reich ter-
> ritory has been finally achieved, the German Reich gov-

72. Logan, p. 74.
73. Townsend, "The German Colonies and the Third Reich," p. 197.

ernment considers the main reason for its resignation from the League of Nations removed. It is therefore willing to rejoin the League. In stating this, it expresses its expectation that in the course of a reasonable time the question of colonial equality as well as the question of the separation of the covenant of the League of Nations from its Versailles basis will be solved by means of friendly negotiations.[74]

In their reply, the other signatories of the Locarno Pact declared their willingness to consider this point at an international conference which they proposed should be called to devise a new over-all European security system. They also asked Hitler some pointed questions on his foreign-policy intentions, the answer to which was evaded in a German memorandum of March 31 that repeated the colonial demand.[75] The whole idea of a new settlement, which might have included colonial revision, eventually was abandoned in the uproar caused by Italy's Ethiopian adventure. The latter also led to a rapprochement between Mussolini and Hitler, which may well have been a factor in the Führer's decision to make renewed colonial overtures to France and Great Britain through that veteran of the colonial cause, Hjalmar Schacht.[76]

We have already mentioned that Schacht was constantly endeavoring to build fires under Hitler's colonial zeal. Without a doubt, Schacht attached a greater importance to colonial revision than any other German leader. He alone seems to have considered war as a means of achieving this goal. In a September 1935 conversation with S. R. Fuller, the American Consul General, Schacht stressed the economic importance of colonies, expressed his hope that they could be got by negotiation, but replied when asked what would happen if the Allies could not be persuaded to return the mandates to Germany: "Colonies are necessary to Germany. We shall get them through negotiation if possible; but if not, we

74. *Hamburger Monatshefte für Auswärtige Politik, 3,* no. 3, 69.
75. Ibid., no. 4, 212–15.
76. Logan, p. 103.

shall take them."[77] It is questionable whether Schacht actually advocated such forcible measures to regain the colonies, especially since he undoubtedly opposed a general war, which would have been the inevitable result. Perhaps he was merely expressing his fear of what *might* happen if the victor powers were unreasonable about the colonial claims, in order to impress the American with the seriousness of those claims.[78] This, at any rate, is what Schacht argued at his trial in Nuremberg and, implicitly, in his memoirs, where he tried to convey the impression that he had pushed his colonial hobby for the sake of peace, in order to turn Hitler's attention away from his plans for forcible expansion eastward.

That this apologia is not without basis is attested to by a letter Schacht wrote to Epp in March 1935 in reply to an inquiry about his attitude toward the colonial claim. Apparently the General had approached several government figures with this question. Schacht's reply, a copy of which was sent to Hitler, is an interesting comment on the deep gulf that separated the thinking of such conservatives as Schacht and Epp from the policies of Hitler.

Schacht pointed out that he was "well aware that the most diverse opinions are held within the National Socialist Party on the colonial question":

> The idea of the *Ostraum* that is to be acquired is un-
> fortunately causing a great deal of trouble. Nothwith-
> standing the need for an adjustment of our eastern
> frontiers, which I too have emphasized time and again,
> it should be clearly understood once and for all that
> Poland is a country not so very much less densely popu-
> lated than Germany and that an advance into the Baltic
> states would render infinitely more difficult the defense
> of an arm stretched out thus far eastward. The deciding
> factor is, however, that along the whole of the eastern
> frontier room could be made for German settlers only

77. International Military Tribunal, *Trial of the Major War Criminals, 36* (Nuremberg, 1947–48), 522–29.

78. Cf. Peterson, p. 270. In a September 1934 conversation with American Ambassador Dodd, Schacht apparently spoke of war as a means to regain the colonies—Logan, p. 71.

by wholly depopulating the area concerned, which no
reasonable person would consider feasible today, however decisive our victory might be.

Moreover, Schacht maintained, a colonial policy would serve the
cause of European peace: "It is [Germany's] purely continental
policy which is ultimately the reason why Germany is always re-
garded by her neighbors as the great threat to peace." Even if
eastern expansion could be carried out with success, it would do
little to enhance Germany's industrial basis. Schacht's economic
mind was revolted by "the romantic idea of turning Germany
into an agricultural nation again," which was basic to the thinking of such *Blut und Boden* enthusiasts as Walther Darré.[79]
    Hitler, by no means a "reasonable person" according to Schacht's
traditional definition of sound political conduct, was of course
not swayed from his dream of a continental empire in the East,
but Schacht and other colonial enthusiasts in his entourage—
there is no question, for instance, that Göring, himself the son of
the first governor of German Southwest Africa, belonged to this
group—were successful in persuading him that this concept did
not exclude a simultaneous colonial policy. We have already
noted that at about this time the formula *Ostpolitik und Kolonialpolitik* became the guideline of public colonial agitation. Similarly, it now appears as the determining factor of German foreign
policy. It must be realized, however, that the *main* territorial
aims of that policy continued to lie to the east. Colonies were
viewed by most Nazi leaders, and certainly by Hitler, as desirable
by-products of continental expansion.
    Schacht, however, was happy when in the summer of 1936 he
received Hitler's permission to raise the colonial matter semi-
officially with the Western Allies. Since he was about to visit Paris
on other business, he asked the French Ambassador in Berlin,
François-Poncet, to arrange for an interview with Premier Blum.
In his conversation with the Ambassador, Schacht did not fail to
mention his fears of Hitler's tendencies toward continental ag-
gressions, especially with respect to Czechoslovakia, which might

79. *German Documents, C, 3,* 1025–27.

still be contained by a colonial concession. About the form such a concession might take, the Minister of Economics made the same suggestions he had first developed in the '20s: "It was not, said Schacht, a question of giving Germany full title to colonial property. But without infringing upon established sovereignty, could not Britain, France, and Belgium concede to the Reich a territory in Central Africa, a territory which might be exploited by a German tenant company?"[80]

In Paris, Schacht's proposals found a friendly reception. "Happily the government of Leon Blum showed considerable understanding for the case I put forward. In principle it was in favor of a friendly discussion of the problem, and it undertook to get in touch with the British Government on the point. The attitude of the French Government filled me with hope which, however, soon changed to depression when the British Government delayed making up its mind on the matter for many months."[81] Perhaps in order to help Britain make up her mind, Hitler himself made his first major public reference to the colonies in his speech before the Nuremberg *Parteitag* of September 9, 1936. In explaining to his audience the economic necessities behind the new Four Year Plan the Führer intimated that this plan might not be necessary if Germany had colonies:

> If the German people and the German Reich had not been exploited for fifteen years, if they had not lost the whole of their international savings and the whole of their foreign capital investments, and above all—if we still had colonies of our own, it would certainly be easier for us to overcome those difficulties . . . [But] quite apart from [these considerations] Germany cannot waive her claim that justice should be done to her colonial demands. The vital rights of the German people are just as important as those of any other nation.[82]

This passage received much attention, especially in Great Britain, where the *Times* argued that a colonial adjustment might well be

80. André François-Poncet, *The Fateful Years* (New York, 1949), pp. 222–23.
81. Schacht, *Account Settled*, p. 94.
82. Johannsen and Kraft, pp. 35–36.

considered in return for "a practical renunciation by Germany of war as an instrument of policy."[83] The attitude of the British government, however, was slow to change from that "resolute opposition" to the colonial claim which the French Ambassador in Berlin seemed to regret.[84] Schacht was most discouraged at the resulting delay, which seemed to bear out Hitler's prophecy that the Western Powers would not hear of Schacht's scheme. Apparently genuinely worried that this negative attitude would encourage Hitler to return to projects of conquest in Eastern Europe which would endanger world peace, he now sought to involve the United States in his project of a European settlement, including colonial revision.

As early as 1936 he had urged, in a conversation with the American Ambassador Dodd, that President Roosevelt, after his re-election, call a "peace conference" to consider, among other questions, a new colonial settlement.[85] He repeated this suggestion in January 1937 to Ambassador Davies, in Berlin en route from Moscow. On this occasion Schacht claimed that he was authorized to offer definite terms to Great Britain and France:

> Stabilization of the present frontiers of European countries; establishment of perpetual peace in Europe; discontinuation of the present arms race; abolition of sanctions, to be replaced by some administrative machinery which would permit the members of this proposed alliance to enforce their decisions; substitution of a workable agreement between powers for the present League of Nations.

Before any such agreements could even be discussed, however, Germany must be given "colonies, access to raw materials, and regions open to settlement and migration."[86]

It seems most unlikely that Hitler really intended, at any time, to agree to the program for European peace set out in these pro-

---

83. Logan, p. 109.

84. François-Poncet, p. 223.

85. William E. Dodd, Jr., and Martha Dodd, eds., *Ambassador Dodd's Diary* (New York, 1941), p. 344—entry for August 18, 1936.

86. Ibid., January 27, 1937.

posals. If they were not in reality merely a scheme of Schacht's —which the Minister of Economics specifically denied—we have to assume that the Führer was here holding out an olive branch, a mere hope for European peace, in return for concrete concessions. This technique he had used before—for example, during the negotiations for the Anglo-German Naval Agreement—and he would use it again, at Munich. The catch in the offer was all too obvious: the colonial claim would have to be satisfied *before* Germany would even talk about a European settlement. The Western Allies, however, while they became increasingly willing to consider colonial concessions as a part of an over-all settlement, would not pay in advance for such a questionable commodity as Hitler's good will. This was the crux of the question of colonial revision in the years from 1937 to 1939.

In February 1937 the British government, although "furious with [the French] for having these conversations with Schacht"[87] in which it felt Leon Blum had been entirely too accommodating about a question that concerned Britain primarily, seems to have finally agreed to start looking seriously into the Schacht proposals. The German Minister of Economics "in February 1937 . . . received confidential information from London which sounded promising,"[88] apparently from the British Chief Economic Adviser Sir Frederick W. Leith-Ross, with whom he was having discussions in Basel about ways to remove trade barriers. Schacht, aware that the French attitude was far more friendly, insisted that a French representative also attend further meetings in which he and Leith-Ross would discuss his August proposals. The French Foreign Minister, Delbos, had high hopes that these conversations might lead to the "reintegration of Germany into the economy of the Western world," thereby perhaps also serving the political cause of peace. In a conversation with the American Ambassador William Bullitt, Delbos outlined his plans, the first step in which would be a general reduction of tariffs.

> The second step would be one which he would ask me to regard as most secret. He and Blum had not discussed

87. *FR* (1937), *1*, 48.
88. Schacht, *Account Settled,* p. 94.

it even with the other members of the Cabinet. They had in mind the creation of consortiums to develop sections of Africa. Germany would not be able to put up much money but a large proportion of the development would be done by the use of German machines. The money would be found in France and England and, if the United States should be inclined to join, in the United States.

To crown the entire proposal Germany would be given a colony, probably the Cameroons. Then all the African colonies except French North Africa and British South Africa would, so to speak, be put into a common pot; British, French, Belgian, Portuguese and German colonies would all be exploited by international consortiums which would in considerable measure favor the use of German products. He felt there was work enough in Africa to consume the energies of the civilized world for the next 50 years. Thus he hoped the manufacturing genius of Germany could be turned from war to peace purposes. At the same time he proposed to attempt to reach agreement with Germany on limitation of armaments . . .

He asked for my opinion and I told him that the ideas he had expressed were close to those of my government and that I was certain you and the President would be glad to know that he was working in this manner.[89]

Nothing came of all these plans. Schacht felt that his policy had been spoiled "by [Hitler's] intervention in the Spanish Civil War, an action which had a most unfavourable effect on our relations with the Western Powers."[90] This may explain why, on March 11, 1937, when Ribbentrop brought up the colonial subject in a conversation with British Foreign Secretary Eden, the latter was once again totally negative in his reply.[91] Furthermore, if Delbos was entirely too optimistic about the British readiness to make con-

---

89. *FR* (1937), *1*, 49–50.
90. Schacht, *Account Settled*, p. 95.
91. *FR* (1937), *1*, 59; cf. 46.

cessions, he misjudged Germany's willingness to give something in return even more severely. It is true that throughout 1937 Hitler and other Nazi leaders became ever more vociferous in their public statements in support of colonial revision. The Führer's speeches of January 30, 1937 (repudiating the War Guilt clause and the German signature to the Versailles Treaty), and May 1, at the 1937 *Parteitag* on September 7, at a harvest festival on October 3, and at Augsburg on November 21 all included passages dealing with the colonial claim, usually in the context of a discussion of Germany's economic difficulties. Other leaders, especially Göring, did not neglect the subject in their public utterances.[92]

This barrage of oratory about colonies did not mean, however, that Hitler considered them important enough to give up any other part of his ambitions in return for Western colonial concessions. While the French government was still optimistic on that point, its ambassador in Berlin was beginning to see things in a different perspective. François-Poncet realized that Schacht was rapidly losing influence and that the negotiations on economic policy and colonies he was still carrying on were "merely a smokescreen behind which Hitler would await the propitious moment to lay hands on Austria and Czechoslovakia."[93] The British government thought along similar lines and doubted that colonial concessions would appease Hitler's appetite for expansion. It took "the position that they would not be ready to return colonies to Germany merely to have Germany make further demands after the colonies were returned. If, however, the question of the return of some portion of the former German colonies to Germany should be the only capstone needed to complete a structure of peace for the world, it would [not] refuse to discuss the question."[94] The German government had just thrown cold water on any hopes for such a colonial settlement when it informed the British Ambassador, Sir Eric Phipps, "that it would be satisfied with nothing less than the return of all the colonies taken from

92. Logan, pp. 118 ff. *Deutscher Kolonialdienst* (September 1937), pp. 1–3. Krumbach, *Franz Ritter von Epp*, pp. 296–97.

93. *FR* (1937), *I*, 92.

94. Ibid., p. 95.

Germany by the Treaty of Versailles,"[95] implying that colonial revision was a German right, not a concession from which the West could expect counterconcessions. With increasing clarity this became the official German line.

In such circumstances, Schacht's renewed visit to Paris in May 1937 remained without practical results. The French expressed their willingness to negotiate about colonies at any time, if the Germans initiated such talks and were willing to offer some quid pro quo. Schacht seemed interested, but the German government took no further action on the French proposals throughout the rest of the year. In December Ambassador François-Poncet handed the record of the Paris conversations to the German Foreign Office but pointed out that by that time it had only historical value, since the German attitude had so much stiffened on other questions pertaining to a general settlement.[96] In talks between Georges Bonnet and Herr von Papen during the latter's visit to Paris in November, the French Finance Minister expressed his disappointment that the talks with Schacht had "unfortunately" had no result.[97]

The summer of 1937 passed without any new diplomatic developments on the colonial question. The new British Prime Minister, Neville Chamberlain, would certainly have acted on any German initiative about a colonial settlement that also promised to contribute to European peace. "I didn't believe myself that we could purchase peace and a lasting settlement by handing over Tanganyika to the Germans, but if I did, I would not hesitate for a moment," he wrote in a private letter.[98] Tanganyika was of course the only part of the former German Empire (with the exception of small strips of Togoland and Cameroons) directly under British control, and Chamberlain could not speak for the Dominions. Instead of capitalizing on Chamberlain's willingness to consider colonial cessions, the German government seems to have let him know that Schacht's ideas did not represent its real policy. "It was implied that about this there was no urgency, that colonies

95. Ibid., p. 84.
96. *Auswärtige Politik*, D, *1*, 78–79, 96–99, 110–15.
97. Ibid., p. 35.
98. Keith Feiling, *The Life of Neville Chamberlain* (London, 1947), p. 300.

were rather an honourable eccentricity of their economic expert, Dr. Schacht."[99] By the end of 1937 Hitler was concerned with other projects; although he still included the colonial claim in his public speeches, he saw little chance of realizing it without having to compromise his Austrian and Czech plans, and therefore let it rest.

> The colonial agitation, certainly after the failure of the August 1936 Blum Conferences, was looked on by Hitler as a diversionary move which would, at least, succeed in muddying the waters of his true aspirations. He would have accepted colonies for their prestige value, but he saw the real solution to the problem of raw materials temporarily in the Four Year Plan and permanently in expansion to the East.[100]

The so-called Hossbach Memorandum, so important for clarifying Hitler's eventual aims in the whole realm of foreign policy, also throws a great deal of light on his attitude toward the colonial problem. At the famous conference on November 5, 1937, attended by Göring, Admiral Raeder, Generals Blomberg and Fritsch, Foreign Minister Neurath, and Colonel Hossbach, who took informal minutes, Hitler clearly indicated that his immediate goals lay in Southeastern and Eastern Europe, that he would not be deflected from these goals by offers of colonies, but also that Germany would eventually seek colonies and would be in a better position to make this demand once it had become more powerful on the Continent.

> As our exports and imports are carried out over those sea lanes which are dominated by Britain, it is more a question of security of transport, rather than one of foreign currency and this explains the great weakness of our food situation in war time.

Thus

> Should the security of our food situation be our foremost thought, then the space required for this can only

99. Ibid., p. 329.
100. Peterson, p. 271.

be sought in Europe, but we will not copy liberal capital-
istic policies which rely on exploiting colonies. It is not
a case of winning people but of winning agriculturally
useful space. It would also be more to the purpose to seek
raw-material producing territory in Europe, directly adjoining the Reich and not overseas. . . .

Two hateful enemies, England and France, to whom a
strong German colossus in the center of Europe would
be intolerable . . . would view the building of German
military strongpoints overseas as a threat to their overseas communications, as a security measure for German
commerce, and indirectly a strengthening of the German
position in Europe.

England could not cede to us anything of its colonial
property due to the opposition of the Dominions. After
the loss of prestige suffered by England due to the transfer of Abyssinia to Italian ownership a return of East
Africa can no longer be expected. In the most favorable
case Britain would propose an accommodation of satisfying our colonial wishes by taking away colonies not
presently owned by Britain, e.g. Angola. French willingness to come to an agreement would be of the same
nature.

A serious discussion regarding the return of colonies
to us could be considered only at a time when England
is in danger and the German Reich strong and well
armed. The Führer does not share the opinion that the
Empire is unshakable.

Resistance against the Empire is to be found less in the
conquered territories than amongst its competitors . . .

Alongside the British Empire today a number of states
exist which are stronger than it. The British mother
country is able to defend its colonial possessions only
allied with other states, not by its own power. How could
England alone, for example, defend Canada against attack by America, or its Far Eastern interests against
Japan?[101]

101. International Military Tribunal, 25, 402–13.

The whole problem of Hitler's attitude toward colonies is shown by these passages to be one of priorities. For the Führer the creation of the continental Greater Germany came first, colonies would be sought after this powerful European bloc had been created, either as the price of an alliance with Great Britain or by joining her other actual or potential enemies. The inclusion of the United States among the latter is an interesting comment on the quality of Hitler's political thinking, especially on non-European matters.

In the light of the Hossbach Minutes the various subsequent efforts of the British government to appease Hitler with colonial concessions, which began with the visit of Lord Halifax to Berchtesgaden in November 1937, were doomed to failure. Indeed, it is highly questionable whether Hitler could have been distracted from his course of aggression against his eastern neighbors even if the British government had been more accommodating on this question earlier, at the time of Schacht's original proposal in August 1936. Certainly, the chance no longer existed at the time of the Halifax visit.

Hitler and the German Foreign Office thought, on the other hand, that they could carry out their eastern program and still reach an accommodation with Britain, in which Germany might receive some colonies in return for some minor concessions which would not compromise her East European plans. In preparation for the Halifax visit the head of the political section at the *Wilhelmstrasse*, Ernst von Weizsäcker, drew up a memorandum that envisaged such an agreement. Realizing that Germany "for a long time to come" would be unable to fight a war against England, Weizsäcker stressed the necessity for a peaceful settlement with the great sea power. "We want from England colonies and freedom of action in the East. England wants from us military nonactivity (*militärisches Stillehalten*), particularly in the West. These wishes are not entirely incongruous with one another." The program Weizsäcker proposed as the basis for the Halifax talks consisted of three points: (1) Consultation between the Locarno powers whenever necessary until a new West European security pact could be negotiated, (2) Publicity of armament programs, and (3) "Institution of a German-English committee to inquire into the German colonial claims. The addition of French delegates would have to be planned."[102]

Such a program was bound to be utterly unacceptable to Britain as well as to France, but for somewhat different reasons. The Western Powers had continued their consultations about a common policy to follow with regard to the colonial claim. As long as Eden continued in office, however, they were quite unable to agree on a formula because the British insisted that they would consider any colonial cession only as part of a general European settlement, while the French government of Camille Chautemps and Yvon Delbos, perhaps even more concerned about Hitler's intentions in Central and Eastern Europe, was inclined to make a down payment for Hitler's good will, in the form of colonial real estate, in order to create an atmosphere in which *later* negotiations on European questions might become possible.

Thus Delbos, the French Foreign Minister, in the fall of 1937 talked to the American Ambassador William Bullitt about his fears that Hitler might soon make a move against Austria, which could cause a war. Complaining about the "exceedingly stiff" British attitude on the question of colonial concessions, he expressed his belief that such concessions offered the "best chance" for beginning negotiations

> which might lead to a peaceful settlement . . . or at least to postponement of war . . . France and England could not offer Germany "concessions" in Austria and Czechoslovakia because in the first place such action would be dishonorable and in the second place the Germans would say that the Austrians and the Germans in Bohemia belonged to them of right and there was no concession whatsoever involved in permitting them to fall into the hands of the Reich. In the colonial domain, on the other hand, France and England had something to give and could therefore demand something in exchange. He felt therefore that through the door of colonial concessions it might be possible to enter into fruitful negotiations.

102. *Auswärtige Politik,* D, *1,* 34.

He believed that if some progress could be made in the colonial field it might not be impossible to begin conversations for a new Locarno.[103]

The Germans were well aware that the French favored a policy of colonial appeasement more than Britain, and had hopes that the French view might eventually win out.[104] The basic differences between the British and the French positions were, first, that Britain wanted to have German concessions before it would consider colonial cessions, while the French would have reversed that order of procedure. Secondly, however, it is implicit in a number of British and French statements and it became increasingly clear through the whole conduct of Western diplomacy in the year before Munich that France, with her primarily continental orientation, was generally more inclined to appease Germany with overseas territory. When Chamberlain, on the other hand, realized that he could not "purchase peace and a lasting settlement by handing over Tanganyika to the Germans," he decided to make an attempt at purchasing peace by giving Germany some of the "freedom of action in the East" that was the other German *desideratum* according to the Weizsäcker Memorandum. Eventually, of course, France went along with British policy. It must be stressed, however, that neither France nor Britain was inclined to give Hitler both—colonies as well as freedom of action in the East. The Hossbach Minutes show that Hitler realized this and decided to concentrate on obtaining the latter.

In the conversations held at Berchtesgaden on November 19, 1937, between Hitler and Chamberlain's emissary, Lord Halifax, the two parties were at cross-purposes. Halifax had come prepared for some serious talk about colonies, which, in view of Hitler's numerous public pronouncements on the subject throughout the year and various soundings that had been made by Ribbentrop, the German Ambassador in London, seemed to be the crux of Anglo-German relations.[105] Hitler, however, turned out to be

103. *FR* (1937), *1*, 158.
104. Ibid., p. 168.
105. *Auswärtige Politik*, D, *1*, 39.

more interested in a discussion of the Austrian and other Central European problems; the colonial claim was discussed, but hardly in an atmosphere of urgency:

> The Colonial question came up in two or three forms in the course of our discussion. If the question could be settled between us, good. If not, he must note and regret. But he hoped that France and Great Britain would examine the question together and arrive at a solution which they could propose. He added:
>
> (1) that if there were countries which for strategic reasons we might not wish to give up, we should offer something in substitution; and (rather humorously)
>
> (2) that he did not want a colony
>
>   (a) at "strategic points which would drag him into trouble"; nor
>
>   (b) in the Sahara; nor
>
>   (c) in the Mediterranean "between two Empires";
>
>   (d) nor in the Far East which was also too dangerous.
>
> To all this I replied that it was quite out of the question for the present or any other Government in England to touch the colonial question except in the setting of a general settlement which would give our people a secure prospect of real understanding and relief of the present tension. But we were perfectly willing to discuss this or any other question, and it therefore ought to be considered what might be the next most useful step. Hitler said that talks and conferences need very careful preparations, and he did not believe in a conference every three months that achieved nothing. The real danger was that of an unsuccessful conference. Let us be content to go slowly. It was the surest way . . .
>
> I definitely got the impression that apart from colonies there was little or nothing he wanted from us, and that as regards European problems he felt time to be on his side . . . He did not give me the impression of being at all likely to go to war with us over colonies; but no doubt

if he cannot be met on this issue good relations, without which the present strain continues, would remain impossible.[106]

Even supposing that Great Britain made concessions in this matter, however, Hitler would not commit himself on the counter-concession Halifax was most interested in, Germany's return to the League of Nations: "Certainly she would not join the League, constituted and functioning as at present."[107]

From his talks with other Nazi leaders, interestingly enough, Halifax received a greater sense of urgency about the colonial problem than he had gathered from his conversation with Hitler. "Blomberg was the only one of the highly placed Germans who admitted to Halifax that it was not the colonial question that was of vital importance to Germany, but Central Europe . . ."[108] Göring and Goebbels, as well as other influential members of the Third Reich, always seem to have attached a greater importance to overseas expansion than Hitler.

Halifax' reflections on the colonial problem in his report on the visit are a most interesting comment on the motives of British foreign policy during this period and especially after Halifax succeeded Eden as Foreign Secretary. Unlike Eden, who had been adamant in his opposition to colonial (or any other kind of) appeasement as late as October 1937,[109] Halifax thought it might be worth trying, although he, too, was not overoptimistic about the chances such a policy offered for European peace:

> The conclusion, I think, is that it will be difficult to make any progress unless we are prepared to make concrete proposals in the one matter that directly arises between us: viz. the colonial issue. Whether or not it is possible, desirable, to try out the line of practical suggestions about the colonies is a question raising many other considerations. The suggestion that we should try to do a bargain on the line of getting him to drop the demand

106. Lord Halifax, *Fullness of Days* (New York, 1957), pp. 189–90.
107. Ibid., p. 188.
108. *FR* (1937), *1*, 184.
109. Ibid., p. 153.

for colonies as a return for a free hand in Europe is neither very moral nor very attractive. There might be more
to be said for the more difficult but sounder bargain of
a colonial settlement at the price of being a good European. But with what collateral security?[110]

Halifax, in this passage, showed a fairly clear understanding
of Hitler's aims and the alternatives faced by British policy. In
accordance with these views he and Chamberlain were to try first
to offer "Hitler a colonial settlement at the price of being a good
European." When this policy signally failed in March 1938, however, they tried the "neither very moral nor very attractive" alternative of continental appeasement—within limits. Eventually,
this policy, too, failed to maintain peace in Europe. Hitler's ambitions were too vast for any policy of accommodation to succeed,
but in the winter of 1937 this was not yet obvious to the Western
statesmen.

Chamberlain considered the proposals Hitler had made at
Berchtesgaden "a fair basis of discussion, though no doubt these
points will bristle with difficulty." Immediate steps were taken to
reach an understanding with the French government about the
form colonial concessions might take. The French, of course, had
for some time been in favor of such a policy. While the Halifax
visit was in progress, Franz von Papen, on a visit to Paris, had
received renewed assurances of French good will about the colonial matter, despite the fact that Papen, acting on instructions,
treated this problem as "secondary" and stressed Central European
problems (i.e., Austria) in his talks with French statesmen.[111]
The latter were far more willing to talk about colonies. Finance
Minister Bonnet assured Papen: "With regard to the colonial
question an appeasement of German demands seemed definitely
feasible to him and he believed that within the British government this opinion was shared . . . But of course one could not deal
with the colonial question as an isolated problem."[112] In the discussions between Premier Chautemps, Prime Minister Chamber-

110. Halifax, p. 192.
111. *Auswärtige Politik*, D, *1*, 83–84.
112. Ibid., p. 35.

lain, Eden, Halifax, and Delbos that took place in London at the end of November, the main French concern was that Britain was trying to make colonial concessions to Germany at the exclusive expense of France and the smaller colonial powers. Apparently Chamberlain suggested that France might, as a starter, "hand the Cameroons to Germany at once without any *quid pro quo*." The French representatives, however, insisted that their country "could not place herself in the position of being the only country to make concessions to Germany in the colonial domain and would do so only if England was prepared to make similar concessions and if such concessions would be part of a general settlement."[113] Chamberlain conceded this point:

> The Prime Minister thought Great Britain would not refuse her contribution in the matter of colonies, though he would not admit a German "right" or allow the principle before Germany made wider concessions; still, the French would perhaps consider an enquiry with Belgium and Portugal for a broad African scheme? He made it clear that we should never swallow the bribe of a separate Anglo-German understanding, or meet her wishes in Central Europe without some satisfaction as to the League and disarmament . . .[114]

Within a year, of course, Chamberlain's insistence on German counterconcessions would virtually vanish. At the close of the Chautemps-Chamberlain talks, the Allies issued a statement which contained the following paragraph on the colonial subject: "A preliminary examination was made of the colonial question in all its aspects. It was recognized that this question was not one that could be considered in isolation and, moreover, would involve a number of other countries. It was agreed that the subject would require much more extended study . . ."[115] This communiqué understandably stirred up quite a storm in the smaller European colonial powers, and especially in Portugal, ever touchy about

113. *FR* (1937), *I*, 186.
114. Feiling, p. 333.
115. Royal Institute of International Affairs, p. 66.

designs on her overseas possessions. The suspicions of those countries that Britain and France were toying with the idea of appeasing Germany with their property had to be calmed by a statement to Parliament, in which Eden denied, not quite candidly, that such plans existed, explaining that the "other countries" mentioned in the communiqué were the Dominions, which were administering mandates.[116]

The Chautemps-Chamberlain conversations also encouraged the Germans to loose a new flood of colonial propaganda and to push the subject through diplomatic channels.[117] They felt that now that they had their foot in the door it might be possible to get the Allies to go one step further and offer colonies as a free gift—without strings attached. Ribbentrop, in separate talks with Chamberlain, Halifax, and Eden during the middle of December, expounded to them the official German view that the colonial question involved a clear, unilateral "legal" claim by Germany which had nothing to do with any European questions.[118] The British statesmen, and especially Halifax and Eden, continued to insist, however, that the Western Powers wanted something in return for any colonies they might give Germany. Eden, obviously still unconvinced of the wisdom of the whole policy of colonial appeasement, stressed that some time would have to pass before concrete proposals could be made to Germany on the basis of the Halifax-Hitler talks. Further study and Anglo-French contacts would be required.[119] Chamberlain, on the other hand, encouraged Ribbentrop by suggesting that definite proposals might be forthcoming by February or March and that parliamentary opinion was favorable to colonial revision.[120] On the French side, François-Poncet informed Papen, during the latter's visit to Berlin in December, that a colonial settlement now hinged merely on Germany's willingness to offer equivalents in the form of assurances for European peace. He particularly urged that Germany consider rejoining a reorganized League of Nations, which might

116. Ibid., p. 67. Logan, pp. 130–31.
117. Logan, p. 132.
118. *Auswärtige Politik,* D, *1,* 102.
119. Ibid., p. 101.
120. Ibid., p. 108.

merely be a clearing house for diplomacy.[121] It is evident that the Allied price for colonies was already going down.

In a German Foreign Office memorandum Weizsäcker pointed out this process of shrinkage. No longer was there talk of a "complicated Pact system" or even of a security pact confined to Western Europe. Even Germany's return to the League seemed no longer a sine qua non in return for colonial concessions. The British were dropping their demands for changes in German economic policy. In effect the demands of the Western Powers had been scaled down to consist merely of an agreement on armaments and German recognition of the principle that political changes in Europe should be brought about by peaceful methods only. Weizsäcker himself thought that the colonies might be worth some concessions on the disarmament question.[122]

Hitler, however, felt that it was only a question of time before the Western Powers would give up their last conditions and he would receive colonies in return for nothing at all. It was only necessary to keep up a constant barrage of demands, and indeed German colonial agitation reached its climax during those months: "We shall voice our demand for living space in the colonies more and more loudly till the world cannot but recognize our claim. What they do not like to hear mentioned today they will get used to in a year's time. What they refuse to concede to-day they will consider in three years' time; and in another three years they will discuss ways and means of settling the problem."[123] Hitler re-

121. Ibid., p. 106.
122. Ibid., pp. 122–23, 142, 148. The process by which the quid pro quo that Britain demanded for colonial concessions tended to become steadily smaller is also noted in a recent work by Martin Gilbert and Richard Gott, *The Appeasers* (London, 1963). In their chapter on colonial appeasement the authors take the traditional view that Hitler lacked all real interest in the colonial claim, which was maintained only as a device to perpetuate a grievance, and thus dislike and distrust of Britain. They do not explain why Hitler, whose statements in *Mein Kampf* they take otherwise very literally, would have been interested in fostering tension between Germany and England, who according to this book were to become allies. Nevertheless, the work adds some interesting points to the story told here. It supports the view that the creation of a German overseas empire was by the late 1930s a distinct possibility, because of the British government's eagerness to remove German grievances.
123. Steer, pp. 18–19.

turned to the colonial topic in a speech on February 20, 1938, which made it quite clear that he refused to consider the colonies as a barter object of the Western Powers. In the course of a description of the successes of the Four Year Plan, he voiced the colonial demand as follows:

> However much we may achieve thus, the hopeless inadequacy of the space allotted to the German nation will not thereby be removed. Therefore our demand will become more and more insistent as the years go by for those colonial possessions of which after all Germany never deprived any other nation, and which are practically worthless to the Powers that hold them but appear indispensable to our own nation. . . .
>
> It is futile to hope that we will bargain away our demand in return for credits. It is not credits that we want, but those fundamental necessities of life which will enable us, by our own efforts, to secure the existence of the nation. Above all, we do not want naïve assurances that we shall be permitted to buy what we need. . . . There is no economic recipe which could be a complete substitute for the possibilities of intensive economic activity within one's own currency area.
>
> I want you to realize that I have the deepest suspicion of all so-called conferences, which may perhaps provide their participants with hours of interesting and stimulating conversation but which generally lead only to the disappointment of the hopes of mankind. . . . Neither can I admit that certain definite natural demands be connected with political bargaining which has no bearing on them.[124]

Along the same lines the German Foreign Minister brusquely informed the British Ambassador Nevile Henderson that Germany was not willing to promise anything in return for colonies, especially before it actually received them. Neurath specifically dismissed the possibility that Germany might return into any kind

124. Ibid., p. 16.

of League of Nations.[125] The same theme—that colonies were a right that Germany was entitled to and that Germany could not be expected to make concessions in return for receiving them back—was sounded in numerous speeches by leaders of the party and of the colonial movement.[126]

That these statements were not without effect on the Allied statesmen is shown by the fact that French Foreign Minister Delbos, during a brief visit to Berlin, conceded to Neurath that he was willing to discuss the various disputes between the Western Powers and Germany—including the colonial claim—separately and one by one, rather than simultaneously.[127] In February 1938, Weizsäcker was convinced that the Western Powers had given up the idea of limiting Germany's freedom of action in Eastern and Southeastern Europe in return for colonies.[128] In London, Eden was anxious to let Hitler know "that the British were sincere in their [approach] to the colonial problem and were not 'stalling.' "[129] Apparently by now the only real counterconcession the Allies demanded from Hitler was a certain amount of good will and restraint in his European ventures, especially on Austria. The Führer, of course, was unwilling to give even that much.

By February 1938 it was known in the German Foreign Office that a generous colonial offer would soon be forthcoming from Nevile Henderson, who had received instructions on the matter during his January visit to London.[130] On March 1, as the Austrian crisis was approaching, Henderson had an interview with Ribbentrop, the new German Foreign Minister, asking him to arrange an audience with Hitler so that the British Ambassador could lay before him "a positive proposal on the colonial question—regarding Africa. On the other hand, the English Govern-

125. *Auswärtige Politik*, D, *1*, 150.

126. Thus, e.g., Epp: "The question must not be involved with other political problems, or there can be no hope of success." Epp was beginning to talk as if Germany were doing the Allies a favor by considering acceptance of colonial concessions! Steer, p. 16.

127. *Auswärtige Politik*, D, *1*, 123.

128. Ibid., p. 140.

129. *FR* (1938), *1*, 136.

130. *Auswärtige Politik*, D, *1*, 161–62. Nevile Henderson, *Failure of a Mission* (New York, 1940), p. 113.

ment must insist on certain counter-concessions [regarding] the securing of peace in Europe." Ribbentrop replied that Germany had a legal claim to colonial revision and that therefore any haggling about a price for colonies must be out of the question. The Ambassador assured him that he didn't intend to insist on any price but merely wanted to ask the Führer if he, in turn, would make "a positive contribution to European pacification."[131] Hitler agreed to receive Henderson for an interview, even though the latter refused to keep the conversation a secret, as the Führer had desired. Eventually it was agreed to publicize the fact that the conversation had taken place, although its content would not be revealed. France received prior advice only to the effect that Henderson was about to launch his *démarche*.[132]

The interview between Ambassador Henderson and Hitler (Ribbentrop and the interpreter Paul Schmidt were the only other persons present) on March 3, 1938, shows how far the Chamberlain government was willing to go to accommodate the German colonial claim, if only Hitler would desist from open aggression on the European Continent.

Henderson opened the conversation by stressing its secrecy. The French, "and even less the Belgians, Portuguese and Italians" (with whose property he was about to tempt Hitler) would not be informed of its content. He pointed out that his proposals were necessarily preliminary ones, since the British government would have to negotiate the details with other powers. Denying that he intended to propose a barter deal, the Ambassador described his mission rather as an attempt to build up a "true and cordial friendship." In order to achieve such a relationship, however, it was required that both sides show genuine willingness to reach agreement. "The positive cooperation of Germany is necessary for the establishment of peace and security in Europe." This did not mean, however, that changes would not take place on the Continent—all the Ambassador asked was that such changes be brought about "in a spirit of reason."

Specifically, Henderson asked Hitler to consider a "limitation of armaments and pacification in Czechoslovakia and Austria."

131. *Auswärtige Politik*, D, *1*, 186–87.
132. Ibid., pp. 192–93.

In this connection he expressed concern about the recent agreements Hitler had extracted from Schuschnigg, which already foreshadowed the *Anschluss,* about to be consummated. In the field of disarmament, the British representative stated, his government was particularly anxious for an agreement to limit the number of bombing planes. Proceeding to the colonial question, Henderson read his instructions verbatim:

> A solution which seemed to them to have many attractions might be found in a scheme based upon the idea of a new regime of colonial administration in a given area of Africa, roughly corresponding to the conventional zone of the Congo Basin Treaties, acceptable and applicable to all the Powers concerned on exactly equal terms.
>
> Each Power, while solely concerned for the administration of its own territories, would be invited to subscribe to certain principles designed to promote the well-being of all.
>
> For instance, there would be the question of demilitarization as well as stipulations for the welfare of the natives, and for freedom of trade and communications. Also, perhaps a commission might be formed consisting of representatives of all the Powers having territory in the area covered by the new arrangements . . .

At the conclusion of his opening statement Henderson asked the Führer whether Germany (1) was prepared, in principle, to participate in a new colonial regime as envisaged by the English proposal, and (2) what contribution she was prepared to make for the general peace and security in Europe.

Hitler began his reply by protesting his friendship for England and expressed his belief that the prohibition of the "international inflammatory press" would be the greatest contribution to the peace of Europe. He compared the relations between Germany and Austria to those of Great Britain and Ireland; he rejected all outside interference in them. Becoming impassioned, Hitler harangued the very cool British Ambassador on Austria and the condition of the Germans in Czechoslovakia. In the case of Austria, Britain should support Germany against Schuschnigg, to show her good will. The denial of self-determination to the Sudeten Germans, moreover, would eventually lead to an "explosion."

Henderson broke in to inquire what Hitler's attitude would be toward the plebiscite on continued independence which the Austrian government had just announced. Hitler evaded this question. On disarmament, he reminded the Ambassador of his proposals of 1935 and 1936 which had been disregarded by the Western Powers. France, instead, had concluded her pact with Russia, who had sabotaged all ideas designed to lead to a limitation of armaments. It was against the Soviets, however, that German armaments were directed. Questioned by Henderson about his views on a limitation of bombers, Hitler was again evasive and referred to his lack of trust in Russia.

The colonial problem, Hitler maintained, would be solved more easily by simply returning her old colonies to Germany than by a "complicated new system."

> He, the Führer, must openly admit, however, that he did not consider the colonial problem ripe for settlement as yet, since Paris and London had declared themselves much too firmly opposed to the return. Therefore, he did not want to press the issue either. One could wait quietly for four, six, eight, or ten years. Perhaps by that time a change of mind would have occurred in Paris and London, and they would understand that the best solution was to return to Germany her rightful property acquired by purchase and treaty. The prerequisite for Germany's collaboration in a new colonial regime was, therefore, the return of the former colonies, which were legitimately acquired but taken away by treaty. Germany did not want to burden other countries not involved in the colonial settlement. Perhaps Belgium and Portugal would not agree, either, and would believe that Germany was demanding something from them to which she was not entitled.[133]

133. Ibid., pp. 201–02.

(The idea of Hitler insinuating to Henderson that the British proposal violated international morality does not lack a certain element of grim humor.) In reply, Henderson again explained his plan, using a globe, and expressed his belief that Portugal and Belgium, as well as France and Italy would eventually cooperate.

Hitler again changed the subject to Central Europe. Pressed by the Ambassador for a firm answer on the colonial proposal, Hitler finally, "in view of the importance of the question" promised a written reply. Ribbentrop broke in to ask if the British government considered returning all of the German colonies, including those administered by the Dominions, a question Henderson confessed himself unable to answer, since he had no authority to speak for the Dominions. To another query by the Foreign Minister he replied that his Congo Basin proposal did not "exclude the return of other German colonies outside of that area." The conference closed on this note.[134]

From this interview, Henderson gained the definite impression that "it was clearly not colonies that interested Hitler" and that the colonial grievance "was merely being exploited for propaganda purposes, partly to keep the claim alive for use later, when Germany's aspirations in Europe—a prior consideration—had been achieved and digested; partly to make the German people believe that it was the want of colonies and not excessive rearmament which was causing the lack of butter and other comforts."[135] This opinion of Henderson's was supported by the fact that the German reply to his colonial proposals, promised once again by Ribbentrop in an interview with Halifax on March 10, was never to be delivered.[136]

Such a reply, it is true, would have been largely pointless after Hitler's march into Austria on March 12, which altered the whole Western position on the question of colonial concessions. These had been offered partly in the hope that they would dissuade Hitler from the use of force in Europe. Now that it had been

---

134. Paraphrased part of the Hitler-Henderson interview based on *Auswärtige Politik*, D, *1*, 196–205.

135. Henderson, pp. 58, 115.

136. Ibid., p. 117.

used, despite Henderson's and Halifax' pleas,[137] there seemed little point in pursuing the colonial matter. Chamberlain stated in the House of Commons on March 16 that "it is obvious that in the present circumstances nothing further can be done about this question."[138] While the official German view held that Austria had nothing to do with colonies and that the German "legal claim" continued to exist,[139] in practice little was done about the colonial question during the spring and summer of 1938. Even the propaganda campaign became somewhat less vociferous. Never again was there to be such a definite possibility of peaceful colonial revision in favor of Germany as in early 1938.

Colonies were still discussed from time to time by the diplomats and governmental leaders of Germany and the Western Allies. In those months of crisis, however, the colonial problem was clearly relegated to a secondary position by all concerned. Hitler himself, through a number of statements, had helped to create this atmosphere in which urgency was lacking by setting a generous time limit for the solution of the colonial problem. Let us note, however, that he *did* set a time limit. To Henderson he had intimated that the colonies could wait for "four, six, eight, or ten years." Later in 1938 he became more specific. In October 1938 Hitler told the departing French Ambassador François-Poncet that the Germans did not intend to raise the question "for five or six years." Ribbentrop mentioned the same period of time to the new French Ambassador Robert Coulondre.[140] Again, in November, Ribbentrop spoke with the visiting South African Minister of Defense, Oswald Pirow, who had always favored the German colonial claim. The German Foreign Minister informed

137. See the accounts of the Ribbentrop-Halifax and Ribbentrop-Chamberlain interviews on March 10 and 11, 1938, in *Auswärtige Politik*, D, *1*, 207–28, which clearly indicate the link between the two questions.

138. Royal Institute of International Affairs, p. 67.

139. *Auswärtige Politik*, D, *1*, 867. German diplomats were instructed to say that there was no connection between the annexation of Austria and the colonial matter. The *Kolonialzeitung* maintained that Germany's economic need for colonies had been made more acute by the addition of six million more people to the "Volk ohne Raum" (*50*, 1938, 134–35).

140. *British Documents*, Third Series, *3*, 310. *Auswärtige Politik*, D, *4*, 399.

Pirow that the colonial question was not acute—it would be "talked about in five or six years."[141] A week later, on November 24, Pirow was received by Hitler, who again brought up the subject of colonies. Pirow assented to the principle of colonial revision: "We wish that Germany get exactly what it had." However, like many South Africans who favored Germany's return to Africa to "strengthen the community of the white master people vis-à-vis the blacks," the Minister of Defense had reservations when it came to the question of restoring to Germany South Africa's own mandate, Southwest Africa, or even Tanganyika, which was often described as belonging to the Union's sphere of interest. Pirow talked vaguely of compensations. "Breaking off [the discussion on] this question, the Führer expressed the opinion that the governments had today all taken such a firm position on the colonial question that it was useless continually to talk about it. One would have to bring it up again in five or six years."[142]

It is possible that this span of five or six years was simply a figure of speech used by Hitler and Ribbentrop to indicate that they did not intend to press the colonial claim in the foreseeable future. There are some indications, however, that Hitler was being quite specific about the time at which he proposed to take steps to get back Germany's colonies: Only in 1944 or 1945 would the so-called Z-Plan of Naval construction enable Germany to face Great Britain at sea. When this plan was formulated at the end of 1938, Hitler had assured his Grand Admiral, Erich Raeder, that there was "no need to expect [a war against England] before 1944." On another occasion, Raeder informs us, Hitler "emphasized that he would not need the fleet for his political purposes until 1946."[143] We must remember that Hitler expected England to stay neutral in a war with Poland, which, according to the Hossbach Minutes, would at any rate take place long before 1944.

141. *Auswärtige Politik*, D, *4*, 290–91.
142. Ibid., pp. 292–94.
143. William L. Shirer, *The Rise and Fall of the Third Reich* (New York, 1960), p. 622; cf. p. 487. Erich Raeder, *Mein Leben* (Tübingen-Neckar, 1956–57), 2, 156. See also "Opinion on the Draft Study of Naval Warfare against England" of September 1938, which states that the "decision to make Germany a world power . . . forces upon us the necessity of making . . . preparations for war" (International Military Tribunal, *3*, 121).

What political purposes, involving danger of war with Great Britain in the mid-forties, could Hitler have had in mind—except overseas expansion? Perhaps this was what Ritter von Epp meant when he said in a speech on October 29, 1938, that "Germany would not allow others to force upon her their own interpretation as for the proper time for the solution of this open question."[144]

If Germany (i.e. Hitler) wanted colonies at all and was not willing to make any concessions to the Western Powers in return for a peaceful solution of the question, the only way that remained to motivate those powers to give up overseas territory to the Reich was force or the threat of it. The proper time for that kind of "solution of this open question," however, would not be at hand until Germany had the power to threaten Britain's command of the sea—five or six years later.

Although there was little action on the colonial matter on the diplomatic front after March 1938—the question was barely mentioned in the talks between Hitler and Chamberlain at Godesberg and Munich[145]—there was now a great deal of public discussion of the matter in the Western countries. Especially after the Munich agreements there was a general feeling that something would now be done about the German colonial claim.[146] This atmosphere gave rise to a good deal of hysteria among British inhabitants of the mandates and of the neighboring territories, who formed themselves into leagues to resist, forcibly if necessary, the return of the colonies to Germany.[147] Chamberlain, as late as October 1938, was willing to consider several colonial concessions if Germany would agree to some kind of disarmament arrangement. The main opposition to such a bargain seems to have come from the Dominions,[148] and there is some evidence that Germany tried to deal with the latter directly in order to overcome this difficulty.[149]

144. *British Documents*, Third Series, *3*, 256–57.
145. Ibid., Second Series, *3*, 635–40. Royal Institute of International Affairs, p. 68. Feiling, p. 370.
146. Steer, pp. 8–9.
147. Roberts, *The Nazi Claim to Colonies,* passim.
148. *Auswärtige Politik,* D, *4*, 267.
149. Ibid., D, *1*, 19–20.

By December 1938 this situation had changed completely. It was becoming increasingly obvious that Hitler refused to be content with what had been given him at Munich, and public opinion was turning against that settlement and the statesmen who had engineered it. Further appeasement was out of the question for the time being. Ribbentrop went to Paris in early December for the signing of a Franco-German Declaration that denied the existence of any territorial dispute between the two countries. He was told by Foreign Minister Georges Bonnet, once an advocate of colonial revision, that the sacrifices France had made in Europe by the Munich agreements precluded doing anything for Germany in the colonial field at that time. The attitude of the French public toward colonial appeasement now was one of "absolute resistance."[150]

This resistance was intensified when the Nazis organized the anti-Jewish pogroms in December 1938. Liberal opinion in Great Britain, which had heretofore been rather favorably inclined toward German colonial ambitions, now turned strongly against the idea of handing over African peoples to the tender mercies of Hitler's "master race." This new attitude found expression in a statement by the Colonial Secretary, Malcolm MacDonald, in the House of Commons on December 7, 1938: "I do not believe that there is to-day any section of opinion in this country that is disposed to hand over to any other country the care of any of the territories or peoples for whose government we are responsible, either as a colonial or as a mandatory power . . . We are not discussing this matter. We are not considering it. It is not now an issue in practical politics . . ."[151] This statement was clear enough for everybody concerned except for such hard-shell imperialists as L. S. Amery, who questioned the meaning of the word "now," which for all practical purposes meant "not any more."

In Germany this hardening of British attitudes was recognized.[152] Ambassador Herbert von Dirksen reported from London

150. Ibid., D, *4*, 415.
151. Roberts, p. 96.
152. See, e.g., a conversation between Ribbentrop and Ashton-Gwatkin, the Director of the Economic Section of the British Foreign Office—*Auswärtige Politik*, D, *4*, 357–58.

that the new German anti-Jewish measures were the main reason for British alienation. The German leaders, recognizing that nothing could be achieved now, put a damper on colonial propaganda. Hitler's statements on this question during late 1938 and early 1939 were remarkable for the mildness of their tone and for the fact that in his speeches the colonies were referred to only in asides.[153]

The only concrete steps taken about the colonial matter during this period were certain discussions between the German Embassy in Paris and the French Foreign Office about the possibility of German firms participating in various African development projects ranging from iron-mining in Guinea to forestry in the Cameroons. No political questions were involved in these talks.[154] In the summer of 1939, however, with the Polish crisis already looming on the horizon and the storm clouds thickening over Europe, Chamberlain may have made one last attempt to realize his aim—European peace—by purchasing it with colonial concessions. In late July 1939 the Permanent Undersecretary of the Treasury, Sir Horace Wilson, contacted Fritz Hesse, then the London Bureau chief of the official German News Agency, with a startling proposal which Wilson requested Hesse to bring to Hitler's attention. He gave him a typed summary of it, "without committing Chamberlain in any way."

Whether or not Chamberlain actually knew of Wilson's move, the latter must have felt that his proposals came close enough to Chamberlain's thinking to be acceptable to him as a basis for a peaceful Anglo-German settlement. Ribbentrop and Hitler, too, took the proposal quite seriously. What Wilson suggested was nothing less than an Anglo-German "defensive alliance for a period of twenty-five years." Chamberlain "would also be ready to make a statement on Germany's former colonies, proposing that they be returned to her by stages." In addition, a way might be found to ease Germany's foreign trade difficulties by making her a "junior partner" in the Ottawa Agreements. Moreover, in an agreement to delimit British and German spheres of economic

153. Gordon W. Prange, ed., *Hitler's Words* (Washington, 1944), pp. 210 ff., 303, 344, 362–63. Logan, p. 162.

154. *Auswärtige Politik*, D, *4*, 434–44.

interest, "Chamberlain was willing to recognize the whole Continent as Germany's special sphere provided British interests were not excluded." In return for these British concessions Hitler would have to "give a binding pledge to undertake no action in Europe (and particularly in Poland) that might lead to war."[155]

Hitler was not inclined to pay this price for British friendship. "Only if he got something tangible at once would he believe that the English were willing to come to an understanding with him and did not mean to destroy him." It was the old difficulty of Hitler's priorities again; Hitler would have his way in the East *before* he would talk about anything else. The success of the negotiations with Russia only encouraged him in this course. Thus on August 14 it was decided to do nothing about the Wilson feeler for the time being—to return to this offer "when the time has come"—i.e. after Hitler's Eastern European ambitions had been achieved.[156]

This was also the tenor of the German peace offer of August 25, which offered Britain a general settlement—*after* the solution of the Polish problem along German lines and in return for the recognition of Germany's limited colonial demands. Hitler elabo-

---

155. Fritz Hesse, *Hitler and the English* (London, 1954), p. 68. I have decided to accept this story, despite the fact that Hesse's credibility has been seriously impugned. The essential core of this account, that a new British compromise approach was made in August 1939, through the efforts of Sir Horace Wilson, which included provision for the settlement of the colonial issue, is confirmed by Herbert von Dirksen, then the German Ambassador in London. According to Dirksen's account, Wilson developed his program through talks between the Minister of Overseas Trade, Hudson, and a Mr. Wohlthat, the German delegate to an international whaling conference, and later in direct talks between Wilson and Dirksen. The Ambassador explicitly states his belief that the proposals outlined on these occasions, which are identical to those described by Hesse, were sanctioned by Chamberlain and the British Cabinet. Similar ideas were also mentioned to Dirksen by a Labor M.P., Charles Roden Buxton. There is no reason why these proposals should not also have been submitted to Berlin through Hesse, particularly in view of the fact that Dirksen was unpopular with Ribbentrop, so that an alternate approach might have seemed more hopeful to the British Government. See Herbert von Dirksen, *Moscow, Tokyo, London: Twenty Years of German Foreign Policy* (Norman, Okla., 1952), pp. 221–28.

156. Hesse, pp. 70–76.

rated upon this in his famous conversation with Nevile Henderson on the 25th. Coming back to his old idea of an alliance between Germany and Great Britain (which had also been a part of Sir Horace Wilson's peace plan), Hitler offered to guarantee the British Empire, provided that "his colonial demands which are limited and can be negotiated by peaceful methods are fulfilled and in this case he is prepared to fix the longest time limit . . ." and that an Anglo-German alliance would not run counter to Germany's obligations toward Italy and the Soviet Union. The whole offer was, of course, contingent on Britain's noninterference in the Polish "settlement."[157]

Although Britain was unwilling once more to purchase peace by continental appeasement she was still willing to pay the colonial price. The British reply accepted Hitler's proposals as a basis for discussion "if the differences between Germany and Poland are peacefully composed."[158] This reply, in effect, made the Wilson offer official. But Hitler would not be bought off with colonial presents. In May 1939 he had once again outlined his political and strategic plans to a group of high-ranking officers at a conference at the *Reichskanzlei*. Colonel Rudolf Schmundt's minutes of that conference show that Hitler would not accept colonies in lieu of continental expansion: "[They are] not a solution of the food problem: Blockade!"[159]

Thus on September 1 Hitler went to war against Poland—to realize his continental goals. When England joined the war—to Hitler's intense surprise and disappointment—the colonial claim, which otherwise might have remained on ice for "five or six years" became an acute war aim for Germany. World War II, begun as a result of *Ostpolitik*, eventually became an instrument of *Weltpolitik* as well.

The colonial enthusiasts immediately saw the war as an opportunity to realize their program. Epp issued a manifesto on the outbreak of the war in which he described "the resurrection of the

---

157. Henderson, pp. 319–21. Otto Meissner, *Staatssekretär* (Hamburg, 1950), pp. 501–02.

158. Logan, p. 176.

159. International Military Tribunal, *37*, 549.

German colonial empire" as one of the aims the Reich was fighting for.[160] The war had not begun over the question of colonies, but now that it had begun, that question too would be settled by its outcome.[161] Hitler himself was more cautious during those early months of the phony war; he still hoped that England and France would eventually accept the fait accompli of the division of Poland and would make peace before they actually started fighting. In that event Hitler would not be unreasonable about colonies. On September 19, announcing the end of the Polish campaign, Hitler suggested that there was still time for the Western Powers to end the state of war with Germany on the basis of the status quo ante in all respects other than Poland. "I have no war aims whatsoever with respect to France or England, nor has the German nation."[162] The colonies remained a question about which one could talk at leisure. In his Reichstag speech of October 6, 1939, he once again offered to call off the war:

> The most important task by far is the creation of a feeling of European security. For this, it is necessary that there be complete clarity about the aims of the foreign policy of the European states. Insofar as Germany is concerned the government of the Reich is prepared to provide complete and full clarity about its foreign policy intentions. In doing so, it prefaces its declaration with the statement that as far as it is concerned the Versailles Treaty is considered to be no longer in existence, i.e. that the German Reich government and with it the entire German people see no reason and no cause for any further revisions whatever, except the demand for colonial property corresponding to the [position of the] Reich and due it, i.e. primarily for the return of the German colonies. This demand for colonies is based not only in the historical legal claim to the German colonies but, above all, in the elementary legal title for a part of the

160. *Kolonialzeitung, 51* (1939), 303.
161. Pfister, *England und die deutsche Kolonialfrage*, pp. 3–4.
162. *Kolonialzeitung, 51* (1939), 324.

raw material sources of the world. This demand is not an ultimatum and it is not a demand behind which stands force, but a demand of political justice and of economic common sense.[163]

There were people in Great Britain inclined to take up the Führer's offer. In November 1939 the Labour Party urged a negotiated peace that would include an "agreed, non-imperialistic settlement of colonies." Chamberlain's mail ran three to one in favor of peace.[164] In December Finland made an attempt to mediate between the belligerents, partly in order to gain more support in her conflict with Russia. The suggested terms included the restoration of Germany's colonies.

When the Western governments failed to respond to such peaceful overtures, the German tone became stiffer. In his speeches of January 30 and February 24, 1940, Hitler made unqualified demands for colonies, no longer offering to negotiate about them. A rather odd episode in the diplomacy of the period would tend to indicate that this demand was a serious one: In February 1940 a German agent, one Maria Radley, was dispatched to South Africa to sound out the government in Pretoria on the possibility of a separate peace with Germany. Obviously Germany would have made the most favorable offer possible in order to detach a Dominion from Great Britain. The German proposal, however, while offering to recognize the Union's position as the "leading white state in the South African *Lebensraum*" and to procure Southern Rhodesia and the High Commission Territories for it in the eventual peace settlement, also maintained the German claim to colonies, which, in view of the Union's position as mandatory for Southwest Africa, could only have an unfavorable effect on the South Africans' willingness to consider the proposition.[165]

Again, on March 18, 1940, Hitler indicated to Mussolini that the colonies were a genuine though not a pressing issue between Great Britain and Germany. Explaining why he had had to make a deal with his proclaimed arch-enemy, the Soviet Union, Hitler

163. Viera, *Kolonien im Blickfeld von Heute,* p. 5.
164. Feiling, p. 424.
165. *German Documents,* D, *8,* 804–05.

said that he would have preferred to work in concert with Great Britain,

> on condition that England would not set limits to Germany's *Lebensraum* eastwards and that Germany would get back her colonies which, after all, were going to waste under England's administration. . . . Moreover, he had not raised his claim in the form of an ultimatum, but had merely pointed out that it was an impossible situation to have to beg for every pound of tea or coffee. Since England, however, had wanted the war, he had been forced to side with Russia.[166]

The German victories of the spring of 1940 naturally made Hitler more determined to insist on a colonial settlement as the price for peace. We must note, however, that the extent of his colonial ambitions remained, for some time, quite modest. General Alfred Jodl testified at Nuremberg that he and Ribbentrop had heard the Führer remark, shortly after the French campaign "that peace could be concluded with England at any time only if part of our former colonies were given back to us."[167] Ribbentrop thought in 1945 that Hitler would have made peace in the summer of 1940 on the basis of the "restitution of one or two German colonies."[168] Some American journalists were told by Hitler on June 17, 1940, "that he intended to take over the former German colonies,"[169] and the "peace plan" which Hess tried to submit to the British government after his spectacular flight to Britain in the spring of 1941 also called for the return of the German pre-World War I empire, with the exception of the islands under Japanese mandate. His plan, Hess claimed, was based on conversations he had had with Hitler after the French campaign, in which the latter had opposed a harsh peace settlement and had argued for an understanding with Great Britain.[170] The Führer

166. Ibid., D, *9*, 8.
167. International Military Tribunal, *15*, 424.
168. Office of the United States Chief Counsel for the Prosecution of Axis Criminality, *Nazi Conspiracy and Aggression* (Washington, 1946), p. 845.
169. Logan, p. 190.
170. International Military Tribunal, *40*, 281 ff.

himself, it thus appears, would have been content to regain Germany's old possessions, and might have taken less, if Britain had been willing to conclude peace in the summer of 1940.

In other quarters there was no such modesty about the potential "fruits of the glorious German victories."[171] The navy and the Foreign Office, quite aside from the professional colonialists, had plans that went far beyond mere colonial restitution and tried to get them adopted as policy. A naval staff document of June 3, 1940, on "Questions pertaining to Territorial Expansion and Bases" advocated a peace settlement that would once and for all end the situation in which Germany, her navy bottled up in the narrow seas, could be easily blockaded. Arguing against a permanent occupation of the Scandinavian and West European countries or the acquisition of bases on their territory, the drafters thought it preferable to leave these areas nominally independent, though closely tied to Germany. Only Iceland should be annexed outright. As for areas outside of Europe, the document recommended the acquisition of

> contiguous possessions in Central Africa—possessions which are made up of the area between Senegal and the Congo and stretch east as far as German East Africa— i.e. they comprise the French possessions, say, south of the line of latitude running through the mouth of the Senegal, the former German colonies of Central Africa, and the Belgian Congo. For purposes of rounding out this area, German Southwest Africa could be considered as exchange territory for British and Portuguese possessions.

In addition to this tremendous African empire, the German navy also would have liked bases on islands off the coast of that continent, plus all of Madagascar or the smaller French islands in the Indian Ocean. Time and the developments of the war would show whether these territorial ambitions should not be further extended at the expense of Great Britain.[172]

171. *Kolonialzeitung, 52* (1940), 145.
172. International Military Tribunal, *34,* 240–42.

Rather similar to this naval program, though based primarily on economic considerations, was a plan worked out in the Economic Policy Department of the Foreign Office. It recommended the economic integration in the German sphere of Denmark, Norway, the Low Countries, Southeastern Europe, and the Baltic countries. This area, however, would still be lacking in fats, sugar, tropical and subtropical vegetable raw material, and certain metals. Therefore Germany must also have colonies: "A colonial empire comprising the German colonies in Africa, the Belgian Congo, French Equatorial Africa (and possibly British Nigeria) after a prolonged period of intensive development could in large measure supply the requirements of Greater Germany and of the greater economic sphere . . ."[173]

It is not easy to say to what extent Hitler adopted these more flamboyant plans of conquest, harking back to the *Mittelafrika* dreams of World War I. In his "peace offer" to Great Britain, made in the course of a Reichstag speech on July 19, he was vague on colonies. Ribbentrop's original draft had been specific in calling for the return of the mandates to the Reich, but it was turned down, according to one informed view, because Hitler no longer really wanted peace with Great Britain but her total defeat.[174] The armistice with France, on the other hand, included nothing which pointed to German colonial ambitions. The inclusion of any such terms in the armistice was apparently not even considered by the Germans,[175] and Hitler talked Mussolini and Ciano out of their demands for Italian occupation of Tunisia and French Somaliland.[176] Again on July 7, when Count Ciano mapped out extravagant Italian demands to be made at the eventual peace settlement, Hitler advocated moderation.

173. *German Documents,* D, *9,* 476–82, 496–501. The similarity of these Central Africa plans to German World War I war aims is striking. See Fritz Fischer, *Griff nach der Weltmacht: Die Kriegszielpolitik des kaiserlichen Deutschlands 1914/18* (Düsseldorf, 1961).

174. Meissner, pp. 548–49. Hesse, *Hitler and the English,* p. 107.

175. A memorandum on the prospective armistice, prepared by Weizsäcker, makes no mention whatsoever of any colonial considerations. *German Documents,* D, *9,* 591–92.

176. Ibid., D, *9,* pp. 608–11, 679–80.

Earlier, while the French campaign was still in progress, the Foreign Office had instructed its ambassador in Madrid to "maintain complete reserve with regard to French Morocco, even if Arab leaders should revolt and ask for German intervention."[177]

The evidence suggests that in the fall of 1940, when it became obvious that England would not make peace and that the war must continue until she had actually been defeated, the German leaders adopted more far-reaching colonial war aims. In September the Spanish Foreign Minister Serrano Suñer visited Berlin to discuss the possibility of Spain's entering the war and to submit a list of Spanish desires predicated on such an eventuality. He was told by Ribbentrop as well as by Hitler himself that Spanish aims in North Africa would not conflict with German plans for a Central African Empire. Spain, however, "could fairly be asked to complete the German scheme by yielding the points that would make the great new German Empire immune to any and all possible future attacks." Specifically, there was talk not only about German bases in French Morocco, most of which would go to Spain, but also about the actual cession of Spanish territory to Germany in exchange for the French North African possessions. Germany claimed to need one of the Canary Islands or Fernando Po, and perhaps some real estate in Rio de Oro, for the establishment of bases to defend the new Central African empire against attack by the United States. Suñer, and Franco, in a letter of September 22, opposed any cession of Spanish territory. This refusal was maintained by Generalissimo Franco when he met with Hitler at Hendaye on October 23. At that time it also became obvious that the extravagant Spanish demands for North African territory might be hard to fit into Hitler's concept for a new order in Europe and Africa, which included a France, friendly to Germany, that would remain a substantial colonial power. Hitler thus declined to make firm promises to Franco.[178]

On his return from Hendaye, Hitler outlined his plans to Marshal Pétain during the meeting at Montoire. The secret *procès-*

177. Ibid., pp. 525–26.

178. William L. Langer, *Our Vichy Gamble* (New York, 1947), p. 91. Herbert Feis, *The Spanish Story* (New York, 1948), pp. 78–79, 93–97.

133

verbal summarized the part of the conversation that dealt with Africa as follows:

> The Führer declared to the Head of the French State that, after the defeat of England and the retrocession of the German colonies, there will be an opportunity, within the framework of a general peace settlement, for a repartition of colonial possessions in Africa, a repartition which, while assuring a harmonization of reciprocal interests, would take account of political necessities and economic needs of the interested European states. This concerns above all the four powers: Germany, Italy, France and Spain. To the extent that this new order in Africa will involve necessary territorial modifications in the existing French colonial domain, the Axis powers will undertake to see that, at the conclusion of peace with England, France obtains territorial compensations and that, in the final accounting, she retains in Africa a colonial domain essentially equivalent to what she possesses today.[179]

According to this statement, then, the retrocession of Germany's former colonies would have been only the first step in a complete redistribution of the African continent, which apparently would have included the creation of a large German colony in Central Africa. The same picture emerges from an entirely different source, namely the conversations between Molotov and the German leaders at the end of November 1940.

The Germans submitted the following draft of a quadripartite agreement for the consideration of the Soviet government:

> 1. Germany declares that, apart from the territorial revisions in Europe to be carried out at the conclusion of peace, her territorial aspirations center in the territories of Central Africa.
>
> 2. Italy declares that, apart from the territorial revisions in Europe to be carried out at the conclusion of

179. Langer, p. 95.

peace, her territorial aspirations center in the territories of North and Northeastern Africa.

3. Japan declares that her territorial aspirations center in the area of Eastern Asia, to the south of the Island Empire of Japan.

4. The Soviet Union declares that its territorial aspirations center south of the national territory of the Soviet Union in the direction of the Indian Ocean.[180]

This staggering plan for the distribution of the world among an expanded Axis was soon abandoned. Russia insisted upon a closer definition of the limit of Germany's aims in Eastern Europe and generally refused to commit herself. Hitler was equally suspicious of Russian activities in the Balkans and elsewhere and made up his mind, shortly after the conversations with Molotov, that the only way to deal with the Russians was to destroy them. Nevertheless, for a short period in the fall of 1940 he actually seems to have considered a policy of overseas expansion as the primary goal of Germany, abandoning, at least for the time being, the idea of continuing his *Ostpolitik* in favor of one of peaceful coexistence with a Soviet Union that would direct its energies toward conquest in Southern Asia. The extensive preparations, to be discussed in the following chapter, which were then being undertaken in Berlin for the acquisition of a colonial empire seem to bear out this hypothesis.

However, once the decision had been made to go to war with Soviet Russia, thereby initiating an *Ostpolitik* on the most gigantic scale, little more was heard of colonies on the diplomatic level. Certainly German ambitions in that field once again became quite limited. Ribbentrop, who had at one time called for a "new organization of Africa," with Germany and Italy in the vanguard,[181] in November 1941, in trying to persuade Japan to enter the war, stated: "In Africa, Germany will be satisfied with roughly those parts which were formerly German Colonies. . . . Germany desires, above all, to control European Russia."[182]

180. Logan, pp. 197–98.
181. Bender, ed., *Kolonien—Ein Kraftfeld Gross Deutschlands*, p. 3.
182. Logan, p. 204.

Hitler himself seems to have lost all interest in a colonial policy after the beginning of the Russian campaign. The subject was no longer mentioned in his speeches. In July 1942, in the course of one of his monologues before his inner circle, he indicated that his attitude had reverted substantially to the line of *Mein Kampf,* which opportunism had led him to abandon temporarily: Coming back to his old ideas of Anglo-German cooperation, the Führer opined that it should be England's role to guard European interests on the sea, Germany's to protect Europe on land.

> Hitler declared further: He had sought the compromise with England on the basis that colonies are not at all necessary for us. Already the problem of maintaining the connection between Greater Germany and such colonies, located perhaps in Africa, created difficulties.
>
> For the maintenance of such a connection, bases for the fleet and even more for airplanes were called for. At this time our geographical position was strategically thoroughly unfavorable for this.
>
> The connection with the occupied Eastern areas, on the other hand, could be created without difficulties, for it could be achieved through the construction of roads and railroads alone.
>
> He could not see an absolute need for colonies in view of the Eastern territories with their extraordinary raw materials potential. We could gain tea, spices, and rubber in them. . . . To pioneer the colonial approach merely because of coffee was unreasonable.[183]

Colonial planning, as we shall see, still went on, in a kind of vacuum, until early in 1943, when all such activities were abandoned. The history of these planning activities clearly confirms, however, that for a number of years the acquisition of an overseas empire had in fact been a major preoccupation of the leadership of the Third Reich.

183. Henry Picker, *Hitlers Tischgespräche* (Bonn, 1951), pp. 123–24.

4

Colonial Planning

It was not until 1939 that systematic preparations were undertaken for the creation of a German colonial empire. Previous to
that time, however, there had been a good deal of discussion
among interested groups and individuals about the policies to
be followed should the former German possessions be restored,
and this discussion is a source of information of the ideas underlying the envisaged colonial policy of the Third Reich.

One of the difficulties the colonial planners encountered was
that no definite understanding ever existed about the extent of
a future German Empire and about the areas that would be included in it. Hitler himself had admitted to Lord Halifax that
this was a matter which could only be viewed in the light of the
specific political circumstances that might surround the fulfillment of Germany's colonial demands, i.e. a question of opportunity. Refusing to commit himself on the extent of his colonial
desires, Hitler distinguished between colonial concessions and
conquest: "There were two possibilities: First, the free play of
powers. What Germany in that case would take could not be
said! The second possibility would be a solution according to

reason"—by which Germany would receive back its former possessions. If the Western Powers felt that simple restitution was not feasible and that certain substitutions must be made for the colonies taken from Germany in 1919, it was up to them to make concrete proposals.[1]

In line with this doctrine of opportunism, colonial agitation during the prewar years concentrated largely on demanding nothing more than the return of Germany's former possessions. There were occasional allusions to larger aims, to a "new division of the world" (in a speech by Goebbels),[2] and to a "moral claim" to colonies over and above the ones Germany had held in 1914, to which it possessed a "legal claim."[3] By and large, however, a statement by General von Epp in the *Europäische Revue* of September 1936 was typical of the line taken by the colonial movement and the government: "When Germany claims colonies she has solely her own colonies in mind, which have been placed under League of Nations mandate."[4] If the mandatories were reluctant about giving up control over one or the other of the mandates, the Reich would not be averse to accepting compensation, including, despite public protestations to the contrary,[5] the property of third parties, such as Belgium and Portugal.[6] (Needless to say, this last possibility was not discussed publicly.) Basically, however, Germany's colonial ambitions in the prewar period were limited to the recovery of its former empire. That this attitude was not, like so many other public pronouncements of Nazi leaders, entirely insincere is shown by documents dealing with the early stages of the preparatory activities for the establishment of a German colonial administration. On October 14, 1939—after the outbreak of the war—a Foreign Office memorandum describ-

---

1. *Auswärtige Politik*, D, *1*, 53.

2. Amery, *The German Colonial Claim*, pp. 16–17.

3. Scheidl, *Deutschlands Kampf um Seine Kolonien*, p. 154.

4. Royal Institute of International Affairs, *Germany's Claim to Colonies*, p. 28.

5. FR (1938), *1*, 447. *Auswärtige Politik*, D, *1*, 75–76, 82. Krumbach, ed., *Franz Ritter von Epp*, pp. 314–18.

6. FR (1937), *1*, 173. Logan, *The African Mandates in World Politics*, pp. 128–29.

ing the progress made on the political preparations as of September 30, 1939, stated that

> In the preparatory work it is assumed that the colonial possessions will be gained by peaceful negotiations, not by a forcible military occupation. Furthermore it is assumed, for the time being, that only the reoccupation of our old colonies is envisaged. The preparations of the OKW [High Command of the Armed Forces] have been carried out according to these presuppositions.[7]

Even in August 1940, when the prospects for German victory had risen considerably, police authorities were still calculating their personnel needs on the basis of the "four old African colonies."[8]

On the basis of all the evidence available, apprehensions about German designs on Liberia, which were seriously entertained by the government of that country as well as by American diplomats,[9] were entirely without foundation. The idea of giving Liberia to Germany as a colony was occasionally voiced in Britain[10] but never in Germany. Suggestions that Hitler had colonial designs on South America[11] were likewise chimerical; if Hitler had occasionally mentioned such ideas, they were not much more than daydreams. Henderson, who characterized Hitler's policy as one of Austrian *Schlamperei* (muddling along) and opportunism wrote that Hitler "had all sorts of general plans in his head but I greatly doubt if he had preconceived ideas as to how they were to be executed."[12]

This element of naked opportunism also explains why, during the early war years, the colonial ambitions of Germany grew far

---

7. Bundesarchiv, Reichsfinanzministerium, *Memorandum from Foreign Office*, dated October 14, 1939, file 11,632.

8. BA, Memo from Chef der Ordnungspolizei, Hauptamt Sicherheitspolizei, dated August 30, 1940, file R 19/245.

9. *FR* (1937), 2, 821–29, 846–47, 852. *FR* (1938), 2, 770–817, 829, 838, 840–42.

10. *The Times* (May 19, 1934), p. 11.

11. Such designs were reported by Hermann Rauschning in *The Voice of Destruction* (New York, 1940), pp. 60 ff.

12. Henderson, *Failure of a Mission*, pp. 196–97.

beyond the original aim of colonial revision; after the victories of 1940 anything seemed to be within the grasp of the Reich, and there was little reason to be modest. Thus J. H. Krumbach, an important figure in the Party's Kolonialpolitisches Amt, declared in 1941, in a brochure produced by the army for the indoctrination of troops, that the time had come for a new "distribution of the space reserve available on the globe," in which more was involved than the reparation of the errors committed at Versailles.[13] H. W. Bauer, one of the leading colonial agitators of the Nazi type and also an official in the KPA, foretold the end of the British Empire, whose place in Africa must be taken by a new order under German leadership. That such statements were not merely outbursts of overly enthusiastic individuals is shown by the fact that the administrative planning section of the KPA showed a suspicious interest in the administrative organization and personnel requirements of the Belgian Congo and "districts of Equatorial Africa adjoining the Cameroons."[14] The economic section of that authority by the end of 1941 had worked out tables of organization for the German economic administration of Nigeria, the Cameroons, French Equatorial Africa, the Belgian Congo, and Tanganyika.[15] This evidence would seem to indicate that the plans of the German Navy and Foreign Office[16] were to be taken quite seriously.

The territorial ambitions of the Reich were, however, limited in one sense: apparently nobody in a policy-making position suggested or thought of acquiring colonies outside of Africa.[17] The old German South Sea colonies were generally conceded to be in the Japanese sphere of influence: "These islands are of importance for the German Reich only as producers of copra and as coaling stations for German steamers in the South Seas. For Japan these

13. Krumbach, *Kolonialpolitik Heute*, p. 7; cf. p. 80.
14. BA, RFM, Letter from Dr. Bielfeld of KPA to Dr. Burmeister of RFM, dated June 10, 1941, file 11,632.
15. KPA, *Tätigkeitsbericht* (1942), p. 32. (Cf. Chapter 1, n. 68.)
16. Cf. above, pp. 131–32.
17. The German claim to "Neuschwabenland," a part of the Antarctic continent, over which a dispute with Norway arose in 1939, is an interesting but minor exception. Ritter, *Der Kampf um den Erdraum*, pp. 333–34.

islands have an inestimable value."[18] The same applied to the German sphere of interest in China. Hitler himself said in a speech in the Reichstag on February 20, 1938, that "Germany has no territorial interest in East Asia . . . We no longer want to return there."[19]

This willingness to give up the claims to non-African areas of the former German Empire distinguished the colonial-minded Nazis from the older colonialists, many of whom had wanted Germany to return to the Pacific, not only to vindicate its claim to full colonial restitution but also out of a specific animosity against Japan. The old "yellow peril" slogan was often used in German colonial agitation until as late as 1938 and Japanese expansion was condemned as a threat to the dominance of the white race.[20] When Japan withdrew from the League of Nations as a result of the Manchurian crisis, there was much speculation whether the islands north of the equator should not automatically revert to Germany.[21] As for the islands under Australian and New Zealand mandate, there were occasional suggestions that they, also, should be returned to Germany or that the Reich should receive suitable compensation for them in other parts of the British Empire, such as Nigeria.[22] With the conclusion of the Tripartite Pact, however, it became the official doctrine that the whole Pacific was Japan's. "What Africa is to Europe, Australia is to Japan."[23] The formerly German island empire thereafter was no longer even mentioned in colonial propaganda, and there are no indications of concrete preparations for its return to German administration.

18. Baravalle, *Deutschland braucht seine Kolonien*, p. 48.

19. Royal Institute of International Affairs, p. 29.

20. *Kolonialzeitung*, *46* (1934), 8–9. Seegert, *Koloniale Schicksalsstunde*, passim. Deutsche Kolonialgesellschaft und Interfraktionelle koloniale Vereinigung des Reichstags, *Deutschland in den Kolonien*, pp. 91–93. Bauer, *Kolonien im Dritten Reich*, *1*, 102–07.

21. *Kolonialzeitung*, *45* (1933), 15, 30. Brenner, *Wem hat Deutschland seine Kolonien Überlassen?* pp. 80 ff.

22. Holtsch, *Die Ehemaligen Deutschen Südseekolonien*, pp. 78–79. Dix, *Weltkrise und Kolonial Politik*, pp. 324–26. Leutwein, *Die Deutsche Kolonialfrage*.

23. *Kolonialzeitung, 53* (1941), 73.

Germany's minimum demands consisted of her former African colonies or comparable territory; her maximum demands were a large bloc in Central Africa, stretching from coast to coast, plus bases in other areas of the continent. However large Germany's empire would be, the Reich intended to be ready to assume the rule over it.

The task of preparing the groundwork of a colonial administration and policy devolved upon the Kolonialpolitisches Amt der NSDAP. This body, nominally a branch of the Party bureaucracy, was in a peculiar position, since it performed functions that would normally be the task of a state agency and was dependent for funds on the Reich treasury. The full story of this agency and its activities has never been told before.

We have already referred to the KPA in its role as the colonial propaganda agency of the Party.[24] Its chief, General von Epp, like so many representatives of the Nazi hierarchy, was anxious to extend the competency of his bureaucratic realm as far as possible; he felt specifically that everything pertaining to colonial affairs fell within his sphere of authority. Thus, when in 1937 and early 1938 the colonial question became so acute in diplomacy that the return of the mandates to Germany could definitely be considered within the realm of possibility, Epp maintained that his agency should be responsible for the administrative preparations necessary in order to enable the Reich to assume control in the colonies with a minimum of delay and difficulty. The General was undoubtedly concerned to hear that others were already poaching on his bureaucratic preserve: Schacht had set up a special department in the Reichsbank to study problems concerning new colonial currencies, and Göring had begun to work out plans for the economic exploitation of the new German empire.[25] Epp, in order to nip this attempt at undermining his authority in the bud, addressed a memorandum to the Führer, in December 1938, apparently requesting that the KPA be reorganized and transferred into the state machinery as a colonial ministry.[26] Hitler refused to go this far, but Epp was authorized by

24. Cf. above, pp. 21 ff.
25. Royal Institute of International Affairs, p. 69.
26. BA, Reichskanzlei, unsigned memorandum, dated June 6, 1940.

a letter of March 9, 1939, from the *Chef der Reichskanzlei,* Hans Lammers, to begin with the preparatory work for the establishment of a colonial administration. Hitler agreed that this task must be performed by a single agency, though in cooperation with all interested parties, and that the agency should be the KPA, not the Foreign Office. The KPA was admonished, however, to stick to its administrative preparations and to let the Foreign Office handle the actual negotiations for the acquisition of colonies.

Since there seems to have been little diplomatic activity in early 1939 which would have justified the belief that the re-establishment of Germany as a colonial power was imminent, it is odd that Hitler should have indicated that the task given to Epp was urgent: He charged the KPA *"to press energetically* [my italics] the preparatory work for a future colonial administration and to make the necessary preparations for the establishment of a Reich Colonial Ministry." Was Hitler already thinking of vindicating the colonial claim by means other than negotiation?[27]

Armed with such authority, Epp set out to create what would in fact be a colonial ministry in substance if not in name. He ran into difficulty when Party Treasurer Franz Schwarz turned down his request for additional funds, protesting that he realized the importance of Epp's task but was unable to support it financially, since Reich Minister of Finance Schwerin von Krosigk was so niggardly with funds for Party activities.[28] This difficulty was solved eventually; from the beginning of the new budget year, October 1, 1939, those activities of the KPA which were essentially public in character, i.e. were performed for the benefit of the state, were supported from the Reich budget.[29] Henceforth, that part of the KPA which carried out the older propaganda and indoctrination functions of that agency was officially referred to as *KPA/Partei,* while the far larger apparatus created to formulate policy and to form the cadre of the new Reich Ministry for Colonies was called *KPA/Staat.*[30]

27. Berlin Document Center, *Reichsorganisationsleiter,* Ordner 311.
28. BDC, Research Section, Ordner 211, Schwarz to Epp, March 31, 1939; Schwarz to Bormann, March 31, 1939.
29. KPA, *Tätigkeitsbericht* (1942), p. 3.
30. Ibid., p. 7.

The scope and rapid growth of the latter are indicated by the budgetary funds allotted to it. For the financial year 1939 the KPA received a mere RM 157,428; in the following year RM 6,379,678 were budgeted; in 1941 this amount rose to RM 29,942,060, parts of which were to be spent on such essentials as "4 eagles, woodcarved" and for a swimming pool for Epp's official residence in Berlin. By that time the expenditures for the KPA were officially referred to as the budget of the *Reichs-Kolonial-Ministerium,* even though the agency technically remained a branch of the Party.[31]

The rapid expansion of the KPA was partly due to a renewed directive stressing the importance and the urgency of its tasks. On June 15, 1940, the Chief of the Chancery, Minister Lammers, addressed a circular to all "Supreme Reich Authorities"—agencies on the cabinet and subcabinet levels—in which he pointed out that the

> situation today demands a speedy conclusion of these preparatory labors. I therefore have to request all supreme Reich authorities, in the name of the Führer, to give their full support within their area of competency to the *Kolonialpolitisches Amt,* and to participate in the task according to their abilities, so that preparations for taking over the administration of our future colonies can be finished within the shortest period.[32]

This document clearly shows that as a result of the victories in the West there was no doubt in anybody's mind that Germany at the conclusion of the war would have an overseas empire, even though there was some confusion as to what areas it would include. Epp's quasi-Ministry (Epp, in September 1940 once again requested that his office be granted the status of a state agency, but was rebuffed),[33] in accordance with this directive established liaison with and drew on the resources of practically all branches of the state and Party hierarchy that might have the remotest interest

31. On the financial aspects of the KPA see the materials in BA, RFM, files 4971–74.

32. Ibid., file 4965.

33. Ibid., file 4969, Lammers to Epp, October 9, 1940.

in colonial activities. It also cooperated with such bodies as the German Red Cross, the *Gruppe Kolonialwirtschaftlicher Unternehmungen*, which represented private business enterprises with overseas interests, and the Colonial Science Section of the Reich Research Council, which was established in September 1940 and equipped with considerable financial means in order to "gather and train colonial experts and to plan for the tasks ahead."[34]

The KPA's own personnel was drawn from various existing agencies; many of its functionaries retained their old positions while they devoted part of their time to their colonial tasks. A definite table of organization for the KPA which had been worked out over many months was submitted to the Office of the Deputy of the Führer in February 1941. It provided for a structure requiring 195 functionaries in addition to secretarial help (see Chart 3).[35] This proposal was rejected by the supreme Party authorities for the following interesting reasons:

1. Such an elaborate organization was unnecessary because the KPA was purely a temporary office, which in a short time would have to be reorganized as a branch of the state hierarchy, i.e. as a Colonial ministry, "since, according to human foresight, the war will be over in the foreseeable future and with the peace will be connected the acquisition of colonies . . ."

2. With its proposal the KPA invaded the domain of *Reichsleiter* Bohle's Foreign Organization (*Auslandorganisation*) of the Party, defined as the "leadership of men," by planning to take charge of Party as well as state organization.[36] Such jealousies were, of course, a constant feature of the totalitarian state.

Notwithstanding its temporary status, Epp's agency became a massive bureaucratic machine. At the beginning of 1942 it was organized as follows:

Under Epp and his *Stabsleiter, Korvettenkapitän* Richard Wenig, there were four major sections: Section I, under Minister Bielfeld, who simultaneously supervised the Colonial Section of the Foreign Office, included four subsections dealing with Ad-

34. KPA, *Tätigkeitsbericht* (1942), pp. 3–6. Bauer, *Koloniale Wende*, pp. 127–35.

35. BDC, *Reichsorganisationsleiter*, file 311.

36. Ibid.

145

CHART 3

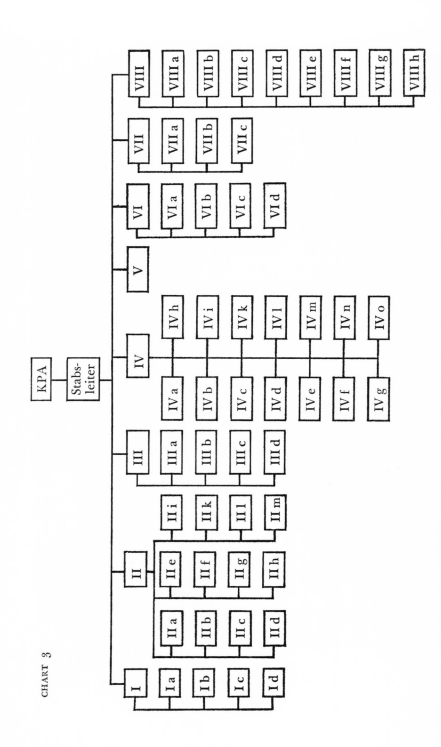

I BUSINESS OFFICE

I a Treasury
I b Personnel
I c Welfare of Colonial Germans
I d Expeditions

II ORGANIZATION FOR THE REACQUISITION OF THE COLONIES

II a Administration
II b Military
II c Police
II d Communications (Traffic)
II e Postal Affairs
II f Economics
II g Currency
II h Racial Affairs Committee
II i Missionary Affairs Committee
II k Academy for German Rights
II l Universities
II m Return of Settlers

III PRESS

III a News Gathering and Propaganda Policy
III b Colonial Press
III c Colonial Archives
III d Speakers' Bureau

IV ADMINISTRATIVE PLANNING

IV a Administration
IV b Personnel
IV c Police
IV d Tariffs and Finances
IV e Justice
IV f Public Health
IV g Schools
IV h Communications (Traffic)
IV i Posts, Telegraph and Telephone
IV k Forests
IV l Cartography
IV m Climatology
IV n Settlement Affairs
IV o Public Contracts

V COLONIAL TECHNOLOGY

VI INDOCTRINATION

VI a Theoretical Indoctrination
VI b Practical Training
VI c Invitations
VI d Reich Seminar

VII SCIENCE AND RESEARCH

VII a Supervision
VII b Central Authority for Colonial Science
VII c Colonial Schools

VIII ECONOMIC PLANNING

VIII a Plantation Agriculture
VIII b Native Agriculture
VIII c Animal Husbandry
VIII d Settlements
VIII e Forestry
VIII f Mining
VIII g Trade
VIII h Banks, Wages, and Insurance

ministration, Personnel, Budgetary and Financial Matters, and Requisitions. Section II, headed by another Foreign Office official, Consul General Rudolf Asmis, was composed of subsections responsible for Justice, Education and Missions, Colonial Science, Native Culture, Health, Heredity and Racial Affairs, Veterinary Affairs, Surveying and Colonial Geography, and a library. A special office, also under Section II, supervised by a Hitler Youth leader, dealt with Youth.

Section III of KPA/Staat included the offices for Economic Planning, Trade, Industry, Banks, Credit and Insurance, Currency and Monetary Affairs, Agriculture, Forests and Timber Economics, Hunting and Conservation, and Mining. It was presided over by an official of the Reich Ministry of Economics, Friedrich Bethke, who simultaneously held positions in Göring's Four Year Plan agency and in the Ministry for Occupied Eastern Areas. Section IV, finally, under the supervision of Karl Remy, a Reichsbahn executive, had separate branches dealing with Traffic, Road Construction and Construction Economics, Railroad Construction and Maintenance, Waters and Harbors, Building Construction, Machine Tools and Electronics, Power, and Postal and Communications Affairs.

In addition there was a Personnel Section with divisions for General Personnel Matters and Applications for Colonial Service, and Individual Personnel Affairs. While the KPA did not have a separate agency for colonial police, a police captain was assigned to it as liaison officer. We shall see that Himmler's police authorities did a good deal of planning on their own. Plans existed for the creation of an additional section on Press, Film, and Radio Affairs, but these were never carried out. A Reich Colonial Institute, designed as a school to train future second echelon officers of the Colonial Service, functioned as a part of the KPA under the direction of Major Paul Schnöckel.[37]

All these agencies of KPA/Staat were located in Berlin. A hot dispute between the KPA and the Ministry for Occupied Eastern areas over the limited office space available in the capital was settled by Hitler personally, who designated the old Marstall

37. KPA, *Tätigkeitsbericht* (1942), pp. 9–13.

Building as the future seat of a colonial ministry, and therefore as the temporary quarters of the KPA.[38] Altogether there were 248 employees of the KPA in January 1942, 209 of whom worked for the agency on a full-time basis. These figures do not include functionaries attached to the KPA offices in Brussels and Paris, which had been established in June 1940 to maintain liaison with French, Dutch, and Belgian colonial agencies and to evaluate—frequently, alas, to loot—the files of the Belgian and French colonial ministries. These offices, supervised by two naval officers with considerable overseas experience, continued to exist even after the KPA itself was forced to suspend its activities.[39]

In view of the fact that by early 1942 Germany was fighting a two-front war and that a critical personnel shortage prevailed, the continued existence of a full-blown colonial ministry without any colonies to administer can only be described as grotesque. The absurdity of the situation was not lost on some members of the Nazi hierarchy. Perhaps, more was involved in the gathering opposition to Epp than merely the sound-enough reasoning that the manpower employed by the KPA could be used in other, more profitable enterprises; we have already had occasion to note that with the beginning of the Russian campaign the colonial dream once more receded into the background of Hitler's plans for the New Order. At any rate, Martin Bormann, who apparently had never been a great believer in overseas colonies (he also made difficulties over the KPA's budget),[40] decided to break up Epp's empire. In a letter of September 1941 he asked Lammers to ascertain whether "in view of the recent developments in the East" (i.e. the beginning and rapid progress of the German attack on Russia) the work of the KPA "still is in agreement with the intentions of the Führer." Should the Führer so desire, Bormann would see to it that the KPA was sharply curtailed "in view of the future plans in the East."

Lammers replied on December 17, 1941, stating that the Führer desired to curtail "drastically the preparatory activities for a future colonial administration." At the same time, however, Lam-

38. Ibid., p. 16.
39. Ibid., pp. 59–63. BA, RFM, esp. file 4965.
40. BA, RFM, file 4974.

mers urged Bormann not to proceed too sharply against Epp's office, especially in view of the fact that the General had already promised him (Lammers) to reduce his staff by one-third by April 1, 1942. For that reason, the Chief of the Reich Chancery recommended that Bormann continue to grant exemptions from military service to Epp's personnel, at least for the time being.

Bormann replied on January 7, 1942. Pointing to the war situation, he expressed hesitancy about the further exemption of Epp's officials: "If we lose the war, even the most beautiful colonial administration won't be any good."[41]

As it turned out, the activities of the KPA were not to be curtailed for another year. Only when, after the defeat at Stalingrad, Hitler ordered a mobilization for total war and the cessation of all work not essential to the war effort and entrusted Bormann with the execution of this decree within the Party was Epp's "colonial ministry" dissolved. Bormann informed Epp in a letter of January 20, 1943, rather high-handedly, that the KPA as well as the RKB must cease all activity by February 15.[42] The General's protests were not altogether in vain; he was able to maintain a fairly substantial remnant administration, which was eventually attached, for budgetary purposes, to the Foreign Office. Essentially, however, colonial preparations and public agitation for colonies came to an abrupt end in early 1943.[43] Whether the suspension—not abolition—of the RKB and KPA would have been lifted if the war had ever again taken a turn more favorable to Germany is a matter of pure speculation. It is clear, however, that by late 1942 or early 1943 colonies were no longer an important German war aim.[44]

By that time the KPA had prepared a substantial basis for an administrative structure and a corps of colonial officials. To begin at the top of the planned administrative pyramid, a draft organizational table for a colonial ministry had been worked out as early as April 1940 by Asmis, the chief of KPA's Section II. Under a

41. Ibid., file 4973.

42. BDC, Research Section, Ordner 211.

43. Ibid., *Reichsorganisationsleiter,* Ordner 768. BA, Epp Papers 37/1. (BA, RFM, file 4974 contains interesting documents on the end of the KPA.)

44. Cf. above, pp. 135–36.

Colonial Minister and a Secretary of State it envisaged a relatively modest establishment of 194 officials. With this draft as a basis, constant discussions about the final form of the central colonial authority took place over the following years. As various committees organized and reorganized the nonexistent ministry, Parkinson's Law operated inexorably. By 1942 a plan for the organization and division of competencies within the planned Section II, the Legal and Cultural Section, called for 209 officials for merely this one part of the Ministry.[45] To convey an idea of the thoroughness with which all details were planned, we include Chart 4,[46] showing the prospective organization of the Economic Section of the Ministry and its executive branches in the field, which is based on a scheme submitted by Asmis on July 21, 1942.

Much of the work of the KPA consisted of the selection and training of a body of bureaucrats to take up the positions established by these administrative schemes. On the highest level, it was universally assumed that General von Epp would become the first Minister of Colonies. An earlier candidate, Wilhelm Keppler, who had been Schacht's successor as Hitler's chief economic adviser, had died.[47] The General was already being addressed in certain documents as "Reichskolonialminister," although there was no legal warrant for the title.[48] Even a successor to Epp had been found; this story furnishes another amusing illustration of the personal jealousies and ambitions hidden under the monolithic façade of totalitarian Germany.

In 1940 "in order to be ready for any eventuality" the KPA had established two "action staffs," skeleton administrations for East and West Africa, so that the transfer of those areas to German sovereignty could proceed with a minimum of friction and delay. The Chief of Staff "Banana"—the cadre for a West African colonial government—was the Stabsleiter of Ernst Bohle's Auslandsorganisation (Foreign Organization of the Party), Ruberg. "Organization Sisal," the corresponding group for East Africa, was

45. BA, RFM, file 9940b.
46. BA, RFM, file 4990a.
47. BA, Epp Papers, 37/1.
48. Ibid.

CHART 4

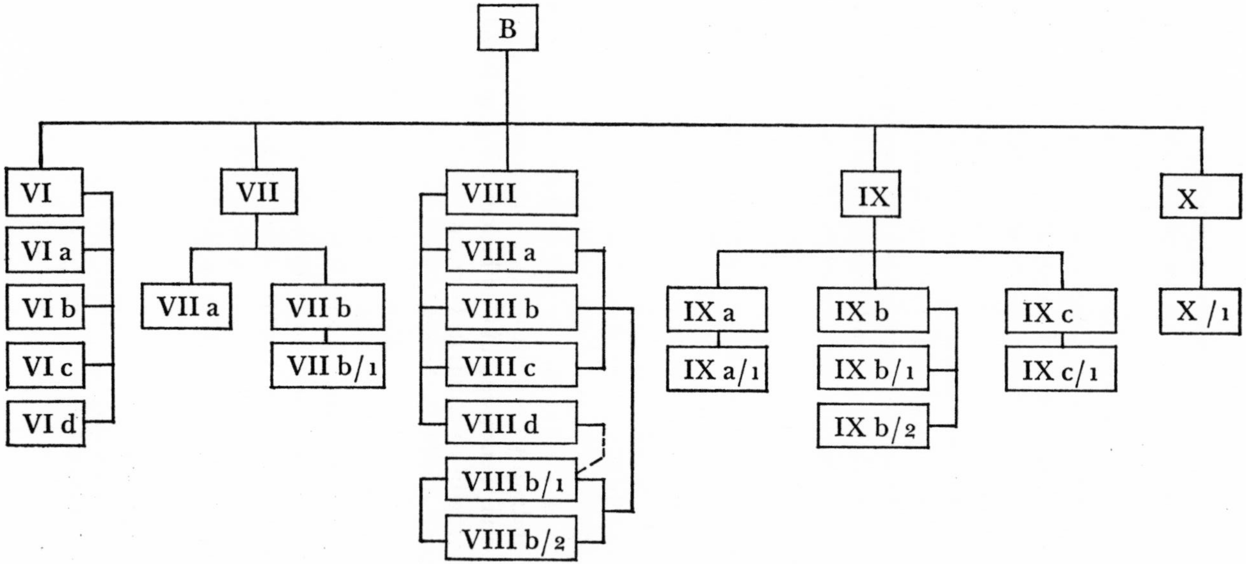
B
VI
VI a
VI b
VI c
VI d
VII
VII a
VII b
VII b/1
VIII
VIII a
VIII b
VIII c
VIII d
VIII b/1
VIII b/2
IX
IX a
IX a/1
IX b
IX b/1
IX b/2
IX c
IX c/1
X
X /1

B ECONOMIC SECTION

VI ECONOMIC PLANNING

VI a   Over-all Planning, Statistics, Direction of Labor
VI b   State-owned Enterprises, Enterprises under Trusteeship
VI c   Geological Survey (Soil Research)
VI d   Economic Training

VII TRADE, INDUSTRY, HANDICRAFTS, BANKS, AND MONETARY AFFAIRS

VII a   Trade, Services, Industrial Handicrafts
VII b   Banks, Monetary Affairs, Insurance
VII b/1   State Bank, Bank of Issue

VIII AGRICULTURE

VIII a   Production: Agriculture, Animal Husbandry, Collection, Practical Training, Schools
VIII b   Marketing: Foods, Industrial Production, Processing, Markets and Supply, Price Regulation
VIII c   Land Law and Land Administration
VIII d   Central Agricultural Experimental Station
VIII b/1   Regional Experimental Stations, Model Plantations and Farms, Agricultural Vocational Schools
VIII b/2   District Agricultural Officers, Agricultural Advisory and Training Service, Market Offices, Fishery Stations

IX FORESTS AND TIMBER ECONOMY, HUNTING AND CONSERVATION

IX a   Forestry
IX a/1   Forestry Experimental Stations
IX b   Timber Economy
IX b/1   Forestry Field Agencies
IX b/2   State-owned Lumbering Enterprises
IX c   Hunting and Conservation
IX c/1   Hunting and Conservation Field Agencies

X MINING

X/1   Mining Offices

headed by Reichsleiter Philipp Bouhler, the Chief of the Führer's personal chancery. "The chiefs of these organizations [had] the task of selecting, in cooperation with the personnel section, the necessary personnel for an administration of the Cameroons and German East Africa and of the neighboring territories belonging to the larger economic areas of these colonies, and to prepare the necessary immediate steps. Preparatory work has been begun for the formation of similar action staffs for other colonies."[49] Bouhler, who had no overseas experience whatsoever, became a colonial expert when virtually all his functions as Chief of the Chancery of the Führer were usurped by Bormann, the Chief of the Party Chancery. Looking around for a new field of activity, he came upon the colonies; Bormann encouraged this new interest, hoping thereby to achieve eventual control of what was left of Bouhler's old office. "One assumes in informed circles that Bouhler will not remain Governor General of East Africa but that he will, after gathering practical experience in the colonies, replace General Ritter von Epp as Colonial Minister." This suited everybody except Ernst Bohle, who feared that his Foreign Organization was being squeezed out.[50] He therefore obtained a special ruling from Rudolf Hess, Hitler's Deputy, specifically delegating to his organization the responsibility for building up the party structure in the colonies.[51]

On a lower level, Asmis worried about receiving the title "Undersecretary of State" as the head of the Economic Section of the Colonial Ministry, for which he had already recruited a full roster of officials among senior civil servants of the Ministry of Economics.[52] It was more difficult to find suitable personnel for service in the field. KPA officials complained about the difficulty of finding persons with colonial experience who "at the same time

49. KPA, *Tätigkeitsbericht* (1942), p. 13.

50. BDC, *Reichsführer SS*, SS 926, letter from Reichssicherheitshauptamt to Himmler. This document shows how Himmler utilized his police apparatus to keep close tabs on the activities and feuds of other leading figures in the Nazi hierarchy.

51. BDC, *Reichsorganisationsleiter*, Ordner 311, letter dated November 2, 1940.

52. BA, RFM, file 9440b; Asmis to Burmeister, December 11, 1940.

are firmly anchored in the National Socialist view of the state and of the world." While colonial experience was definitely desired— in a circular to local party branches the KPA invited applications from persons with such experience who might be up to 60 years old[53]—the right political outlook was more important, and applicants were selected on the basis of their "National Socialist élan and colonial enthusiasm." Thus only eight of twenty-four prospective top officials had any colonial experience.[54]

In order to overcome this handicap a training program was set up. A large number of officials would be needed—a draft plan for the administration of German Southwest Africa called for no less than 790, and larger numbers would be needed in the Cameroons, Tanganyika, and Togoland, for which similar plans had been prepared[55]—and while there was no lack of applications (the KPA had more than 3,700 on file by the summer of 1942) politically impeccable attitudes alone were apparently not judged sufficient preparation for colonial service. As early as 1938 the *Reichsbund der Deutschen Beamten* had begun to hold training courses for colonial officials.[56] In March 1940 the KPA took over the responsibility for such training. Courses were originally conducted at Ladeburg, where there already existed a school for colonial agitation, and later in a newly acquired estate in Berlin-Grunewald.

Under the leadership of SS *Standartenführer* Major Paul Schnöckel, the director of the new Colonial Institute, fifty-nine four-week courses were held from March 1940 until the end of 1942. The curriculum of these sessions, based on instructions approved by Epp and by Alfred Rosenberg (who was responsible for all *Schulung* within the Party) included these topics:

1. Bases of the National Socialist World View
2. The Comportment of the German in the World
3. History and Politics
4. Geography of the "African Complementary Space"

53. BDC, Research Section, Ordner 211.
54. BA, RFM, file 9440b. *Tätigkeitsbericht* (1941).
55. BA, RFM, files 4985a and 5990a.
56. *Deutscher Kolonialdienst* (July 1938), pp. 14-15.

5. Colonial Policy and Administration
6. The African and Native Policy
7. The European as the Instrument of Colonial Policy in Africa.
8. Colonial Economics and Economic Policy
9. Communications and Communications Policy [*Verkehrspolitik*]
10. Colonial Policy and Its Teachings
11. Colonial Policy and World Policy[57]

In addition to providing this rather cursory training, heavily interlarded with political indoctrination, for which it had provisionally earmarked 2,200 of the thousands of applicants for colonial service,[58] the KPA also screened applicants medically[59] and had initiated preparations for the training of such specialists as engineers, technicians, and lawyers. Its education office had already trained some 100 teachers for native schools from among suitable educators nominated by the Reich Ministry of Education, while working on the principles that were to govern native schools, the structure of the school system of the colonies, and syllabuses.[60]

Other governmental bodies were carrying on their own training programs for personnel selected for the colonies. Göring's Forestry Office was ready to furnish a fully trained Colonial Forest Protection Detachment.[61] Preparatory work for the establishment of a Colonial Police Force was carried on by a Colonial Police Office in the Hauptamt Ordnungspolizei and by a division of the Hauptamt Sicherheitspolizei, both in Himmler's domain.[62] It was the former of these two agencies, much to the chagrin of the Security police,[63] which carried out most of the colonial police preparations.

57. *Kolonialzeitung, 54* (1942), 281.
58. KPA, *Tätigkeitsbericht* (1942), pp. 33–34.
59. Ibid., p. 27.
60. Ibid., p. 19.
61. BA, Epp Papers, letter from the Secretary of State in the Reich Forestry Office to Epp, of November 30, 1940.
62. KPA, *Tätigkeitsbericht* (1942), p. 47.
63. BA, Epp Papers, letter from Dr. Zindel to Dr. Schachinger, of September 7, 1940.

Applications for colonial service were solicited from all local police units as early as March 1939.[64] Unsolicited applications had been received and filed as far back as November 1935.[65] Virtually none of the candidates who offered themselves, possessing the ability "to treat the natives with severity but with paternal good will and unimpeachable justice"[66] had any colonial experience. One applicant in describing his qualifications for colonial service stressed the facts that he had "worn an SS or political leader's uniform for eight years and I know how to wear it . . ." and that he was "already the father of five children, have thus done my share in regard to population policy and could therefore very well live separated from my wife . . ."[67] Another gentleman wanted to go to the colonies because he had failed to get a promotion and wanted "damned well to get ahead instead of getting stuck here as a Secretary."[68] Apparently the main consideration in selecting candidates for training, aside from health qualifications, was prior military service. Most aspiring colonial police officers had no knowledge of foreign languages.

The training of these candidates was begun in 1940 when three courses for German police officers were held at the Italian Colonial Police School in Tivoli. Courses in African languages were also given in Germany.[69] The Colonial Police Office, established by Himmler's decree on January 14, 1941, and headed by Lieutenant-General Pfeffer-Wildenburg,[70] established its own training center at Berlin-Oranienburg in March of that year.[71] The director of that institution was immediately responsible to Heinrich Himmler in the latter's capacity as Chief of German Police. A similar center was established in Vienna in January 1942.[72] Train-

---

64. BA, Hauptamt Ordnungspolizei, file R/19/15, circular from Reichsführer SS und Chef der deutschen Polizei im Reichsministerium des Innern (Himmler) of March 6, 1939.

65. Ibid., file R/19/248.

66. Ibid., circular from Himmler of July 22, 1940.

67. Ibid., file R/19/246, letter to Polizeidirektor, Troppau, of July 8, 1940.

68. Ibid., file R/19/247, letter from Polizeisekretär Vogel, of July 20, 1941.

69. Ibid., file R/19/15. *Kolonialzeitung, 53* (1941), 156.

70. BA, HO, files R/19/36 and R/19/245.

71. Ibid., file R/19/15.

72. Ibid., file R/19/245.

ing courses for officers lasted for four months, for those of other ranks, five and a half. African languages (Haussa, Ewe, and Kisuaheli) were included in the curriculum, which also placed special emphasis "on infantry weapons training . . . as the best means of education toward hardiness and comradeship and as a test of character." By July 1942 a total of 167 officers and 700 sergeants and other ratings had undergone this training. Most of them were subsequently sent to serve in the North African Theater and in the Balkans. Ten police medical officers had received special training at the Hamburg Institute for Tropical Diseases.[73] Despite the fact that Himmler in a directive of March 25, 1942, ordered the cessation of all colonial preparatory activity,[74] the training of personnel at Vienna continued until August 1942 while courses at Berlin-Oranienburg were still being held in February 1943.[75]

Other organizational preparations already completed included an incredibly detailed pay scale for colonial officials—the salaries planned were quite small, smaller in some instances than those paid to colonial officials in 1910[76]—and a draft law on the status of colonial officials. Interestingly enough, Bormann's Party Chancery took a considerable interest in the latter, insisting on the right to screen all colonial officials.[77] A pay scale had been devised for colonial military forces, but Hitler himself decided in October 1940 that there should not be a separate colonial army. Rather, army units would be assigned to colonial stations on a rotating basis.[78] Maps were being prepared of the former German colonies and, significantly, of Gabon and Moyen Congo. The Cartography Section of the KPA also had gathered a large library of maps of Africa, many of them "secured and acquired" in Paris and Brussels, and was feuding with the Armed Services over competency in surveying.[79] Suitable persons were also available to take over

73. KPA, *Tätigkeitsbericht* (1942), p. 48.
74. BA, RFM, file 4970.
75. BA, HO, files R/19/10, R/19/240.
76. BA, RFM, files 4969, 9440b.
77. Ibid., file 4968, Memorandum dated May 19, 1941.
78. Ibid., file 4969, Memorandum by Bursche, dated October 25, 1940; cf. file 4980.
79. KPA, *Tätigkeitsbericht* (1942), pp. 28 ff.

colonial businesses belonging to nationals of enemy countries as trustees.[80]

In addition, files were being kept of firms eligible to receive public contracts in the colonies, the structure and procedure of a system of courts had been worked out, details of colonial budgetary matters were under discussion, preparations had been completed by the Navy for the medical care of "natives in all tropical naval bases and harbors which shall be occupied by the navy or taken under military or civilian administration"[81] and draft bills had been prepared for the control of animal epidemics and on other veterinary matters. The Traffic Section of the KPA had made a thorough survey of all motor vehicles available in the colonies and of all railroads and roads, while also gathering information on wages, railroad tariffs, available and needed personnel for the communications services, and procedures used in the training of native personnel. The Cameroons and Tanganyika had already been subdivided into Road Maintenance and Construction Supervision Districts. Railroad specialists were planning the standardization of the gauges of all African roads and had prepared, at the request of the High Command of the Armed Forces, a detailed study on a railroad from Tripoli to Lake Chad. Endless correspondence and meetings between the representatives of virtually all cabinet offices (at one such meeting, on July 20, 1941, sixty-two persons were present!) culminated in a plan for a prefabricated sectional structure suitable for various government buildings in the tropics. A special tropical automobile had also been developed, preparatory work had been undertaken "on the standardization of the machine tool inventory in the colonies," the question of the best method of organizing repair shops for railroads and other communications services had been studied in detail, along with the problem of spare parts and fuel supply.

A linguist was employed in working out a proposal for a lingua franca for West Africa and work was in progress on the standardization of the orthography of Kisuaheli. The Native Culture section had prepared a memorandum on positions for and the tasks

80. Ibid., p. 36.
81. BA, RFM, file 4973, letter from Oberkommando der Wehrmacht to RFM, dated September 1, 1941.

of government ethnologists, whose role was considered to be of special importance in view of Nazi doctrines on native policy, which stressed the maintenance of tribal patterns. The Labor Laws section had prepared executive orders for Directed Labor (*Arbeitseinsatz*) "of natives and aliens of similar status," proposals for the administration of Directed Labor, and details on a "labor book" for natives, on wages and hours; and had written laws for the protection of both female native employees and minor employees.[82] It may well be questioned whether at any time in history a nonexistent empire had been so well administered!

Unfortunately, the files of the KPA disappeared at the end of the war, so that we do not know all the details concerning the Nazis' colonial policy. Enough documentary material is available, however, to fix the broad outlines of this policy, and many members of the KPA have furnished us with glimpses of their colonial doctrines in their publications which appeared before and during World War II.

Basic to all colonial planning was a set of principles summed up in a "Colonial Catechism," which apparently had been worked out by the head of the KPA's Section II, Asmis.[83]

German Colonial Catechism

[Deutscher Kolonial Katechismus]

1. The German Reich takes over the colonies with unlimited sovereignty, free of all international obligations, but it is willing to cooperate with other colonial powers.
2. The German colonies are parts of the Reich, not foreign territory. They enjoy the full military protection of the Reich. They have their own legislation and finance.
3. Every German called to work in the colonies, whether for the government or not, has to prove himself

---

82. KPA, *Tätigkeitsbericht* (1942), passim. BDC, *Reichsministerium für Volksaufklärung und Propaganda*, Ordner 443. BA, RFM, file 4973.
83. BA, RFM, file 4990b, Asmis to Burmeister, April 22, 1940.

worthy of the great task given there to the German people. He who fails to fulfill this duty will not be tolerated there.

4. The power of the Reich (sovereignty) in the German colonies is in the hands of the Führer and *Reichskanzler*. He is represented by the governor of the colony. In his hands lie the supreme powers in the colony in all areas.

5. The principle of the separation of races applies in the German colonies. Aiding the welfare of the natives is one of the primary tasks of all German colonial activity. The separate folkish nature of the natives, their customs and mores and legal institutions, will be honored insofar as they do not offend the German concept of morality.

6. For non-natives German law is principally applicable; for natives, native law. Regular courts have jurisdiction over non-natives, the administrative authorities over natives.

7. The natives are protected in their landed property and their other rights. Landed property may be transmitted from natives to non-natives only with permission of the competent authority.

8. The German government strives for the participation of natives in the administration.

9. Freedom of conscience prevails in the German colonies. All facilities and institutions of worship enjoy the equal protection of the German government.

10. The German government takes a special interest in the education of the natives. All private institutions of education are under the supervision of governmental authorities.

11. The natives' health will be guarded. For this purpose diseases and epidemics will be combated and the hygienic conditions among the natives improved as far as possible. Securing the sufficient nutrition of the natives is an important task.

12. The colonies will be economically developed. Their economic value will be made available to the German over-all economy, of which the colonial economy is a part. Scientific research in all fields will be supported.

This set of principles was to form the basis of Colonial Law, a kind of constitutional document for the future German Empire. The provisions of that Law were debated within the hierarchy of the Reich from the spring of 1940 until August 1941. By that time virtual consensus had been achieved on its final form, and General von Epp ordered further work on it to cease until he could get a definite decision from Hitler on its principles.[84] The colonial policy doctrines set out in the cited document owe much to those of Bismarck's empire. The judicial system envisaged here, the stress on native education and medical facilities as well as the statement on religious policy, are clearly based on pre-1914 ideas and practices. The additional factors of racism and the greater stress on the direct participation of the state in colonial development are new. Here the totalitarian philosophy of the Third Reich becomes clearly visible.

Point 1 of the Colonial Catechism is clear enough. It merely restates the position that the German colonialists had taken for years and which Hitler, for example, stressed in his talk with Henderson—that Germany would not consider a mandate or similar arrangement but would insist on owning colonies outright. The cooperation mentioned in this paragraph would include such items as common measures against "African Bolshevism" (which in Nazi terminology included all movements striving for greater autonomy—not to mention independence) and the sharing of research in tropical medicine, technology, etc. The provisions of the Congo Act with regard to the limitations on the trade in arms and alcoholic beverages might also be re-enacted in a new treaty between the colonial powers. The distinctions between the native policies of the various European powers, on the

84. Ibid., file 4966.

other hand, were to be preserved as a positive value. They were considered to preclude any common "cultural work."[85]

An elucidation of Part 2 of the Colonial Catechism is provided by a statement of the Ministry of Interior on the planned Colonial Law, which stressed that the Law must be framed in such a manner and the administration of the colonies organized in such a way "that their development into a mere *Schutzgebiet* or 'protectorate' in the English sense or even into an autonomous entity" would be impossible.[86] The colonies, in short, would simply be a political and economic annex of the Reich.

High on the list of those who would not be tolerated in the colonies were, of course, Jews. Nazi writers charged that Jews had been responsible for what they considered the shortcomings of the Bismarckian colonial policy, especially for its exploitation of the natives.[87] They also were accused of undermining the natives' respect for the white race.[88] Finally, an official of the Propaganda Ministry alleged, they stood behind "those powers who further, or even make appear tolerable, the equality of the Negro with the White Race, the mixing of peoples and races and the introduction of black peoples into world politics . . ."[89] Aside from excluding Jews, the Nazis wished to protect their colonies against the formation of an element of "poor whites" whose economic performance—possibly inferior to that of some Africans —and low standard of living and morality also would undermine the myth of white superiority.[90] This consideration undoubtedly played a role in the general opposition on the part of National Socialists to the idea of mass settlement of whites in the colonies,

85. Westermann, *Beiträge,* pp. 23–24, 45–52 (articles by Reinhold Schober and Consul General Rudolf Karlowa); cf. Karlowa, *Deutsche Kolonialpolitik,* p. 28.

86. BA, RFM, file 4966, letter from Reichsministerium des Innern to KPA, dated August 21, 1940.

87. *Deutscher Kolonialdienst* (December 1938), pp. 1–4. Krumbach, *Kolonialpolitik Heute,* p. 37.

88. *Deutscher Kolonialdienst* (December 1937), pp. 2–3.

89. Brüsch, *Kolonien—ein Kapitel Deutscher Ehre,* p. 38.

90. Ibid., pp. 76–77. Leutwein, p. 30.

which we have already noted.[91] The settlement that would take place would be tightly controlled. One official of the KPA suggested that land should not be granted to settlers outright but only by a copy-holding arrangement under which the state would receive a fixed percentage of each settler's agricultural production, the proceeds from which would then be used to set up and equip new farms.[92] Similarly, a memorandum dated July 2, 1942, from the Chief of the KPA's Section for Communications and Technology suggested the creation in the colonies of "culture centers," to prevent random settlement. These centers, following the Italian example, would consist of schools, hospitals, party headquarters, etc., and would serve as the nucleus for a surrounding German settlement.[93] The question of white settlement is, of course, an important consideration in land and native policy and will therefore have to be discussed further in connection with these terms.

Part 4 of the Colonial Catechism speaks for itself. Its author had undoubtedly been mindful, in formulating it, of the unhappy situation that had existed in the prewar German colonies, in which the commanders of the *Schutztruppe* often acted quite independently of the German government. The principle embodied in this point also would prevent the establishment in the colonies of a welter of party organizations without proper coordination.[94] A proposal for the organization of local governments in the German colonies envisaged the following structure:

The Governor (in the case of his absence or incapacitation the Vice Governor) of the colony was to have absolute authority over all officials in the colony. The Central Administration headed by him was to consist of six functional divisions.

The first two of these would be responsible for Personnel and General Administration, including land policy. The Division of Native Affairs and Labor Policy would be in charge of the activities of the Labor Front, race policy, and Protestant missions. (The available documents have nothing to say about Catholic missions.)

91. Cf. above, pp. 49–51.
92. Wangenheim, *Kolonien des Dritten Reiches*, pp. 60–61.
93. BA, RFM, file 4990a.
94. Cf. Wangenheim, p. 46.

Labor Commissars, to be stationed in the most important plantation and recruiting areas, would be responsible to this office. The fourth major division was to handle financial and budgetary affairs; the fifth, the colonial press, propaganda, radio, party affairs, arts and sciences, the affairs of foreigners resident in the colonies, and a number of minor functions. Finally, a judicial office was projected, whose head, the Chief Prosecutor, would also function as the chief legal adviser to the Governor of the colony.

Technical Services would form a part of the central administration in that their chiefs would be responsible to the Governor. The representatives of the services in the field, however, would operate independently of the administrative hierarchy, responsible only to the chief of their service. These technical services would include the following sections:

a. Agriculture
b. Animal husbandry and Veterinary Affairs
c. Forestry
d. Geology and Mining
e. Health
f. Education
g. Technology (construction, road, air and water transport and maintenance, etc.)
h. Railroads

Local administrative districts would be in charge of a *Landrat,* who would be responsible for all administrative tasks as well as local police, tax collection, roads, etc. Jurisdiction over natives would be vested in this official.

It was apparent already from Himmler's insistence on his sole responsibility for carrying out colonial preparations within his own domain that the new colonial administration would not be able to include the police within its sphere of authority. The principle of centralization thus was already violated. The KPA seemed ready to accept this fact, merely suggesting that the police, while under its own administration, be under the executive control of local officials. But jails and the assignment of prisoners to forced labor were conceded to fall within the police sphere of responsibility.[95]

Native policy must be the heart of all colonial policy. Racism was the heart of the National Socialist world view and would therefore determine the policies Nazi Germany would follow as a colonial power in Africa. For these reasons an examination of the ideas and attitudes of Point 5 of the colonial program we are discussing is particularly interesting. In view of the fact that the German colonial claim was often attacked abroad on the grounds that Nazi racial attitudes made them unfit to rule over people of different races, a great deal was written by German colonialists to refute this allegation and to picture racism as a principle which could, in fact, form the basis of a colonial policy beneficial to native populations. Only rarely was the racist point of view (as in Hitler's famous characterization of Negroes as "born half-apes")[96] expressed in its more brutal formulations.[97]

Most of the colonialists purported to see in the African a race destined by its natural characteristics to be ruled by the white master race, yet for this very reason entitled to just and humane treatment.[98] Many, however, were inclined to concede to the Negro and his culture special unique racial values which should be protected and preserved. Every race in this view had such values—except the Jews, the only people who were altogether inferior in every respect and whose treatment by the Nazi rulers therefore did not imply similar treatment for the African: "With the colored people overseas there does not connect a past filled with hatred and strife. The German colonial pioneers worked and fought shoulder to shoulder with the natives of the country."[99]

The colonial policies of other powers were often sharply con-

95. BA, RFM, 4990a, undated memorandum.

96. Hitler, *Mein Kampf,* p. 430.

97. It would be a mistake, of course, to ascribe all manifestations of racism in German colonial thought to Nazi ideology. Certain racist assumptions, after all, were basic to all European colonialism. Views held by Peters and his followers in the 1880s, for example, could easily be taken for those of National Socialists. See, e.g., Müller, p. 184.

98. See, e.g., Rohrbach, *Deutschlands Koloniale Forderung,* pp. 124 ff.

99. Viera, *Kolonien im Blickfeld von Heute,* p. 132. Cf. Baravalle, pp. 4, 54–55.

demned by Nazi writers. The French were scored for their egalitarian theory of assimilation as well as for their oppressive and exploitative practice—especially in connection with the raising of native troops. The abolition of the color bar in the French mandates, moreover, was declared illegal, since the mandates were not the property of the mandatory powers. It is interesting to note that the Portuguese, toward whose authoritarian regime the Nazis felt a certain affinity, were never condemned as sharply for not making a colonial policy principle out of racial prejudice as were the French. The administrative and other aspects of Portuguese policy were, in fact, lauded.[100]

Criticism of British colonial policy ranged from accusations that England had established a system of "soft negrophilism" in Tanganyika, Togoland, and the British Cameroons[101] to condemnations of Anglo-Saxon "racial snobbery" which treated the Negro as an inferior while "coddling and cultivating a truly and entirely inferior people, the Jews."[102] Britain was also accused of providing few concrete benefits for its native populations.[103] As for South Africa, it is interesting that its racial policies, to which the proposed Nazi policies would seem to bear a close resemblance, were not always wholly approved. Thus Oskar Karstedt, in a volume published by the Reichsforschungsrat, condemned the Union's "brutal" pass laws, whose application could create "monstrous wrong."[104] Italian policy was condemned, prior to 1938, for allowing mixed marriages,[105] and New Zealand's capitulation to the Maoris was cited as an example of exaggeratedly good treatment of natives,[106] while the United States was

---

100. *Kolonialzeitung, 47* (1935), 57–58, 149–50. Ritter, *Der Kampf um den Erdraum,* pp. 70, 358. Karlowa, p. 33. Rohrbach, *Deutschlands Koloniale Forderung,* p. 43.

101. Rohrbach, pp. 36, 41–42, 45. Wangenheim, p. 35.

102. Baravalle, p. 4.

103. *Kolonialzeitung, 47* (1935), 176.

104. Oskar Karstedt, *Probleme afrikanischer Eingeborenenpolitik, Kolonialwissenschaftliche Forschungen 8,* Herausgegeben im Auftrage des Reichsforschungsrates und der deutschen Forschungsgemeinschaft von Günter Wolff, Leiter der Kolonialwissenschaftlichen Abteilung (Berlin, 1942), p. 54.

105. Brüsch, pp. 80–81.

106. Holtsch, pp. 16 ff.

denied any right to criticize German racial policies in view of its treatment of American Negroes, "who through their work helped develop the resources of the country," and of the natives of the American Pacific islands, especially those of Guam.[107] (Their almost total neglect with respect to medical care was sharply criticized.) Germany, it was claimed, would avoid all these extremes and would certainly not treat its Africans worse than other colonial powers.[108]

What emerges as the basis of a Nazi colonial policy is a mixture of the racial and *Blut und Boden* aspects of Nazi ideology and the paternalistic practices of the German colonial administration prior to World War I. In the first place it was assumed that the various races were absolutely different in their capabilities and style of life. These differences must be accepted, cultivated, and preserved. The European, whose racial heritage provided him with a special talent for organization and technical invention was destined to rule over other races, who were not therefore to be considered inferior in all aspects of their culture—merely different. In its most idealistic as well as intellectually respectable form, this view was expounded by the noted African historian and anthropologist Diedrich Westermann in *Der Afrikaner heute und morgen*.[109] The same view, however, can also be found in articles by Walter Gross, Director of the Party's "Office for Race Policy,"[110] and by Günther Hecht, also a representative of that agency,[111] who summed up the Party's official dogma as follows: "The colored man has his own value; he is neither more nor less valuable than we, but he is largely and deeply different from us. We as the intellectual superiors psychologically explore his essence, his being. When we know that, we know what is necessary for him and what he can truly grasp and understand. We have to treat him accordingly."[112]

---

107. Abs, *Der Kampf um Unsere Schutzgebiete*, pp. 284, 295.
108. For a statement to this effect by Hermann Göring see Logan, p. 141.
109. (Berlin, 1937), passim.
110. Brüsch, *Kolonien—Grossdeutschlands Anspruch*, pp. 102–06.
111. Brüsch, *Kolonien—ein Kapitel Deutscher Ehre*, pp. 66–82.
112. Ibid., p. 82.

Specifically, the National Socialists proposed to cultivate "a native *Volkstum* living and working in a healthy social community"[113] by two broad policies: the prevention of physical mixing of the races and the rejection of a Europeanizing and civilizing mission in favor of the maintenance of native cultures, laws, and ways of life.[114] Racial mixing was considered dangerous because mixed blood populations were alleged to be inferior to both parent races[115] and because as uprooted, proletarian elements they furnished a breeding ground for "Bolshevism," i.e. all forms of political and economic discontent.[116] The proper way of life for the Negro was considered to be a rural, agricultural one, which would preserve the "group directedness" of African civilization and such values as the African family, native dances, handicrafts, etc.[117] Christianity, the Western concept of freedom, a money economy, and military service were all considered to be unfit for adoption by the Negro race,[118] which instead should be given an opportunity "to seek its development in accordance with its own ideas and ideals."[119] Specifically, this meant the preservation in its essence of tribal society,[120] and its agricultural basis: "The negro robbed of his field is like a plant taken out of the earth."[121] Minister Hans Frank summed up the whole concept in a speech delivered in May 1939 before the Academy for German Rights:

> In place of the economic exploitation of Africa it would be necessary to substitute a just and planned development of the natural resources and the encouragement of the native peasants and husbandmen. It will be a

113. Wüst, *Kolonialprobleme der Gegenwart,* p. 10.

114. See, e.g., Schmitt, *Kolonien für Deutschland,* pp. 42–43.

115. E.g. Ritter, *Kampf um den Erdraum,* p. 20.

116. Scheidl, p. 255. Bauer, *Kolonialforderung,* p. 74.

117. *Kolonialzeitung,* 52 (1941), 157–60. Rohrbach, *Afrika—Beiträge zu einer praktischen Kolonialkunde,* p. 135.

118. Karlowa, p. 60.

119. Johannsen and Kraft, *Germany's Colonial Problem,* p. 50.

120. See, e.g., Bender, *Kolonien—ein Kraftfeld Grossdeutschlands,* pp. 122–31; Westermann, *Beiträge,* pp. 91–110.

121. Bauer, *Koloniale Wende,* p. 56.

special task to stop the continuing dissolution of tribalism taking place under the influence of degenerating
liberalism and to carry out a division of black and white
living space, through which alone the distinctive
(*artgemäss*) development of the natives under the strict,
just leadership of the whites could be guaranteed.[122]

Frank's speech shows that the Afrikaner Nationalists have no
monopoly with respect to the idea of territorial *apartheid*. This
notion was a definite part of the German colonial plans. While
some observers doubted that the ideal—total territorial separation—could be achieved,[123] others held that it *must* be achieved
under any circumstances, economic considerations, such as the
need for industrial labor, notwithstanding.[124] In that way there
could never be a colored proletariat and a danger of Communism.[125] Clearly, a policy of territorial separation of the races
must run counter to economic considerations. This incompatibil-
ity between the demands of a racist policy and economic exploitation, painfully evident in present South African racial policies, was
already implicit in the discussions of Nazi colonialists—even
though Germany did not actually have an empire—and will be
discussed below.

True colonial experts were not unaware of the changes oc-
curring in Africa—urbanization, industrialization, the breakdown
of tribalism—but generally they considered these changes as evils
to be arrested and even to be undone as far as possible: "The
'good African' . . . is not the black inhabitant of Johannesburg
or the student at Achimota College . . but the black peasant."
Even if it should prove impossible to maintain the tribes and
tribal culture—and with it indirect rule—the African tradition
must somehow be preserved or re-established, a tradition in which
urbanism and industrial civilization had no place.[126] This could
be achieved by changing the whole colonizing approach so as to

---

122. Schmitt, *Funktion und Bedeutung*, p. 160.
123. Bender, *Kolonien—ein Kraftfeld Grossdeutschlands*, p. 51.
124. *Kolonialzeitung*, *51* (1939), 18–20. Cf. Karlowa, p. 35.
125. Scheidl, p. 255.
126. Karstedt, *Der Weisse Kampf um Afrika*, pp. 8–35, 91–92.

stop all attempts at Europeanizing the Africans[127] and by assuring that they had sufficient land to live on. Diedrich Westermann was realistic enough to realize that "the further progress of the Europeanization of the African cannot be halted" but proposed to lead it into "healthy paths"—not really specifying what he had in mind.[128] Even more liberal and thoroughly untypical of Nazi attitudes were the views of Walter Pahl, who in an article in the *Kolonialzeitung* pointed out "that the entry of civilization into Africa is an unstoppable process" and called for a new relationship between the European and the African, to be based on cooperation of the separate racial spheres (the author also seems to have envisaged territorial segregation). The "master and servant relationship" between the races that prevailed in South Africa he described as a seedbed of communism.[129]

It is only when we proceed from the philosophical discussion of a native policy to be adopted by the Third Reich to an examination of some examples showing what its application would mean in practice that the full meaning of what the Nazis had in mind becomes apparent. Thus a draft of a Kolonialblutschutzgesetz prepared by the KPA in effect made the Nuremberg laws applicable to Africans. It forbade all marriages between Germans and persons of African or mixed ancestry and declared invalid such marriages that had been concluded in contravention of the law, especially abroad. The law would have forbidden and provided punishment for illicit sexual relations between white and colored persons; for such relations between a white woman and an African man—but not vice-versa—the death penalty was provided.[130] Apparently it had not yet been decided whether the Nuremberg definition of an Aryan (a person with three Aryan grandparents) would also apply in the colonies.[131] As for other discriminatory legislation, an article in the *Kolonialzeitung* recommended corporal punishment for natives, the prevention of the "rise of great fortunes and their influence and power in the

127. Kühne, *Das Kolonialverbrechen von Versailles,* pp. 126–27.
128. *Kolonialzeitung, 51* (1939), 4–8.
129. Ibid., *48* (1936), 211–42.
130. BA, RFM, file 4965.
131. *Kolonialzeitung, 53* (1941), 5–7.

hands of colored persons" and segregation of all facilities.[132]
A "certain compulsion to work" was considered necessary, for
physical labor by whites would be out of the question in view of
the need to maintain an absolute color bar.[133] Natives would
not be citizens of Germany but merely "protected persons." As
a reward for especially meritorious conduct, they might be made
"protectorate citizens."[134] Mixed-blood elements, such as the
"Cape Boys" in Southwest Africa, would be considered undesir-
able in German possessions and pushed out.[135] Native policy
would be flexible enough to provide for different approaches to
different peoples.[136] Standards applied to a "master race," such
as the Watusi in Ruanda-Urundi,[137] would be different from
those that would govern the Bantu population. Apparently the
racial experts of the Party even had ways to make Aryans out of a
whole people. The Samoans seem to have achieved such status.[138]

The application of racist principles to the administration of
justice would mean that natives would not be treated with kid
gloves, as they were by British colonial courts.[139] Corporal
punishment was praised as a "truly educational measure," be-
loved by the natives, who were quite unable to understand other
forms of punishment.[140] Their racial characteristics, moreover,
were said to demand immediate punishment for a misdeed, so that
plantation owners in remote areas should be equipped with some
kind of judicial authority over their employees.[141] The ordinary
judicial procedure for a native would consist of a hearing before
the District Officer, possibly assisted by a native assessor. Persons
of mixed blood would also be tried in this fashion, not before
the regular courts, which would be reserved for whites. Apparently

132. Ibid., *52* (1940), 152–56.
133. Wangenheim, p. 57.
134. Ibid., p. 55.
135. *Kolonialzeitung, 53* (1941), 5.
136. *Deutscher Kolonialdienst* (June 1937), p. 1.
137. Ibid. (November 1937), pp. 4–8.
138. Hans Ernst Pfeiffer, *Unsere schönen alten Kolonien* (Berlin, 1941), p. 110.
139. Diehl, *Die Kolonien Warten*, p. 183.
140. Ibid., p. 61. Bender, *Kolonien—ein Kraftfeld Grossdeutschlands*, p. 78.
141. *Deutscher Kolonialdienst* (June 1937), p. 8.

the purpose was to deny natives any possibility of initiating pro-
ceedings against their employers. The Labor Front alone could
act in cases where African workers had a legitimate grievance.[142]

In the case of land policy the Nazis' racial attitude and *Blut und
Boden* ideology might actually have worked in favor of the African. If the African was to develop his true nature as a farmer, not
as a proletarian, and if his whole sphere of life was to be kept
separate, territorially as well as spiritually, from that of the European, then he must be given sufficient land. German colonial
planners thus condemned British policy in East Africa, where
"native interests [were] subordinated to those of a handful of
whites,"[143] and stated that in a German colony two great principles would be applied: the African's right to maintain his own
"racial life" and his right to keep the soil necessary for this.[144]
This right to soil, to be sure, would exist only where such soil
was used and culture values were created, but the African would
be helped in improving his agricultural methods and in fighting
soil erosion. In addition to territorial separation of the African
and white areas of settlement, specific crops and other activities
might also be segregated in order to prevent economic competition
between Africans and whites.[145] Thus Africans might be forbidden to raise coffee[146] but have stock-raising left to them exclusively.[147] In order to raise the level of native agriculture, African farmers might be organized into cooperatives or similar corpo-
rate groups in which membership would be mandatory.[148] Such
organizations were considered especially suitable in view of the
group-directedness of African culture.

It is interesting that in this area of land policy Nazi ideologues
espoused a policy more favorable to the African than did the conservatives, especially those with African experience. The settler
mentality of the latter was opposed to the concept of an independ-

142. Wangenheim, p. 54.
143. Karstedt, pp. 58 ff.
144. Kühne, p. 113.
145. Brüsch, *Kolonien—Grossdeutschlands Anspruch*, p. 128.
146. Diehl, p. 44.
147. Schultze, *Der Wirtschaftswert Unserer Kolonien*, p. 24.
148. Brüsch, *Anspruch*, p. 128. Karstedt, pp. 119 ff., 129–34.

ent African peasant population. Thus Paul Rohrbach, who had once been Reich Settlement Commissar for Southwest Africa, described Africans as hopelessly incapable of working independently and considered native reservations merely a transitory stage in the integration of the Africans into the white economy.[149] Another old Southwest African proposed to limit native reservations in the territory to such an extent that they could not provide more than "homesteads for old people and those incapable of work."[150] Southwest Africa, with its fairly large white population, its territory and climate suitable for further white immigration, seems to have been considered a special case even in the KPA. One of its officials, Paul Ritter, deplored the Mandate Administration's policy of allowing the natives to keep cattle and their own land and maintained that, since only the technical ability of Europeans had made a large part of the dry country suitable for habitation, it should belong to Europeans alone.[151] The conflict between a liberal land policy and the demands of European plantations, mining, and industry for African labor was recognized in an article by Geo A. Schmidt, a member of the *Kolonialwirtschaftliches Komitee*. Demanding, as usual, a clear territorial separation of African and European settlement, Schmidt suggested various criteria on the basis of which land would be assigned to natives. One important consideration was that not too much land should be given to Africans, so that not all available labor would be required for its cultivation. European enterprises had to be assured of a plentiful labor supply.[152] In line with this philosophy, one proposal was to allot about 45 per cent of the available land in the colonies to the Africans, the rest to Europeans.[153] In view of the emphasis that was placed on economic development and exploitation of the colonies, it is likely that this kind of thinking would soon have prevailed over the idea of creating a native peasantry. In South Africa, at any rate, where a similar conflict exists between racist attitudes and the facts of an

149. Rohrbach, *Afrika—Beiträge*, pp. 108 ff.
150. *Kolonialzeitung*, 52 (1940), 172.
151. Bauer, *Koloniale Wende*, pp. 67–79.
152. Bender, *Kolonien—ein Kraftfeld Grossdeutschlands*, p. 91.
153. Schultze, p. 14.

industrial economy, the latter have (until very recently) determined the actual policies adopted.

It is hard to see how the colonial policy envisaged by National Socialist planners could have provided for "the participation of natives in the administration." Apparently this phrase merely meant that Germany would make use of African chiefs for purposes of local administration. The model to be imitated here was not, however, the British system of indirect rule, which allowed chiefs a fair degree of autonomy, but the Portuguese administrative practice, whose adaptation of "Bantu despotism" to its own purposes was considered exemplary.[154] Natives would also be employed in the lower ranks of the administrative hierarchy. Thus a circular (dated March 6, 1941) from the Chef der Ordnungspolizei stated that only the officers of colonial police forces would be recruited in Germany. The lower ranks were to consist of "suitable colored men." This regulation would not apply to the settler colony of Southwest Africa, where the whole police force would be European.[155]

The National Socialist attitude toward the missions was far less favorable than Point 8 of the Colonial Catechism would seem to indicate. The missions were condemned for trying to Europeanize the natives, thus making them "impertinent" and prone to Communism. Missionaries, according to this view, had failed to maintain proper racial attitudes:

> Nobody denies that the mission has created great values. Social service, hospitals, and many other things are real values. But if these missionaries had at all times looked upon themselves solely as Europeans, having come out not merely to baptize, but obligated, as white men, to stand in a human capacity between the administration and the natives and to mediate, while also maintaining their dignity—if they had done that, then the missions would not have solely torn down the barriers which are now down . . . [156]

154. *Kolonialzeitung, 54* (1942), 174–76.
155. BA, HO, file R/19/245.
156. Brüsch, *Kolonien—ein Kapitel deutscher Ehre,* p. 76. Quoted from an article by Günther Hecht, a functionary of the Office for Race Policy.

In the future only such missionaries would be admitted to the colonies who had "proved at home their National Socialist attitudes."[157] Missionary work in the colonies would be under the strict control of the Central Administration's office of Native Affairs. The task of the missionary would be to counteract the growth of Islam[158] and to indoctrinate the Africans "to live and work with and under whites, as is necessary in a colonial country administered along modern lines." Their influence should also be brought to bear to counter "agitation" among the natives.[159] Missionaries were not allowed to take any part in colonial planning. In 1937, a directive by General von Epp forbade local units of the *Reichskolonialbund* to cooperate in any form with missionary societies.[160] The literature of National Socialist colonial agitation is full of attacks against missionaries. Clearly the Third Reich intended to minimize the humanizing influence missionaries had had on the colonial practice of other powers and, for that matter, on the Bismarckian empire's colonial policy.

The viciousness of the racial policy the Third Reich proposed to follow in Africa becomes fully apparent in discussions about the kind of education to be given to natives. To be sure, Africa experts like Diedrich Westermann and Martin Schlunk argued against "closing the road to higher education" to Africans and condemned the kind of attitude that lay behind the unfavorable comparisons that were often drawn between "niggers in pants" and "the unspoiled bush negro." While Westermann was in favor of limiting access to higher education in order to prevent the formation of an academic proletariat, he was not completely opposed to granting the Africans such opportunities.[161] The typical National Socialist attitude, however, opposed higher education for Africans on the grounds that it merely created a "caricature of European culture." The University College at Achimota was criticized as an example of an "unnatural" British racial and edu-

---

157. *Deutscher Kolonialdienst* (June 1937), p. 8.

158. Wangenheim, p. 52.

159. Diehl, pp. 249–54.

160. BDC, Research Section, Ordner 212, *Mitteilungsblatt der Bundesführung des Reichskolonialbundes* (June 15, 1937), pp. 22–23.

161. Westermann, *Beiträge*, pp. 32, 91–110. Wüst, pp. 67–81.

cation policy: "The blacks are in the end the sufferers. They give up their African character without realizing that after all they can never become Europeans."[162] Speakers were instructed to point out in colonial indoctrination lectures that National Socialism condemned all such attempts to assimilate peoples of other races or to bring European civilization to them. "National Socialism thus denies a 'cultural mission' . . ."[163] In conformity with this philosophy, the schooling of natives in German colonies would be confined to the elementary level: "The simple fundamentals of reading, writing, and arithmetic" would suffice for the education of a class of peasants and artisans.

In addition, the curriculum would stress "obedience to and respect for parents and educators, manual skills, and personal hygiene." German would be taught only to clever pupils. A little extra education might be given to an "elite," i.e. schoolteachers and minor administrative officials, in accordance with local demands.[164] Thus it was decided in a number of conferences between representatives of state, party, and armed forces agencies to train natives as lower-echelon health personnel, but not as physicians.[165] The Nazis, in short, would not have allowed the training of an African leadership that might have challenged their power. The kind of advancement "along their own racial lines" that the African could look forward to under Nazi rule is starkly described by Paul Rohrbach: "He will not read books or carry on correspondence, he will not eat in the European manner, he will be less demanding with respect to furniture, tools, and the daily small needs of life; he will not take trips, spend no money for the education of children, need no expensive machines."[166]

He would, however, be taken care of medically. A great deal of stress was placed in the colonial literature as well as in actual planning on public health, especially on programs to reduce in-

162. Ritter, *Kampf um den Erdraum*, p. 353. *Kolonialzeitung*, *48* (1936), 378–79.

163. BDC, Research Section, Ordner 212, *Mitteilungsblatt* (June 15, 1937), pp. 31–32.

164. *Deutscher Kolonialdienst* (June 1937), p. 7. Wangenheim, pp. 50–51.

165. KPA, *Tätigkeitsbericht* (1942), p. 25.

166. Rohrbach, *Deutschlands Koloniale Forderung*, p. 142.

fant mortality and improve the Africans' diet.[167] Hitler, to be sure, was "furious" at the idea of pampering the natives by setting up "kindergartens and hospitals for [them]."[168] But the main reason behind the interest shown in the health of the Africans was far from humanitarian. It was rather the fact that German economic planners were concerned about a shortage of labor brought about by a stagnant or only slowly growing African population.[169] Provisions for medical measures were primarily designed to overcome this difficulty in developing the German Empire. Public health thus was considered to be a part of economic development and labor policy.[170]

Given a shortage of manpower, moreover, the Nazis felt that a system of forced labor would be indispensable in the development of the colonies.[171] We have already referred to the legal framework that had been created for the "organization of labor."[172] The Reich Labor Service and the Labor Front were slated to play important roles in the labor administration.[173] To make sure that all Africans would be "organized" for labor, the KPA had already drafted a law that introduced a workbook to be carried at all times by "all male workers over the age of 16 who are organized for labor purposes." Natives not so organized—i.e. those incapable of work, those with jobs outside German possessions, and women— would have received identification cards. Even the form of the booklet had already been prepared. It was to contain a record of the bearer's employment, his tax payments, and his health. Natives found not to be in possession of this book would be punished. Since employers were to keep the pass in their possession for the

---

167. See, e.g., Bender, *Kolonien—ein Kraftfeld Grossdeutschlands*, pp. 92 ff.; Wangenheim, pp. 47–48; Brüsch, *Kolonien—ein Kapitel deutscher Ehre*, pp. 58 ff.

168. Henry Picker, *Hitlers Tischgespräche*, entry for February 19, 1942.

169. See, e.g., Diedrich Westermann, *Der Afrikaner heute und morgen*, pp. 339 ff.

170. See, e.g., Karlowa, p. 51.

171. Bauer, *Koloniale Wende*, p. 66. Schultze, p. 6. Bauer, *Kolonien im Dritten Reich, 1,* 73.

172. Cf. above, p. 160.

173. KPA, *Tätigkeitsbericht* (1942), p. 15. Karlowa, pp. 51–52. Viera, pp. 133–34.

duration of the native's work contract, an employee was bound to his place of work by the force of law. This system would have been even more vicious than the pass law in force in the Union of South Africa, which requires Africans to carry a similar passbook at all times.[174]

With respect to the more general aspects of economic policy in the colony, we find that the overseas possessions of the Reich would have been absolutely subordinated to the mother country economically as well as politically:

> We define [colonization] in such a way that the German colonial economy can only be considered as a special branch of the German national economy as a whole, that it is out of the question that the aim of the economic development of a colony could be to create, now or in the future, an organism standing by itself and existing according to its own vital principles, which finally could be connected with the mother country only administratively and would claim against it "rights" of whatever sort.[175]

The colonies were to be solely producers of raw materials for the German economy. No industrialization would be allowed to take place. This kind of colonization was seen to require central planning as the basis for success. Accordingly, economic action by the state would play a large role, especially since the state would not be bound by considerations of short-range profitability in making investments. Part of the need for investment would also be supplied by the "forced savings" of the natives, whose consumption would be held to a minimum.[176]

This thoroughly oppressive neo-mercantilistic system was de-

174. BA, RFM, file 4982, the draft law and a sample workbook are included in a letter, dated September 6, 1941, from the chief of the KPA Dienststelle Berlin to Ministerialrat Burmeister of the Finance Ministry. The latter's reply contains a refreshing bit of common sense: in refusing to comment on the draft law, Burmeister observed that in his opinion this would be "neither important to the war effort, nor useful."

175. Rohrbach, *Afrika—Beiträge*, p. 103.

176. Haag, *Kolonien und Industriewirtschaft*, pp. 67–89. Rohrbach, pp. 104–05. Karlowa, p. 51.

scribed in the odd terminology of the totalitarian state as the opposite of exploitation, since it would benefit not a few individuals and private companies, but the whole nation.[177] The new colonialism, in the view of the Nazis, created an economic symbiosis from which the Africans would benefit also, by being provided with leadership, security, and welfare programs.[178]

It is obvious that in this kind of thinking there could be no room for the evolution of colonies toward independence. National Socialist publicists recognized the signs of a growth of African nationalism but saw in them merely a result of mistaken British and French policies and of Bolshevist propaganda. Britain and France were accused of pursuing a policy of "colonial suicide" by providing the natives with higher education:[179] "The guilt of the English and French in having awakened the self-consciousness of the colored people will one day avenge itself, especially on those nations themselves."[180] The native African press was described as being "in the pay of Moscow,"[181] and "Bolshevist disintegrative propaganda" was alleged to be supporting African nationalism in an effort to push the white man out of Africa as a necessary precondition for the victory of Bolshevism in Europe.[182] The Nazis seemed content to see the end of World War II result in the end of the British Empire and in independence for its peoples in Asia and the Near East.[183] But in Africa, the future German colonial sphere, independence movements would not be tolerated: "If colonial policy manifests unpleasant aspects in the solution of [this problem], if it is proven that it cannot be handled any more with the same ease as formerly, then we must seek the causes in the great colonial guilt of the Western Nations."[184] Africa must forever remain under European control as an "economic reserve area" of Europe. Its populations "according to their racial mental

---

177. Karlowa, pp. 8, 51–52. Krumbach, *Kolonialpolitik Heute*, p. 8.
178. Krumbach, p. 8. Viera, pp. 133–34.
179. *Deutscher Kolonialdienst* (May 1938), p. 20.
180. Baravalle, p. 91.
181. *Deutscher Kolonialdienst* (March 1938), p. 12.
182. Karlowa, p. 57.
183. *Kolonialzeitung*, 52 (1940), 21–22. Westermann, *Beiträge*, p. 28.
184. Paul Schnöckel, *Das deutsche Kolonialproblem* (Berlin, 1937), p. 7.

giftedness are behind us not merely temporarily but forever, and are thus destined to be led by us."[185]

Despite the fact that Nazi rule over non-European areas never became an actuality, and that therefore our study must be viewed at least in part as an excursion into the never-never land of history as it might have been, it does provide us with certain conclusions of some importance to any attempt to gain a clear view of Nazi foreign policy aims, the nature and state of imperialism in the thirties, and the phenomenon of appeasement.

In the first place, the facts we have outlined suggest that Hitler's policy was based far less on any master plans or undeviating ideological convictions than most historians of the period have assumed. If *Mein Kampf* had indeed contained the complete recipe for Hitler's foreign policy, colonial agitation and planning would have had no place in the Nazi scheme of things. It may, of course, be argued that the colonial issue was taken up only as a diversionary tactic, as a smoke screen behind which Nazi plans for European aggression could be carried out more efficiently. That was, for example, the view finally taken by Nevile Henderson. But our analysis of the Hossbach Minutes, of the significance of German naval plans, and of the German-Russian conversations of November 1940 suggest that this view, too, must be revised. It indicates that overseas expansion had become during the late 1930s and the early war years a real objective of the German leadership— though a long-term one. In November 1940 Hitler would have been ready to sacrifice even continued Eastern expansion for the realization of a new global plan of aggrandizement, in concert with the other dictatorial regimes, in which Germany's share would have been Africa south of the Sahara. If we accept the possibility that Hitler was sincere in his overtures to Molotov—as I am inclined to do on the basis of documents showing that plans for the invasion of Russia were held in abeyance until it became clear that Russia was not willing to cooperate on German terms— then we must readjust our whole view of the motives of Hitler's actions.

185. Rohrbach, *Deutschlands Koloniale Forderung*, p. 73.

We have to conclude that his development of a program for an aggressive foreign policy in a book he wrote as an obscure politician did not prevent him from changing his mind about that policy when circumstances had changed and when an important precondition for the success of eastward expansion failed to materialize. This was, of course, the alliance with Great Britain, which constituted a vital part of the policy concepts developed in *Mein Kampf*. In short, our study would tend to indicate that we should view Hitler less as a mad prophet, motivated in his actions entirely by the wild dreams and imaginings of a warped mind, proceeding to carry out his plans in the teeth of objective reality, but more as a realistic, opportunistic, albeit utterly ruthless and murderous politician whose only fixed aim was the increase of German national—and therefore his own personal—power, in whatever area and by whatever means seemed most convenient as dictated by the circumstances of the moment.

Once we fully realize this *dynamic* nature of Nazi foreign policy, it becomes obvious that there is absolutely no reason to assume that even the full realization of Hitler's continental New Order would have meant the end of the process of aggrandizement. This study indicates clearly that it would have been only a step toward the extension of German dominion to overseas areas.

To summarize: Nazi ideologues such as Darré believed in Eastern expansion for its own sake; the colonial enthusiasts believed in the acquisition of overseas territories as an alternative to that policy. Hitler, however, as the arbiter of actual German policy, was willing, in the final analysis, to adopt the program of either group, or both, in his quest for ever-increasing power, emphasizing one or the other in accordance with opportunity. The formula *Ostpolitik und Kolonialpolitik* expresses this attitude.

It is only when Hitler's aims are seen in that fashion that the futility of the Western policy of appeasement becomes apparent. Appeasement was a definite and positive policy, not merely a response to German actions. In the colonial field, where no direct and immediate German pressure existed, this becomes very clear. The proposals for a colonial settlement came from Paris and London, not from Berlin. Such a policy could succeed only if German objectives, no matter how large, were limited and more or less clearly defined. Such was not the case. Our survey of the history of appeasement with regard to colonial matters indicates that Hitler was simply not willing to give up his policy of continental aggrandizement in return for colonial concessions. It also shows, however, that he would not shelve his non-European objectives in return for a free hand in Europe. Chamberlain was unable to buy peace in Europe with Tanganyika (or, among others, the Congo basin proposal). There is no reason to suppose on the other hand that he could have bought the security and integrity of the British Empire by agreeing to Hitler's conception of a New Order in Europe. The colonial claim was maintained by Germany after Munich. It was maintained even during the Polish crisis of August 1939, when tactical considerations might have dictated that it be muted.

A rough negative correlation seems to have existed between the willingness of Britain and France to make concessions to Germany on the colonies, and to permit her expansion eastward. The greatest willingness to give up colonial territory was shown before the annexation of Austria and before Munich, while the Western Powers were still resisting Hitler's European program. When they gave in on these questions, their attitude on the colonial question stiffened. They were not willing to pay a double price for peace. It is interesting to note, however, that during the Polish crisis British plans for a colonial settlement were revived. The old policy of the age of imperialism, which had often solved European crises with the expedient of colonial "compensation," was not yet dead.

The willingness of the Western Powers to barter African territories and populations in the grand style of the nineteenth century for the sake of peace in Europe, and to do so in full realization of the nature of the German dictatorship, must cast the strongest doubt on the claim, frequently made today, that British policy in Africa foresaw and consciously aimed at the political emancipation of the colonies. This retroactive explanation of the events of the 1950s must be viewed as a variant of the truth expressed in the fable of the sour grapes. The Western Powers, far from being solicitous about the political development of Africa toward independence, were willing to hand over African territories to a

German Empire, whose plans for a colonial administration combined all the most illiberal and oppressive aspects of the colonial practices of the European powers, allowing no possibility whatsoever for Africa's emergence into freedom.

On the other hand, it must also be stressed that the plans drawn up for the administration of Germany's African possessions as well as the rationale for the aims of the colonial movement were hardly different in kind from the theory and practice of the imperialism of other colonial powers. The dictatorial nature of the German government, of course, would have led to a greater stress on the more flagrantly illiberal aspects of an inherently illiberal system. Nazi ideology merely influenced the German colonial plans insofar as it provided an explicit rationale for the racialist assumptions implicit in every system of European colonial rule over non-Europeans. It may be said that the schemes of the German colonial planners reflect an attitude more in accordance with the colonialism of the turn of the century than with the more liberal variety practiced in Africa in the thirties. This kind of lag has characterized German history in many instances. Here it may be explained by the fact than the experience on which the Germans drew in mapping their future policies lay several decades in the past. Even so, German attitudes and proposed policies were not totally out of touch with current realities. The similarity between the proposed German regime—to be characterized by total political and economic subordination of the African populations, the total separation of the native from white civilization, as well as by a quasi-paternal interest in their material welfare—and current theories and practices in South Africa is indeed striking.

This investigation can therefore be viewed as a case study of colonial ideology and a colonial system per se. Since it was never put into practice and thus created no vested interests, it will find few defenders. But in condemning that system, we essentially condemn the whole ideology which justified European rule over non-European areas. The relative ease with which colonialism could be fitted into the structure of Nazi ideology must be considered an indictment against the whole colonial system. In the final analysis the same forces and ideas that brought about the defeat of National Socialism also overthrew imperialism.

Bibliography

BIBLIOGRAPHICAL AIDS

Kolonialpolitisches Amt der NSDAP, *Koloniales Schrifttum in Deutschland* (Munich, 1941).

Reichskolonialbund, *Kolonien im deutschen Schrifttum* (Berlin, 1936). These two bibliographies of German colonial literature proved very helpful. Neither claims to be complete. The KPA bibliography expressly excludes all works by "non-Aryan" authors. A supplementary list of German works on the colonial question was gathered from the *Deutsche Kolonialzeitung* (see below).

UNPUBLISHED DOCUMENTS

The bulk of the files of the Kolonialpolitisches Amt der NSDAP and of the Reichskolonialbund seems to have been destroyed at the end of World War II. The Bundesarchiv of the German Federal Republic has so far been unable to get any definite information on the fate of that material. A substantial amount of documents on the activities of the KPA, the RKB, and other agencies concerned with German overseas plans is, however, available in the Bundesarchiv, scattered among the files of various German government agencies: Reichsfinanzministerium, Reichsministerium für Wissenschaft, Erziehung und Volksbildung, Reichskanzlei, and Hauptamt Ordnungspolizei. Of particular value were also the Epp Papers, now in the Bundesarchiv, and the papers of the former Colonial Secretary Solf, which provided interesting insights into the problems of the colonial movement of the 1920s. The U.S. State Department's Berlin Document Center contains scattered material, some of which proved to be of the greatest importance. *Ordner* 211 and 212 (Research Section) contain various documents on the organization and finances of the KPA and RKB. The Hauptarchiv has, in file 266, the highly revealing Activities Report of the KPA referred to frequently in Chapter 4. File 1294 includes instructions by Ribbentrop and Goebbels for the public discussion of the colonial question and Hitler's 1930 statement on the colonial claim, which is quoted in the text. *Ordner* 311 and 768 of the files of the Reichsorganisationsleiter contain a great deal of material on the organization, personnel, and finances of the KPA. File SS 936 (Reichsführer SS) contains the amazing report on the colonial ambitions of Bouhler, Bohle, and others.

The Institut für Zeitgeschichte in Munich has copies of some of the material in the Berlin Document Center, as well as incomplete files of the KPA's official organ, the *Deutscher Kolonialdienst*.

DOCUMENT COLLECTIONS

Akten zur deutschen Auswärtigen Politik 1918–1945 (Baden-Baden, 1950–   ).

Documents on German Foreign Policy 1918–1945 (Washington, 1950–   ).
The British and German documents (both German and English versions were used of the latter) are indispensable in tracing the role played by the colonial claim in prewar diplomacy.

Foreign Relations of the United States; Diplomatic Papers (Washington, 1954–59).
The volumes for 1936–41 proved very helpful, since American diplomats in Europe took a considerable, and often sympathetic, interest in colonial revisionism, often touching on the subject in their reports to Washington.

International Military Tribunal, *Trial of the Major War Criminals* (Nuremberg, 1947–48).

Office of the United States Chief Counsel for Prosecution of Axis Criminality, *Nazi Conspiracy and Aggression* (Washington, 1946).
The Nuremberg documents are exceedingly useful in complementing the Foreign Office material on prewar diplomacy and in providing a fuller picture of Schacht's role in 1936 and 1937.

Woodward, E. L., and Butler, Rohan, eds., *Documents on British Foreign Policy,* (London, 1950–   ).

BIOGRAPHIES AND MEMOIRS

Amery, L. S., *My Political Life* (London, 1953–55).
Amery in 1919 played an important role in drafting the part of the League Covenant that established the Mandatory System. As Colonial Secretary he was the main proponent of Closer Union. In the 1930s he was the leading British opponent of a policy of colonial revisionism.

BIBLIOGRAPHY

Das Deutsche Führerlexikon, 1934/1935 (Berlin, 1934).
   Biographical reference work.
Feiling, Keith, *The Life of Neville Chamberlain* (London, 1947).
   Shows that Chamberlain seriously considered colonial concessions.
François-Poncet, André, *The Fateful Years* (New York, 1949).
   Contains information on Schacht's negotiations with the French
   government in 1936 and 1937. Shows that France was willing to
   consider colonial concessions.
Halifax, Lord, *Fullness of Days* (New York, 1957).
   Contains a good account of Halifax' interview with Hitler in the
   fall of 1937, which shows British willingness to consider colonial
   concessions.
Henderson, Sir Nevile, *Failure of a Mission* (New York, 1940).
   Very full on the negotiations in the spring of 1938, which convinced
   Henderson that colonies were not among Hitler's primary objectives.
Hesse, Fritz, *Hitler and the English* (London, 1954).
   Hesse, a German newspaperman, was the intermediary through
   whom the British offer of the summer of 1939 was allegedly made,
   which contemplated a colonial adjustment in return for a peaceful
   solution of the German-Polish conflict.
Kordt, Erich, *Nicht aus den Akten* (Stuttgart, 1950).
   A German diplomat's account of Anglo-German relations in the
   prewar years. Some reference to colonial questions.
Krumbach, Josef H., ed., *Franz Ritter von Epp: Ein Leben für Deutsch-
   land* (Munich, 1940).
   The official Party biography of Epp.
Meissner, Otto, *Staatssekretär* (Hamburg, 1950).
   Interesting because of the evidence the former Secretary of State
   in the Reich Chancery presents on the diverging views among the
   Nazi leadership.
Raeder, Erich, *Mein Leben* (Tübingen-Neckar, 1956–57).
   Contains an account of German naval preparations for a war with
   Great Britain, to be waged in the mid-1940s.
Rauschnigg, Hermann, *The Voice of Destruction* (New York, 1940).
   This not always dependable work includes accounts of conversations
   with Hitler dealing with the dictator's overseas ambitions. The
   author views Hitler as an opportunist.
Schacht, Hjalmar, *Account Settled* (London, 1949).
   In his apologia Schacht reiterates his views on the necessity of free
   access to raw materials for Germany's economy and defends his
   attitude toward the colonial claim.

Stresemann, Gustav, *Vermächtnis* (Berlin, 1932–33).
> Essential for its account of the Locarno negotiations, in which the question of colonial revision played a role.

Weizsäcker, Ernst von, *Memoirs* (Chicago, 1951).
> Seems to show that in the German Foreign Office colonial revision was not a major preoccupation.

COLLECTIONS OF SPEECHES, ETC.

Hess, Rudolf, *Reden* (Munich, 1938).
> Hess, in justifying the Four Year Plan, repeatedly stressed the necessity of colonial areas as raw material providers.

Hitler, Adolf, *Mein Kampf* (Boston, 1943).
> At the time the book was written Hitler opposed overseas expansion as a waste of German energy.

Picker, Henry, *Hitlers Tischgespräche* (Bonn, 1951).
> Some illuminating passages on Hitler's views on colonial policy. Shows that, as the war in Russia progressed, Hitler lost all interest in overseas projects.

Prange, Gordon W., ed., *Hitler's Words* (Washington, 1944).
> Many of the passages in this collection deal with the colonial question.

Rosenberg, Alfred, *Schriften und Reden* (Munich, 1943).
> The chief Nazi theoretician and advocate of *Ostpolitik* occasionally also advocated overseas colonies.

THE LITERATURE OF THE COLONIAL MOVEMENT

> The analysis of the colonial argument contained in Chapter 2 as well as parts of the discussion of projected German colonial policies in Chapter 4 are based largely on the following works, which are typical of the propaganda efforts of the German colonialists.

Abs, P. Josef Maria, *Der Kampf um unsere Schutzgebiete* (Düsseldorf, 1930).

Baravalle, Robert, *Deutschland braucht seine Kolonien* (Graz, 1939).

Bauer, H. W., *Deutschlands Kolonialforderung und die Welt* (Leipzig, 1940).

———, *Kolonien im Dritten Reich* (Cologne, 1936).

———, ed., *Koloniale Wende; Das deutsche koloniale Jahrbuch, 1942* (Berlin, 1942).

Bender, Hans, ed., *Kolonien—ein Kraftfeld Grossdeutschlands; Das deutsche koloniale Jahrbuch, 1941* (Berlin, 1941).

Brüsch, Karl, ed., *Kolonien—ein Kapitel deutscher Ehre; Das deutsche koloniale Jahrbuch, 1938* (Berlin, 1938).

————, *Kolonien—Grossdeutschlands Anspruch; Das deutsche koloniale Jahrbuch, 1939* (Berlin, 1939).

Cramer, Ernst Ludwig, *Wir kommen wieder* (Potsdam, 1940).

Deutsche Gesellschaft für Völkerrecht und Weltpolitik, *Raw Materials and Colonies* (Berlin, 1940).

Deutsche Kolonialgesellschaft und Interfraktionelle koloniale Vereinigung des Reichstags, *Deutschland in den Kolonien* (Berlin, n.d.).

Diehl, Louise, *Die Kolonien warten* (Leipzig, 1939).

Dix, Arthur, *Weltkrise und Kolonialpolitik* (Berlin, 1932).

Forstreuter, Adelbert, *Der endlose Zug*, Kampfschriften der Obersten SA-Führung; Band 14 (Munich, 1939).

Fritz, Georg, *Kolonien?* (Berlin, 1934).

Jacob, Ernst Gerhard, *Deutsche Kolonialkunde; 1884–1934* (Dresden, 1934).

————, *Das koloniale Deutschtum* (Bayreuth, 1939).

Johannsen, G. Kurt, and Kraft, H. H., *Germany's Colonial Problem* (London, 1937).

Karlowa, Rudolf, *Deutsche Kolonialpolitik* (Breslau, 1939).

Karstedt, Oskar, *Der weisse Kampf um Afrika* (Berlin, 1938).

Krumbach, J. H., *Kolonialpolitik heute*, Tornisterschriften des OKW, Abt. Inland, Heft 25 (Munich, 1941).

Kühne, Lothar, *Das Kolonialverbrechen von Versailles* (Graz, 1939).

Kuntze, Paul H., *Das neue Volksbuch unserer Kolonien* (Leipzig, 1942).

Leutwein, Paul, *Die deutsche Kolonialfrage* (Berlin, 1937).

Onnen, Jakobus, ed., *Deutsche Kolonialprobleme*, Reichsberufswettkampfsarbeit der Kolonialschule Witzenhausen (Berlin, 1940).

Pfeiffer, Hans Ernst, ed., *Unsere schönen alten Kolonien* (Berlin, 1941).

Pfister, Bernhard, *England und die deutsche Kolonialfrage* (Tübingen, 1939).

Reichskolonialbund, Bundesführung, *Koloniales Taschenbuch 1942* (Munich, 1942).

Ritter, Paul, *Der Kampf um den Erdraum* (Leipzig, 1936).

Rohrbach, Paul, *Deutschlands koloniale Forderung* (Hamburg, 1935).

————, ed., *Afrika—Beiträge zu einer praktischen Kolonialkunde* (Berlin, 1943).

Schacht, Hjalmar, "Germany's Colonial Demands," *Foreign Affairs* (Washington), *21* (January 1937), 223–34.

This article, a rather routine presentation of the German arguments for colonies, aroused considerable interest in 1936. It was the first important instance in which the colonial claim had been raised by a member of the German ruling group for the benefit of a non-German audience.

Scheidl, Franz J., *Deutschlands Kampf um seine Kolonien* (Vienna, 1939).

Schmitt, Matthias, *Kolonien für Deutschland,* Der Neue Stoff, 8 (Stuttgart, 1939).

Schnee, Heinrich, *German Colonization Past and Future* (London, 1926).
This work may be described as a classic of the colonialist cause. In it Schnee coined the expression Colonial Guilt Lie.

Schnöckel, Paul, *Das deutsche Kolonialproblem,* Schriften der Hochschule für Politik, Herausgegeben von Paul Meier—Benneckenstein; I. Idee und Gestalt des Nationalsozialismus, Heft 24 (Berlin, 1937).

Schön, Walter von, *Deutschlands Kolonialweg* (Berlin, 1939).

Schreiber, Hermann, *Deutsche Tat in Afrika* (Berlin, 1941).

Seegert, Joachim, *Die dritte Heimat* (Berlin, 1933).

——, *Koloniale Schicksalsstunde der weissen Rasse* (Berlin, 1934).

Steinhoff, Ilse, *Deutsche Heimat in Afrika* (Berlin, 1941).

von Stuemer, Willibald, *Kolonial—Fibel* (Berlin, 1936).

Viera, Josef, *Kolonien in Blickfeld von heute* (Düsseldorf, 1940).

Wangenheim, Hans Ulrich Freiherr von, *Kolonien des Dritten Reiches* (Berlin, 1939).

Wagener, Georg, *Das deutsche Kolonialreich* (Potsdam, 1937).

Wüst, G., ed., *Kolonialprobleme der Gegenwart* (Berlin, 1939).

Zadow, Fritz, *Koloniale Revision* (Leipzig, 1941).

von Zastrow, G., ed., *Deutschland braucht Kolonien* (Berlin, 1925).

Unlike these purely propagandistic efforts, the works listed in the following section make some claim to scientific objectivity. In effect, however, they often state the same arguments on a somewhat higher intellectual level.

Brenner, Harro, *Wem hat Deutschland seine Kolonien aufgrund des Versailler Diktats überlassen?,* Völkerrechtsfragen; Herausgegeben von Max Wenzel; 45 (Berlin and Bonn, 1938).
The author comes to the conclusion that Germany technically retains sovereignty over the African mandates.

Dresler, Adolf, *Die deutschen Kolonien und die Presse,* Forschungen zur Kolonialfrage; Herausgegeben vom Kolonialgeographischen Institut der Universität Leipzig, K. H. Dietzel, ed., 11 (Würzburg, 1942).

A cursory survey of the German colonial press and of press attitudes toward colonialism from the 1880s to 1940.

Haag, Herbert, *Kolonien und Industriewirtschaft*, Vol. 5 of the same series as Dresler (Würzburg, 1940).
Expounds on the importance of overseas raw material sources for German industry.

Holtsch, Maria, *Die ehemaligen deutschen Südseekolonien in Wandel seit dem Weltkrieg* (diss., Marburg, 1934).
Notable for its positive discussion of Japanese accomplishments.

Karstedt, Oskar, *Probleme afrikanischer Eingeborenenpolitik,* Kolonialwissenschaftliche Forschungen; Herausgegeben im Auftrage des Reichsforschungsrates und der Deutschen Forschungsgemeinschaft von Günter Wolff, Leiter der Kolonialwissenschaftlichen Abteilung, 3 (Berlin, 1942).
Karstedt, an old colonial and member of the KPA, favored a "strong" native policy, based purely on the interests of German settlers and the German economy.

Mellem, Wilhelm, *Der deutsche Kolonialanspruch* (diss., Erlangen, 1938).
Denounces the colonial clauses of the Versailles Treaty as contrary to international law, thus developing a German legal claim to colonial restitution.

Nachrodt, Hanswerner, *Der Reichskolonialbund,* Schriften der Hochschule für Politik; Herausgegeben von Paul Meier—Benneckenstein II. Der organisatorische Aufbau des Dritten Reiches, Heft 30 (Berlin, 1939).
Brief sketch of the organization and aims of the Reichskolonialbund.

Pfister, Bernhard, "Die britische Kolonialdiskussion," *Zeitschrift für die gesamte Staatswissenschaft,* 99 (1939), 23–63.
Surveys British opinion on the colonial question, stressing voices favoring revision.

Schmitt, Matthias, *Funktion und Bedeutung der Kolonien,* Forschungen zur Kolonialfrage; Herausgegeben vom Kolonialgeographischen Institut der Universität Leipzig, K. H. Dietzel, ed., 9 (Würzburg, 1940).
Stresses raw materials as the main reason for German colonial desires. Denies that mass settlement is possible or desirable.

Schultze, Joachim H., *Der Wirtschaftswert unserer Kolonien* (Berlin, 1940).
Discussion of the economic potential of the African mandates.

Westermann, Diedrich, *Der Afrikaner heute und morgen* (Berlin, 1937).
Good discussion of social changes taking place in Africa: urbaniza-

tion, detribalization. The author believed that these developments could not be halted but should be controlled.

————, ed., *Beiträge zur deutschen Kolonialfrage* (Essen, 1937).
A symposium by various colonial experts on political and economic aspects of the colonial claim. Moderate in tone.

Winkelmann, Friedrich W., *Die deutsche Kolonialfrage als Vökerrechtsproblem* (diss., Göttingen, 1936).
Similar in argument to the Mellem work. Also concerns himself with the question of sovereignty over the mandates.

The following memoirs of old colonials are surprisingly free of propaganda appeals for colonial revisionism. However, they undoubtedly contributed to the growth of interest in this cause.

Hahl, Albert, *Gouverneursjahre in Neuguinea* (Berlin, 1937).

Lettow-Vorbeck, Paul Emil von, *Meine Erinnerungen aus Ostafrika* (Leipzig, 1920).

————, *Was mir die Engländer über Ostafrika erzählten* (Leipzig, 1920).

Riedel, Otto, *Der Kampf um Deutsch-Samoa* (Berlin, 1938).

Colonial fiction was often an instrument of revisionist propaganda. Some examples follow:

Grimm, Hans, *Volk ohne Raum* (Berlin, 1932).
The classic novel of German colonization. It propagated a kind of social imperialism wedded to racial doctrines. The author had been expelled from South Africa in 1914. The work first appeared in 1926 and was an instant success.

Grumpelt, Werner, *Im Herzen von Deutsch—Südwest* (Berlin, 1939).
Short stories of farm life and native wars in Southwest Africa, written for adolescents.

Pfeiffer, Heinrich, ed., *Heiss war der Tag* (Berlin, 1933).
Similar to the above.

Voigt, Bernhard, *Du meine Heimat Deutschsüdwest* (Berlin, 1925).

————, *Auf dorniger Pad* (Berlin, 1926).

————, *Das Herz der Wildnis* (Berlin, 1940).

————, *Die Farmer vom Seeis Rivier* (Potsdam, 1943).

————, *Heinz Fuhrmann findet heim* (Potsdam, 1943).

————, *Die Vortrecker* (Potsdam, 1943).

————, *Die deutsche Landnahme* (Potsdam, 1944).

All these works deal with South and Southwest Africa, which the author knew personally. They protest against the colonial clauses of the Treaty of Versailles and especially against the confiscation of German private property in the colonies. The three last works form a cycle covering the whole history of German colonization in Southwest Africa.

The work of Hans Grimm, who concerned himself almost exclusively with colonial topics in his novels and short stories, is discussed from a National Socialist viewpoint in the following monographs:

Hoffknecht, Alfred, *Hans Grimm; Weltbild und Lebensgefühl* (diss., Munich, 1934).
Kirsch, Edgar, *Hans Grimm und der nordische Mensch* (Munich, 1938).

The German colonial claim was endorsed by some non-German authors. Examples are:

Dawson, William Harbutt, "Hitler's Challenge," *The Nineteenth Century and After, 710* (April 1936), 401–16.
    Dawson was the most vocal British advocate of colonial revisionism. To some extent he also favored appeasement with regard to European questions.
Gilwicki, Constantin von, *Die Enteignung des deutschen Kolonialbesitzes* (Hamburg, 1937).
    This Polish author endorsed the German colonial claim partly in order to justify a similar Polish claim.
Toynbee, Arnold J., "Koloniale Revision," *Hamburger Monatshefte für Auswärtige Politik, 3,* Heft 3, pp. 81–86.
    The British historian favored colonial revision as part of a general settlement.

NEWSPAPERS AND PERIODICALS

Deutsche Kolonialzeitung (Leipzig, 1933–36, Munich, 1936–43).
    A basic source for any discussion of the German colonial movement.
Deutscher Kolonialdienst, Ausbildungsblätter der Reichsleitung des Kolonialpolitischen Amtes der NSDAP (Munich, 1935–43).
    An official publication of the KPA, this monthly furnishes interesting insights into the colonial policies which this agency was developing for the envisaged new German empire.
The Times (London, 1929–43).
Völkischer Beobachter (Munich, 1924–43).

Secondary Works

The only postwar work dealing with the German colonial ambitions of the period discussed in this monograph is Rayford W. Logan's *The African Mandates in World Politics* (Washington, 1948). Concerning himself only with the diplomatic aspects of the colonial claim, Professor Logan wrote too early to be able to avail himself of the mass of German, British, and other documents published or made otherwise accessible in later years. The book is particularly useful for its full discussion of political and public reaction to the German claims in Britain, France, and other countries. Contemporary analyses of the German colonial movement and its aims include:

Henderson, H. D., *Colonies and Raw Materials,* Oxford Pamphlets on World Affairs, 7 (Oxford, 1939).
Concludes that a redistribution of colonies would not significantly improve the economic position of the have-not nations.

Kuczynski, R. R., *"Living Space" and Population Problems,* Oxford Pamphlets on World Affairs, 8 (Oxford, 1939).
Denies that colonies can provide a solution for the problems of overpopulated countries.

Royal Institute of International Affairs, *Germany's Claim to Colonies,* Information Department Papers, 23 (London, 1939).
An excellent contemporary survey and appraisal of the German colonial campaign and British and continental reaction to it, based mainly on newspaper sources and speeches.

Townsend, Mary E., "The Contemporary Colonial Movement in Germany," *Political Science Quarterly, 43* (1928), 64–75.
A discussion of the colonial groups of the Weimar period. The author tended perhaps to exaggerate the importance of these groups and the impact of their agitation. This is virtually the only discussion of German colonialism that appeared outside Germany during the Weimar period.

———, "The German Colonies and the Third Reich," *Political Science Quarterly, 53* (1938), 186–206.
A perceptive brief discussion of the work of the RKB and of Nazi leaders' statements on the colonial problem.

The following works are essentially polemics, directed against the German colonial claim. A few, especially the Bennett work, contain some interesting factual information on Nazi activities in Africa.

Amery, L. S., *The German Colonial Claim* (London, 1939).

Bennett, Benjamin, *Hitler over Africa* (London, 1939).
Bullock, A. L. C., ed., *Germany's Colonial Demands* (London, 1939).
Lewin, Evans, *The Germans and Africa* (London, 1939).
Macauley, Neil, *Mandates—Reasons, Results, Remedies* (London, 1937).
Ritchie, Eric Moore, *The Unfinished War* (London, 1940).
Roberts, Granville, *The Nazi Claims to Colonies* (London, 1939).
Steer, G. L., *Judgment on German Africa* (London, 1939).
It is interesting to note that virtually all these books, which strongly opposed colonial revision, appeared in the immediate prewar period, after the policy of appeasement had signally failed. In earlier years the German claims had often been discussed sympathetically in the British press.

The following miscellaneous works provided insights on various aspects of this investigation:

Feis, Herbert, *The Spanish Story* (New York, 1948).
Shows that African questions played a major role in German-Spanish negotiations in 1940.
Langer, William L., *Our Vichy Gamble* (New York, 1947).
Outlines the German attitude toward the French Empire and gives some insight into German postwar plans for Africa in the author's account of Franco-German negotiations in 1940/41.
Meyer, Henry C., *Mitteleuropa in German Thought and Action 1815–1945* (The Hague, 1955).
This work, which focuses on the period just before and during World War I, shows that a certain tension has always existed between continental and overseas expansion as possible aims of German policy. It indicates, however, that many individuals favored a combination of both policies—a formula that seems to have been adopted by the leadership of the Third Reich.
Rudin, Harry R., *The Germans in the Cameroons* (New Haven, 1934).
Contains a good sketch of the colonial movement in the Bismarckian and Wilhelminian periods. The attitudes and argumentation of the colonialists of the 1930s are quite similar to the ones described here, a fact which tends to bear out the analysis of the colonialists as an essentially conservative group, in which Nazi Weltanschauung played only a secondary role.
Schacht, Hjalmar, *The End of Reparations* (New York, 1931).
———, *Grundsätze deutscher Wirtschaftspolitik* (Oldenburg, 1932).
In both books Schacht reiterates his views on the German need for colonies.

Schnee, Heinrich, *Geschichtsunterricht im völkischen Nationalstaat* (Bochum, 1936).

Describes how colonial propaganda was introduced into the school curriculum.

Zimmermann, Emil, *The German Empire of Central Africa* (London, 1918).

This World War I propaganda pamphlet, less polemical than one might expect, contains excerpts from German writers who advocated the creation of a large German *Mittelafrika*. The project was revived in World War II.

Index

INDEX